Controversies in Classroom Research

A Reader edited by
Martyn Hammersley
at the Open University

Open University Press

Milton Keynes • Philadelphia

Open University Press
Open University Educational Enterprises Limited
12 Cofferidge Close
Stony Stratford
Milton Keynes MK11 1BY, England

and
242 Cherry Street
Philadelphia, PA 19106, USA
First Published 1986

British Library Cataloguing in Publication Data
Controversies in classroom research.
  1. Education——Research 2. Teaching
  I. Hammersley, Martyn
  371.1'02'072   LB1028

  ISBN 0-335-15248-1
  ISBN 0-335-15247-3 Pbk

Library of Congress Cataloging in Publication Data
Controversies in classroom research
  Includes index.
  1. Interaction analysis in education.   2. Observation (Educational
method).   3. Education——Research.
  I. Hammersley, Martyn.
  LB1025.2.C636 1986   370'7'8   86-12717
  ISBN 0-335-15248-1
  ISBN 0-335-15247-3 (pbk.)

Text design by Carlton Hill
Typeset by Colset Private Limited, Singapore
Printed in Great Britain by St. Edmundsbury Press, Bury St. Edmunds, Suffolk

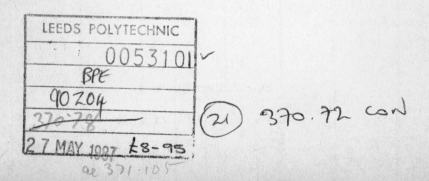

Contents

Part Two: Studying Classroom Language

Part Three: Macro and Micro Analysis

Part Four: Case Study and Action Research

Contents

Acknowledgements

Essays in this collection come from the following sources, to whose publishers grateful acknowledgement is made:

'Interaction analysis in informal classrooms: a critical comment on the Flanders' system', by Walker, R. and Adelman, C., *British Journal of Educational Psychology*, Vol. 45, pp. 73–6, (1975).

'Revisiting classroom research: a continuing cautionary tale', by Delamont, S. and Hamilton, D., in Delamont, S. (ed.), *Readings on Interaction in the Classroom*, Methuen, London, pp. 3–24, (1984).

'Revisiting Hamilton and Delamont: a cautionary note on the relationship between "systematic observation" and ethnography', by Hammersley, M., *Research Intelligence*, 20, October, pp. 3–5, 1985.

'The characteristics and uses of systematic classroom observation', by McIntyre, D. and Macleod, G., in McAleese, R. and Hamilton, D. (eds.), *Understanding Classroom Life*, NFER, pp. 111–129, (1978).

'Language in classroom interaction: theory and data', by Furlong, V.J. and Edwards, A.D., *Educational Research*, Vol. 19, No. 2, pp. 122–8, (1977).

'Scratching the surface: linguistic data in educational research', by Stubbs, M., in Stubbs, M. *Educational Linguistics*, Basil Blackwell (1986).

'Talking and teaching: reflective comments on in-classroom activities', by Sharrock, W. and Anderson, R., in Payne, G.C.F. and Cuff, E.C. (eds.), *Doing Teaching: The Practical Management of Classrooms*, Batsford, (1982).

'Putting competence into action: some sociological notes on a model of classroom interaction', by Hammersley, M., in French, P. and MacLure, M. (eds.), *Adult–Child Conversation: Studies in Structure and Process*, Croom Helm, (1981).

'Whatever happened to symbolic interactionism?', by Hargreaves, D., in Barton, L. and Meighan, R. (eds.), *Sociological Interpretation of Schooling and Classrooms: A Reappraisal*, Nafferton, (1978).

'Self-contained ethnography or a science of phenomenal forms and inner relations', by Sharp, R., *Boston University Journal of Education.*, Vol. 164, No. 1, pp. 48–63, (1982).

'Ethnography: the holistic approach to understanding schooling', by Lutz, F.W., in Green, J. and Wallat, C. (eds.), *Ethnography and Language in Educational Settings*, Ablex., (Vol. V in the series *Advances in Discourse Process*, ed. Freedle, R.), (1981).

'Some reflections upon the macro–micro problem in the sociology of education', by Hammersley, M., *Sociological Review*, Vol. 32, No. 2, pp. 316–324, (1984).

'The micro–macro problem in the sociology of education', by Hargreaves, A., in Burgess, R.G. (ed.), *Issues in Educational Research: Qualitative Methods*, Falmer, (1985).

'The conduct of educational case studies: ethics, theory and procedures', by Walker, R., in Dockrell, B. and Hamilton, D. (eds.), *Rethinking Educational Research*, Hodder and Stoughton, (1978).

'An adversary's account of SAFARI's ethics of case study', by Jenkins, D., in Richards, C. (ed.), *Power and the Curriculum: Issues in Curriculum Studies*, Nafferton, (n.d.).

'Democractic evaluation as social criticism: or putting the judgment back into evaluation', by Elliot, J., in Norris, N. (ed.), *Theory in Practice: SAFARI Papers 2*, Centre for Applied Studies in Education, University of East Anglia, (1977).

'Bread and dreams or bread and circuses? A critique of "case study" research in education', by Atkinson, P. and Delamont, S., in Shipman, M. (ed.), *Educational Research: Principles, Policies and Practices*, Falmer, (1985).

Thanks must go to my colleagues John Scarth and Peter Woods for their help in compiling this book.

Introduction

M. Hammersley

Over the last thirty years there has been substantial growth in the amount of research on classrooms, both in North America and in Britain. Besides a sharp increase in the *number* of studies produced, there has also been a diversification of approach and an intensification of debate about theoretical and methodological issues. In the 1950s the most influential discipline within the field of classroom research was psychology, at a time when that discipline was less internally divided and disputatious than it is today. The approach adopted was very much an applied one, building on a longstanding concern with 'teacher effectiveness'. But there was also a reaction against some of the methods used in earlier research, notably the reliance upon global ratings of teacher effectiveness or classroom climate (Walker 1971; Dunkin and Biddle 1974; MacIntyre 1980). Emphasis came to be placed upon objective, systematic observation of classroom events using low-inference observation schedules, and there was increased use of statistical analysis.

Since that time, psychology itself has become more disparate in character, for example through the growing influence of cognitive psychology, revitalised by work in artificial intelligence, and through the development of ecological, ethogenic and phenomenological approaches in social psychology (Barker 1968 and 1978; Harré and Secord 1972; Armistead 1974; Valle and King 1978; Rosnow 1981; Sampson 1983; Harré, Clarke and De Carlo 1985). The dominant experimental and correlational paradigms have been strongly challenged, as have the theoretical orientations associated with them. As part of this there has been increased advocacy of naturalistic study of everyday settings employing relatively unstructured, qualitative methods.

To varying degrees, these developments within psychology have impinged upon classroom research over the last twenty years. However, in addition, other disciplines have come to have a major impact upon it. In the United States cultural anthropology has probably been the most influential disciplinary influence outside of psychology. While anthropological work on education and schools has a long history (Delamont and Atkinson 1980; Vierra, Boehm and Neely 1982; Eddy 1985), the specific focus upon the classroom is rather more recent and has been particularly important for its contribution to sociolinguistic research (Dumont and Wax 1969; Cazden, Hymes and John 1972; Green and Wallat 1981; Wilkinson 1982). Social anthropology has been much less influential upon classroom research in Britain. While some work on education has been done by British anthropologists (Middleton 1970; Mair 1972), little of it has focused upon classroom processes. However, anthropology did have an indirect effect on classroom research through Liam Hudson's recruitment of social anthropologists to the Centre for Research in Educational Sciences at Edinburgh University in the late 1960s and early 1970s (Hudson 1977; Delamont and Hamilton 1984 [Reading 1.3 this volume]).

Sociology has also become an important source of classroom research in recent years. Before 1970 there was little or no sociological work on classrooms. Since then the situation has changed dramatically, particularly in Britain, to a lesser extent in North America. The main reason for this change was the resurgence of interest in various forms of interpretive sociology in the late 1960s and 1970s. Particularly important here were two versions of interpretive sociology which stressed the study of face-to-face interaction: symbolic interactionism and ethnomethodology.

Symbolic interactionism arose as a distinctive approach to sociological work in the 1940s and 1950s in the writings of Herbert Blumer, though its origins can be traced back to the social psychology of earlier writers like George Herbert Mead, William I. Thomas and Charles Horton Cooley, and to the tradition of case study and life history research which flourished in the Department of Sociology at Chicago University in the 1920s and 1930s (Rock 1979; Bulmer 1984). Blumer reacted against the growing influence, both within Chicago and elsewhere in North American sociology, of theoretical and methodological work which portrayed human actions as mere *responses* to psychological conditioning or social forces. He argued that human actions are actively constructed on the basis of complex processes of interpretation through which people *make* sense of the world. These processes derive from, but also act back upon, perspectives which are developed in the course of social interaction. He argued that given the nature of human action the appropriate methodology in sociology is ethography: the study of social interaction in natural settings through observation and informal participation and conversation (Blumer 1969).

Ethnomethodology shares some similarities with interactionism. Both emphasise that human actions cannot be understood without taking account of the processes of interpretation which generate them. However, where interactionism sees the meanings embedded in action as the product of relatively stable perspectives shared by social groups, ethnomethodology treats meanings as context-dependent. From this point of view, agreement among actors is not produced by a commonality of meanings but rather by the collective use of shared methods to create intelligible behaviour and to find meaning in others' actions (Garfinkel 1967; Heritage 1984). Thus where interactionists investigate the perspectives and practices shared by groups of actors, ethnomethodologists are concerned rather with documenting the methods by which actors produce and understand everyday behaviour. Both orientations, however, encourage the detailed qualitative analysis of patterns of social interaction, including those taking place in classrooms. (For reviews see Hammersley 1980 and 1982, Delamont 1981 and Woods 1983 and 1985).

While some anthropological and sociological research on classrooms has been particularly concerned with classroom language, there has also been an important input into classroom research from linguistics. In Britain this has emerged from a distinctive British linguistic tradition with its origins in the work of Malinowski and Firth, but developed particularly by Michael Halliday (Coulthard 1977; Burton 1981). The major contribution to classroom research here is the work of Sinclair and Coulthard (1975). These researchers were concerned with developing a form of linguistic analysis, modelled upon that already available at the levels of morphology and syntax, which would capture the structure of discourse, including the dialogical patterns to be found in classrooms (see also Stubbs 1975 and 1976, and Willes 1983).

Not surprisingly, given its recent history, classroom research has been the site for some major theoretical and methodological debates. To some degree this is the product of the clash of different disciplines, but at least as important has been the character of the particular intra-disciplinary perspectives which have been applied to classroom research. Indeed, there are some striking similarities between ecological, ethogenic and phenomenological approaches in psychology, interpretive approaches in sociology, and linguistic analyses of discourse. The growth in influence of these approaches has produced a cross-disciplinary shift away from quantitative analysis of large samples towards detailed, qualitative investigations of smaller amounts of data, even of single lessons. Associated with this shift have been attacks upon attempts to describe the world of the classroom in quantitative terms and to test explanations of it by means of statistical techniques. This is exemplified in arguments between ethnographers and systematic observers. However, there have also been arguments among representatives of the new approaches to classroom research, for example over how classroom language is to be analysed, about whether macro or micro explanations are the most appropriate, and about the merits and legitimacy of theoretical and applied research.

This volume collects together key articles in these debates about the methodology of classroom research. The remainder of this introduction will summarise each debate and sketch the content of the articles included.

Ethnography versus Systematic Observation

By the 1960s, systematic observation had become the dominant method of research on classrooms. This approach typically involves the observation of large samples of teachers and pupils by observers using a coding scheme in which the activities taking place at regular points in time or in particular time intervals (say every 3 seconds or every 25 seconds) are checked off. Undoubtedly the best known coding system of this kind is that developed by Ned Flanders (Flanders 1970). FIAC (Flanders Interaction Analysis Categories) was designed to measure variations in the level of control exercised by the teacher over classroom events. However, this system of coding is by no means the only one. There are over 100 systematic observation coding schemes currently available, focusing on various aspects of classroom interaction (Simon and Boyer 1974; Galton 1978).

There has been considerable debate within the systematic observation tradition, both about the validity of the results produced, and also about particular techniques employed (Rosenshine 1971; Flanders 1973; Dunkin and Biddle 1974; MacIntyre 1980). However, in the late 1960s and 1970s this tradition also came under sharp attack from those working in other research traditions (Coulthard 1974; Hamilton and Delamont 1974; Walker and Adelman 1975; Stubbs 1975). The main criticisms were that:

> 1 The use of pre-established categories prevents recognition of the complexity of classroom behaviour and obstructs the development of theories that are sensitive to this complexity.
> 2 That by using arbitrary time sampling, systematic observation neglects natural patterns in classroom interaction.
> 3 That classroom interaction is studied without any attempt to understand the context in which it occurs and in particular the perspectives of the teachers and pupils involved.

These criticisms are presented in this volume in the articles by Walker and Adelman (Reading 1.1) and Delamont and Hamilton (Reading 1.3). (Though in addition see Stubbs, Reading 2.2.) Also included is a reply to the criticisms by two representatives of the systematic observation tradition, McIntyre and Macleod (Reading 1.2), and a brief response of my own to Delamont and Hamilton (Reading 1.4).

Classroom interaction as discourse

Classroom interaction is predominantly verbal and there has been some
debate about the methodological implications of that fact. On the face of it
this might seem like an issue on which disagreement would simply follow
disciplinary lines. However, while the linguists certainly do argue that the
verbal nature of much classroom interaction should shape our whole
approach to analysing it, there are sociologists who advance the same argument (Mehan 1979; Atkinson 1981).

What the implications of studying classroom interaction as language use
are depends, obviously, not just upon whether one thinks that linguistic
analysis can be applied above the level of the sentence but also upon how one
believes language should be studied in the first place. There is considerable
diversity within linguistics on this issue, in addition to differences among
linguists, anthropologists, sociologists and psychologists. In Reading 2.1
Furlong and Edwards sketch the approaches to language to be found in the
systematic observation, ethnographic and sociolinguistic traditions, and
argue that we must understand the theoretical assumptions which underly
these approaches before we can assess them effectively. Stubbs (Reading 2.2)
provides a powerful argument from the linguistic side of the fence, suggesting that studies which ignore the organisation of language, and of discourse in particular, run a serious risk of misinterpreting what is going on in
classrooms and why. He uses the work of Labov on the social distribution of
linguistic variation as a model for the kind of linguistically sensitive research
that is required (Labov 1972).

As ethnomethodologists Sharrock and Anderson (Reading 2.3) also point
to the importance of classroom talk, but they recommend a different
approach to Stubbs. They renounce the pursuit of generalisations, whether
about the structure of discourse or of society. What they propose is the
analysis of instances of classroom interaction as everyday activities, looking
in detail at how participants construct these activities. And they give particular emphasis to the content of teachers' classroom talk, which they portray as
the inculcation of subject knowledge.

In Reading 2.4, I adopt a more conventional sociological approach,
arguing that what is required is a synthesis of those approaches to classroom
talk, both ethnomethodological and sociolinguistic, which try to document
the cultural competence involved in its production with those sociological
approaches, especially interactionist ethnography, which treat it as a process
of action constructed by the actors in the pursuit of particular goals. (Brazil
1981 is a response to this article by a linguist.)

Macro versus micro research

Within sociology, and to a lesser extent within anthropology and psychology, there has been considerable debate about the appropriateness of macro and micro explanations. Unfortunately, there has also been some confusion about what the terms 'macro' and 'micro' mean. Their root meaning refers to differences in the scale of the phenomena which are held to explain the events under study. For example, an explanation of the prevalence of formal teaching in secondary schools in terms of its advantages over informal methods in dealing with the maintenance of classroom order would be a *micro* explanation (though explanations for why classroom order was important, or needed to be maintained, might be macro explanations). On the other hand an explanation for the prevalence of this teaching style in terms of the demands of the examination system or the needs of capitalism would be a *macro* explanation. In debate, this distinction between types of explanation has become associated with a number of other issues, notably the relation between different theoretical approaches, such as interactionism, ethnomethodology and Marxism.

The articles by Lutz and Sharp (Reading 3.1 and 3.2) present arguments from within anthropology and sociology, respectively, for the priority of macro-analysis. Lutz makes a distinction between ethnography and ethnographic methods. He argues that much use of ethnographic technique in the field of education takes the form of micro-ethnography, the study of face-to-face encounters in particular settings. He claims that this is not true ethnography, since that involves the study of a whole society through a complete cycle of events that regularly occur as it interacts with its environment. Micro-ethnography, he suggests, fails to shed light on the more complex issues that account for 'much of what goes on (or doesn't go on) in schooling' p. 109). The narrower the focus of a study, he suggests, the more likely it is that important variables will be omitted.

Sharp also argues that micro-studies are inadequate. But she goes further. She claims that ethnography, by its very nature, must adopt a micro focus and is limited to documenting the perspectives of the people under study and reporting what can be observed by the ethnographer him or herself. She labels this the world of 'appearances', or of 'phenomenal forms', and argues that explanations for why this world takes the forms it does must appeal to 'deeper social structural causal mechanisms' (p. 120). Understanding of these causal mechanisms can, she claims, only be provided by a theory based upon 'an historical analysis of the development of the capitalist mode of production throughout its various stages, in different national situations' (p. 130). Unlike Lutz, Sharp believes that what is essential is not just macro research, but a particular macro theory, namely Marxism, whose validity she clearly believes is already well-established.

There are those who reject the very possibility of macro-analysis.

Sharrock and Anderson's article (Reading 2.3) seems to come close to this view, with its emphasis on the importance of descriptions focused upon local contexts. However, most interactionists accept the value of both macro- and micro-analysis; though they would not accept the claim that macro-analysis has priority or is the only source of explanations for social phenomena. David Hargreaves' article (Reading 3.3) represents a reaction against some earlier work by Rachel Sharp. In the course of a study of teachers in a 'progressive' primary school (Sharp and Green 1975), she had argued, much in the manner of her later article, that symbolic interactionism and social phenomenology can provide only descriptions of, not explanations for, the perspectives and practices of teachers, and that they fail to take adequate account of the role of power and social structural factors in shaping patterns of schooling. Hargreaves accepts the value of both macro and micro levels of analysis and of attempts to synthesise Marxism and interactionism. However, he rejects Sharp and Green's criticisms of interactionism as false, and criticises their ethnographic work for failing to substantiate the claims they make on the basis of it. He argues that the defects of their research stem from a neglect of the particular strengths of interactionist ethnography.

The other articles in this section, by Andy Hargreaves (Reading 3.4) and myself (Reading 3.5), both involve attempts to disentangle the different issues in the macro–micro dispute. Hargreaves discusses three questions: the relationship between theory and evidence, between macro and micro theory, and between school and society. He argues that what is required if progress is to be made in resolving the macro–micro problem are sustained attempts to relate theory and evidence, especially at the meso level, in the borderland between macro and micro. Linked studies of different settings, for example of local authority decision-making and of decision-making in schools and classrooms within that authority, are recommended as ways of developing meso-level theories and thus linking macro and micro levels of analysis. He gives particular emphasis to the development of bridging concepts like 'coping strategy' (Westbury 1973; Abrahamson 1974; Woods 1979; A. Hargreaves 1978 and 1979; Pollard 1982).

In my article (Reading 3.4) I start from a similar recognition of multiple issues, but suggest that resolution of any one of these does not resolve the others, and I focus upon what seems to me to be the macro–micro problem proper: can social events be best explained by appeal to features of the local situation in which they occur, current or historical, or is it necessary to appeal to larger scale causes, such as the nature of the national, or even international, context in which they are located? In my view this issue, and the question of whether some kind of synthesis like that proposed by Hargreaves is required, cannot be answered by philosophical argument alone but also depends upon assessment of the fruits of attempts to develop valid macro and micro theories. It seems to me that both the futility of the macro–micro debate and the relative absence of well-established theories in the sociology of education stem from the same source: the organisation of the discipline around approaches rather than around research problems.

Theoretical versus action research

Alongside developments within the disciplines of psychology, anthropology and sociology, in recent decades there has also been a growth of interest in classroom processes on the part of curriculum specialists and evaluators. Moreover, here too there has been a shift away from quantitative techniques towards approaches similar to those of ethnographers (Taylor and Richards 1979). However, curriculum researchers have found it necessary and desirable to modify ethnographic techniques in some important respects. In his article 'The conduct of educational case studies' (Reading 4.1) Rob Walker outlines the approach adopted by some of the curriculum researchers associated with the Centre for Applied Research in Education at the University of East Anglia. This involves two important departures from ethnographic methodology. First, the amount of time spent in a setting is reduced, on the grounds that it is necessary to produce results rapidly if they are to be usable by practitioners. If there is delay, the information becomes out of date. Secondly, access is to be negotiated on the basis that those studied control the data collected, and must give their permission for its publication. This contrasts with the more conventional ethnographic practice in which the ethnographer maintains control of the data but promises in any publication to try to preserve the anonymity of the setting and of the people he or she has studied. There were two reasons for this modification. First, it was felt that without it condensed fieldwork of the kind advocated would not be feasible, since there would not be sufficient time for the researcher to build up trust with participants. Secondly, Walker argues that, from an ethical point of view, people own the facts about their own lives, particularly where these facts are their perceptions and definitions of the situation, the primary data in case study research of the kind he is advocating.

This reconceptualisation of case study has led to much debate. Some commentators, represented by Jenkins (Reading 4.2) and Elliot (Reading 4.3) in this volume, have argued that the ethical position adopted by Walker involves internal contradictions. Thus Jenkins claims that in practice the negotiative procedure adopted by Walker results in the case study researcher obtaining all the information he or she requires and then putting pressure on participants to allow its release and dissemination. Elliot reinforces this argument, but adds a different point. He argues that the release of some kinds of information is in the public interest and should be published whether or not participants agree. However, information in the private domain should not be published without the explicit and uncoerced permission of participants. Elliot argues that the distinction between public and private information can be determined on the basis of criteria available in Rawls' analysis of the principles of justice (Rawls 1972).

These criticisms arose from within the field of curriculum research. However, there has also been some debate between curriculum case study researchers on the one hand and sociologists and anthropologists on the other (Delamont 1978; Barton and Lawn 1980–1; Ozga 1980–1; Lawn and Barton 1980–1). Included here is an article by Atkinson and Delamont (Reading 4.4.) which charges exponents of curriculum case study with neglecting to apply the canons of ethnographic methodology in their research. The result, the authors suggest, is accounts of educational settings which are simply descriptive, offering little insight or analysis, and which are also of doubtful validity.

Conclusion

Underlying the controversies in classroom research debated in this book are some genuine and difficult problems concerning the study of the social world: for instance, whether anything approximating the understanding we now have of physical phenomena is possible in the realm of human behaviour; or whether there is any role for theoretical, as opposed to applied, social science. However, at present, and for the foreseeable future, such issues do not seem resolvable in any convincing manner. Different, equally reasonable, views can be taken. And in part this is because such arguments rest upon assumptions about what it is and is not possible for social science to achieve, and these can only be assessed on the basis of the present and future work of social scientists themselves. Even then we must be careful not to assume that what is produced through the use of a particular research strategy is all that *could* be produced by that strategy. In light of this, the tone of some of the debates among classroom researchers is unfortunate. Often, the impression is given that the answers to the big philosophical questions are not only already known, but are obvious to anyone intelligent enough, or unbiased enough, to see them.

However, it would be a mistake to treat these debates about classroom research as simply the collision of conflicting philosophical positions. To some degree they are battles for control of territory and status among disciplines and disciplinary sub-groups. More charitably, they represent clashes among researchers with different purposes who tend to see others as engaged in the same enterprise as themselves, but simply doing it badly. Clearly, how one thinks classroom research should be done will depend upon what one takes to be its main functions. And as with social science generally, the purposes underlying classroom studies are manifold. If one is investigating the possibility of applying linguistic analysis above the level of the sentence, one will set about research differently from someone who is attempting to document the extent to which a particular teaching style enhances pupils' levels of achievement. While researchers pursuing these two goals will encounter many of the same methodological problems, they will approach them from different angles because of their different purposes. However, they may be tempted to erect their solutions to these problems, and the principles underlying them, into an abstract philosophy of classroom research which is contrasted with the philosophies of others.

There seems to be a growing trend for social scientists to become locked into competing 'paradigms', and this includes classroom researchers. Within these paradigms certain fundamental assumptions are taken as beyond question; other paradigms being dismissed as 'positivist', 'empiricist', 'reductionist', 'individualistic', 'impressionistic', 'subjective' etc. Argument degenerates into abuse. Differences between research practice in the various paradigms are exaggerated. The standard of rigour assumed in critiques of work in other traditions is far higher than that applied within the paradigm. Serious debate about methodological issues is closed down both within and between research traditions (Hammersley 1984).

There is no doubt that classroom researchers face difficult methodological problems, whatever the tradition in which they work. Moreover, in my view, none of the strategies currently available in any of the different research traditions is very successful. Given this, it seems essential to approach these problems with some humility, examining the arguments of those in other traditions with an open mind, being willing to search for common ground and to try to understand different views. It is in the hope of stimulating productive debate among the various traditions of classroom research that this volume is offered.

References

ABRAHAMSON, J. (1974). 'Classroom constraints and teacher coping strategies', unpub. Ph.D. thesis, University of Chicago.

ARMISTEAD, N. (ed.), (1974). *Reconstructing Social Psychology*. Harmondsworth, Penguin.

ATKINSON, P. (1981). 'Inspecting classroom talk', in Adelman, C. (ed.), *Uttering, Muttering, Collecting, Using and Reporting Talk for Social and Educational Research*, London, Grant McIntyre.

BARKER, R.G. (1968). *Ecological Psychology: Concepts and Methods for Studying the Environment of Human Behaviour*. Stanford University Press.

BARKER, R.G. and Associates (1978). *Habitats, Environments and Human Behaviour*. San Francisco, Jossey Bass.

BARTON, L. and LAWN, M. (1980-1). 'Back inside the whale: a curriculum case study', *Interchange*, 11, 4.

BLUMER, H. (1969). *Symbolic Interactionism*. Englewood Cliffs, N.J., Prentice Hall.

BUCHER, R. and STRAUSS, A. (1961). 'Professions in process', *American Journal of Sociology*. 66.

BULMER, M. (1984). *The Chicago School of Sociology*. Chicago, University of Chicago Press.

BURTON, D. (1981). 'The sociolinguistic analysis of spoken discourse', in French, P. and MacLure, M. (eds.), *Adult–Child Conversation*, London, Croom Helm.

CAZDEN, C.B., HYMES, D.H. and JOHN, V.P. (eds.) (1972). *Functions of Language in the Classroom*. New York, Teachers College Press.

COULTHARD, M. (1974). 'Approaches to the analysis of classroom language', Educational Review, 26, 3, 2.

COULTHARD, M. (1977). *An Introduction to Discourse Analysis*. London; Longman.

DELAMONT, S. (1981). 'All too familiar? A decade of classroom research', *Educational Analysis*, 3, 1.

DELAMONT, S. and ATKINSON, P. (1980). 'The two traditions in educational ethnography: sociology and anthropology compared', *British Journal of Sociology of Education*, 1, 2.

DELAMONT, S. and HAMILTON, D. (1984). 'Revisiting classroom research: a continuing cautionary tale', in Delamont, S. (ed.) *Readings on Interaction in the Classroom*, London, Methuen.

DUMONT, R.V. and WAX, M.L. (1969). 'Cherokee school society and the intercultural classroom', *Human Organisation*, 28, 3.

DUNKIN, M.J. and BIDDLE, B.J. (1974). *The Study of Teaching*. New York, Holt Rinehart & Winston.

EDDY, E.M. (1985). 'Theory, research and application in educational anthropology', *Anthropology and Education Quarterly*, 16, 2.

FLANDERS, N.A. (1970). *Analyzing Teacher Behaviour*. Reading, Mass., Addison Wesley.

GALTON, M. (ed.) (1978). *British Mirrors: a collection of Classroom Observation Systems*. School of Education, University of Leicester.

GARFINKEL, H. (1967). *Studies in Ethnomethodology*. Englewood Cliffs, N.J. Prentice Hall.

GREEN, J.L. and WALLAT, C. (1981). *Ethnography and Language in Educational Settings*, Vol. V. in the series, *Advances in Discourse Processes*, Norwood, New Jersey, Ablex.

HAMILTON, D. and DELAMONT, S. (1974). 'Classroom research: a cautionary tale', *Research in Education*, 11, 1–15.

HAMMERSLEY, M. (1980). 'Classroom ethnography', *Educational Analysis*, 2, 2.

HAMMERSLEY, M. (1982). 'The sociology of classrooms', in Hartnett, A. (ed.), *The Social Sciences in Educational Studies*, London, Heinemann.

HAMMERSLEY, M. (1984). 'The paradigmatic mentality: a diagnosis', in Barton, L. and Walker, S. (eds), *Social Crisis and Educational Research*, London, Croom Helm.

HARGREAVES, A. (1978). 'The significance of classroom coping strategies', in Barton, L. and Meighan, R. (eds.), *Sociological Interpretations of Schools and Classrooms*, Driffield, Nafferton.

HARRE, R. and SECORD, P.F. (1972). *The Explanation of Social Behaviour*. Oxford, Basil Blackwell.

HARRÉ, R., CLARKE, D. and DE CARLO, N. (1985), *Motives and Mechanisms: an Introduction to the Psychology of Action*, London, Methuen.

HERITAGE, J. (1984). *Garfinkel and Ethnomethodology*. Cambridge, Polity Press.

HUDSON, L. (1977). 'Picking winners: a case study of the recruitment of research students' *New Universities Quarterly*, 32, 1, 88–106.

LABOV, W. (1972). *Sociolinguistic Patterns*. University of Pennsylvania Press.

LAWN, M. and BARTON, L., (1980–1). 'Recording the natural world: dilemmas in educational research', *Interchange*, 11, 4.

MACINTYRE, D. (1980). 'Systematic observation of classroom activities', *Educational Analysis*, 2, 2, pp 3–30.

MAYER, P. (ed.) (1970). *Socialisation: the Approach from Social Anthropology*, London, Tavistock.

MEHAN, H. (1979). *Learning Lessons*. Cambridge, Mass., Harvard University Press.

MIDDLETON, J. (ed.) (1970). *From Child to Adult: Studies in the Anthropology of Education*, New York, Natural History Press.

OZGA, J. (1980–1). 'Educational fiction: illuminating or blind alley?', *Interchange*, 11, 4.

POLLARD, A. (1982). 'A model of coping strategies', *British Journal of the Sociology of Education*, 3, 1.

RAWLS, J. (1972). *A Theory of Justice*, Oxford, Clarendon Press.

ROCK, P. (1979). *The Making of Symbolic interactionism*. London, Macmillan.

ROSENSHINE, B. (1971). *Teaching Behaviours and Student Achievement*, Slough, National Foundation for Educational Research.

ROSNOW, R. (1981). *Paradigms in Transition: The Methodology of Social Inquiry*. New York, Oxford University Press.

SAMPSON, E.E. (1983). *Justice and the Critique of Pure Psychology*. New York, Plenum Press.

SHARP, P. and GREEN, A. (1975). *Education and Social Control*. London, Routledge & Kegan Paul.

SIMON, A. and BOYER, B.G. (ed.) (1974). *Mirrors for Behaviour III: An Anthology of Observation Instruments*. Wyncote Penn., Communication Materials Center.

SINCLAIR, J. McH. and COULTHARD, M. (1975). *Towards an Analysis of Discourse: The English Used by Teachers and Pupils*, London, Oxford University Press.

SMITH, L. and GEOFFREY, T. (1968). *The Complexities of the Urban Classroom*, New York, Holt, Rinehart and Winston.

STUBBS, M. (1975). 'Teaching and talking: a sociolinguistic approach to classroom interaction', in Chanan, G. and Delamont, S. (eds.), *Frontiers of Classroom Research*, Slough, National Foundation for Educational Research, 1975.

STUBBS, M. (1976). 'Keeping in touch: some functions of teacher talk', in Stubbs, M. and Delamont, S. (eds.) *Explorations in Classroom Observation*, London, Wiley.

TAYLOR, P.H. and RICHARDS, C. (1979). *An introduction to Curriculum Studies*. Slough, NFER.

VALLE, R. and KING, M. (1978). *Existential-Phenomenological Alternatives for Psychology*. New York, Oxford University Press.

WALKER, R. (1971). 'The social setting of the classroom: a review of observational studies and research', M. Phil. thesis, University of London.

WALKER, R. and ADELMAN, C. (1975). 'Interaction analysis in informal classrooms', *British Journal of Educational Psychology*, 45, 73–6.

WESTBURY, I. (1973). 'Conventional classrooms, "open" classrooms and the technology of teaching', *Journal of Curriculum Studies*, 5, 2.

WILKINSON, L.C. (ed.) (1982). *Communicating in the Classroom*. New York, Academic Press.

WILLES, J. (1983). *Children into Pupils*. London, Routledge & Kegan Paul.

WOODS, P. (1979). *The Divided School*. London, Routledge & Kegan Paul.

WOODS, P. (1983). *Sociology and the School: An Interactionist Viewpoint*, London, Routledge & Kegan Paul.

WOODS, P. (1984). 'Educational ethnography in Britain', *Journal of Thought*, 19,2, pp 75–94.

PART ONE
Systematic Observation and Ethnography

Interaction Analysis in Informal Classrooms: A Critical Comment on the Flanders' System

R. Walker and C. Adelman

Summary: Recent attempts to use Flanders' FIAC system to observe teacher-pupil interactions in primary school classrooms had indicated severe limitations in this approach. The method is useful in a formal situation, but it contains an implicit 'theory of instruction.' If this technique is applied to those informal classrooms, whether primary or secondary, in which the teaching-learning situation is defined more in terms of interpersonal communication than of transmission of information, the coded observations will miss out the very processes which define informal methods. Alternative procedures of observation should be adopted to take account of the context within which teachers talk to pupils and hence to assess the meaning of an interaction, as well as recording its occurrence.

Introduction

Since 1968 we have been collecting recordings of school classrooms where teachers have been attempting to put into practice some form of curriculum innovation. Although these recordings have been made within the context of a number of research projects, at least one general problem has constantly recurred. To what extent do changes in *what* is taught relate to changes in the *way* it is taught? In what ways do changes in curriculum involve changes in pedagogy?

Because these recordings have been made over a period of time, and as parts of research projects pursuing related, but different, problems, the sample we have is not a controlled experimental sample; rather it is an archive

which has been selectively added to according to a set of developing principles. Nevertheless, we now have well over a hundred hours of audio visual
recordings (Adelman and Walker, 1974) of classroom situations which can
be broadly characterised as being 'open' or 'informal' situations. This
includes recordings of teachers in primary and secondary classes, in a wide
range of subject areas, and working according to a number of different
educational philosophies, ideas and plans.

The problem we started with was that of trying to map varieties in the
teacher's 'role' in a number of innovating classrooms, but in time this led us to
look not just at the teacher's performance but at the context within which the
teacher acted, not just in physical and social terms, but also in intellectual
and ideological terms. In other words, we shifted our interpretive framework from the psychological into the sociological, linguistic and anthropological areas as our accumulating material caused us to view our problems
as more complex than we had at first realised.

A critical point in this change of approach came as we realised the
inadequacy of the processing techniques we were using to translate our
recordings into data. The methods we were using were those developed in
the USA by Withall (1949), Medley and Mitzel (1958), and Flanders (1970). It
was, however, around the use of Flanders' method that the problems crystal-
lised.

In this paper we have attempted to report the nature of the difficulties we
encountered in using this sophisticated and increasingly widely used technique in the exploration of classroom manifestations of educational issues.
Given that educational research is increasingly becoming involved in the
study of problems commissioned by practitioners, rather than in the study of
its own discipline-generated problems, our attack is not on the technique
itself so much as on the uses to which it may be put. Our concern is that
particularly in its use in evaluation and teacher development there is a distinct danger of elevating the assumptions of a research method to a theory of
teaching.

Problems in Using the Flanders' System

Perhaps the first thing we realised about using the FIAC system was that
although it is possible to use it in a large *number* of classrooms, only a
narrow *type* of classroom provides satisfactory coding conditions. Even
when (on a suggestion of Flanders) we used radio microphone equipment to
overcome acoustic and perceptual difficulties, we found that in many
classrooms the talk did not fit the categories available to code it. It seemed to
us that the coding system was only appropriate when classroom talk was of a
public dialogue form. In the informal situations we recorded, teachers and

children simply did not talk in ways which the *a priori* coding system could cope with. For example, the 'question-answer' sequence, which is a central feature of the Flanders category system, makes little sense when applied to some of those intimate conversations between teachers and children where both are talking but where the only questions that are being asked are those asked by the children. In fact, from our research we are tempted to suggest that it is virtually a feature of 'open' classroom situations that simple patterns of statements and responses – such as are implicit in FIAC – are rarely observed.

We would stress that this is not simply a problem calling for new or different categories, but for a different concept of talk. Talk has connotative as well as denotative meanings – what is said often depends for its significance on shared meanings which are hidden from the casual observer.

A casual observer cannot understand what is being said in a way that allows him to hear the talk as it is heard by the pupils. What he hears are the meanings available to anyone in the culture; what he misses are the meanings only available to a participant in the relationship. In some classrooms it is often just those local, immediate and personal meanings that are educationally most significant – and any research technique that designs them out of consideration runs the risk of completely misunderstanding and misrepresenting the reality.

One dramatic example of this we observed was in a class where a student called out 'strawberries, strawberries' after another student had been rebuked by the teacher for not doing his homework adequately. All the class laughed but the observer could not see the joke. Later the observer discovered that the connotative meaning of 'strawberries' was dependent on the antecedent teacher's witticism: 'Your work is like strawberries. Good as far as it goes, but it doesn't last nearly long enough' (Walker and Adelman, 1976).

For the observer attempting to follow the meanings communicated by talk this incident is problematic but the Flanders observer could handle it because he does not need to understand the meanings of what is being said to participants; he only needs to understand it in terms of his own frame of reference. ('Is it a direct or indirect question?'). But our point is that in more complex incidents it is not only 'meanings' but also the structure of the talk itself, for example, the nature of 'questions,' that is an item of the immediate culture. Teachers and students develop ways of talking to each other which, though at surface level may appear rambling, elliptical, jokey, anecdotal or metaphorical, may be interpreted by them as theoretical or substantive. In some classes, teachers develop ways of talking, ways of listening, and ways of enquiring ('asking questions'), where it does not seem as though they are being serious or asking questions at all, but careful inspection of their talk in relation to actions reveals that very often they are exploring difficult and complex areas in a sensitive way.

Our impression is, from reading the research, that Flanders' technique is suited to the study of classrooms where talk is used merely as a *transmission* coding, as part of a communication system where one person transmits messages while others receive. But to discover what makes a question a question in the kind of talk we have described means looking beyond *what* is said to how, why, where and to whom it is said. It means looking beyond the immediate action to its antecedents and consequences. In other words, on-the-spot analysis is theoretically impossible for it demands some account of the prospective and retrospective elements of action. Theoretically it also demands that we look at any incident in terms of continuously changing relationships between talk and identity-for-self and identity-for-others within their social context, and this is something that can only be guessed at from the observation of the surface facets of action.

The second major problem we have found with the Flanders system relates strongly to the first. We find it is useful as a survey instrument but find that it does not stand up to ethnographic documentation. Some researchers have recently used FIAC as a basic outline to 'fill-out' by ethnographic methods (Delamont, 1973; Nash, 1972). Our experience is that the underlying dichotomies inherent in the system will not stand up to this kind of data saturation. In the classrooms we have observed and recorded the FIAC system does not fit and its underlying theoretical basis is inadequate. The distinction between 'direct' and 'indirect' teaching *styles* did not help us in conceptualising a set of classrooms where 'teaching style' seemed less significant than either the structure of the classroom situation in communication terms, or the teacher's beliefs and values concerning knowledge. Such individualistic behavioural notions can only be applied within taken-for-granted contexts. We believe that the classes we have recorded are radically different forms of social situation from those reflected in the literature on interaction analysis in that they involve talk as a reflective activity. The implication of this, we believe, is that research has been continued with the idea that classrooms have a peculiar common structure which they need not necessarily possess.

In the classes we have recorded, people talk to each other in a way that appears quite different from that normally heard in schools. Their talk is not simply based on what Halliday (1969) calls 'a representational model' but exploits other quite different forms. The talk is not simply 'informal' in *style* – it corporates radically different conceptions as to the relationship between role and identity which can only be elucidated by moving into areas of research quite different from those which underly Flanders' technique.

The limitation of the applicability of the FIAC system to one model of classroom talk restricts its use in the evaluation of curriculum innovation – where the intention is often to create or introduce changes in role and concomitant talk (Humanities Curriculum Project, Nuffield Science, etc.). For the assumptions built in to FIAC appear very similar to those rejected by the innovators – the problem is not simply seen as being one of trying to get from a 'direct' to an 'indirect' style of teaching within a didactic conception of education – but as trying to create quite new social contexts within which teacher and students can communicate.

The same problem arises again in teacher education – FIAC incorporates a set of values about teaching, which, if treated as a total theory, have the effect of crippling the teacher's actions. Instead of opening alternative options, it is used to close and to control. For instance, conventional micro-teaching is often based on a rather narrow instructional model of teaching buttressed by self-fulfilling assessment based on FIAC.

Summary and Suggestions

Flanders' system for the analysis of classroom interaction is limited by its inherent conception of talk. This limits it to seeing teacher-student inter-action in terms of the *transmission* of information, sometimes one-way, sometimes two-way. It does not concern itself with talk as the expression and negotiation of meanings; as the medium through which people see them-selves as others see them. The underlying concept is simply one of informa-tion-exchange, it does not touch on the relationship between talk and knowledge, between talk and identity, both for oneself and for others. In short, it sees talk as transmission, not as communication.

The descriptions it produces of classroom situations are, to borrow two technical terms from anthropology, *etic* not *emic* (see Harris 1968). That is to say, their meanings are totally dependent on the outsider's frame of refer-ence – they make no concessions to the immediate cultural milieu. There is no attempt to account for, or to explore, the alternative perspectives avail-able to teachers or students – to take their realities as an essential element of the situation.

There is no distinction drawn between *action* and *behaviour*, *praxis* and *process*. As a result behaviours are simply seen as produced by 'actors' in a mechanical way. In choosing to reject intentionality as an area for descrip-tion the technique has no way of discovering *why* people do things, or of accounting for the large amount of time in some classes that is taken up in the exploration of motives.

Its concern with *denotative* meanings leads it to see talk as a surface feature of action and to miss the many, and often paradoxical, meanings that emerge from seeing talk in its full context.

These limitations restrict the use of the FIAC system to that of a survey instrument in the study of certain types of formal classroom situatiion. It is a valuable initial research tool – just as IQ tests can be useful in the context of particular research problems. Its use is dangerous where the technique is used as a substitute for educational theory – for its theoretical basis is weak, unsound and inadequate.

Finally we would like to note what we feel needs to be taken into account when classroom situations are to be analysed within the different kinds of demands that are more usually typical of educational situations.

First, talk needs to be considered in terms of the structure of its situation. When classroom situations are formal, or centralised, talk has character-istics quite different from when the situation is informal or decentralised.

Second, talk needs to be considered in relation to the tasks being defined and the resources available for their resolution. Sometimes talk will itself define the task and be the resource, but on other occasions task and resource may lie outside the realm of talk.

Third, talk needs to be considered in relation to the set of relationships it encompasses.

Taken overall these three conditions constitute a demand for viewing talk within its context; for substituting a more complex reality for the 'verbal behaviour' studied by interaction analysis.

Modern methods of recording, particularly in the audio-visual field, have made available a whole new source of data for educational research that allow it, as never before, to overcome technical problems of reliability, validity and design and so to address a range of problems and issues that are not simply derived from its constituent disciplines but which are of general educational interest. But if research is to enter direct study of education in action then it is essential that the methods and technique used do not isolate the researcher from the situation under study. As Flanders himself has warned: 'The procedure makes no sense at all when what is lost by the process is more important than what is gained' (1970, page 30).

Acknowledgements

This research grew out of three separate projects: (i) the Classroom Research Project, Centre for Science Education, Chelsea College, 1968–72, funded by Chelsea College and the SSRC, supplementary grants from the Ford Founda-tion and the University of London Central Fund; (ii) Ford Teaching Project, Centre for Applied Research in Education, University of East Anglia, 1973–5; (iii) Ford SAFARI Project, Centre for Applied Research in Educa-tion, University of East Anglia, 1973–76.

References

ADELMAN, C.L., and WALKER, R. (1974). Stop-frame cinematography with synchronised sound: a technique for recording in school classrooms. *J. Soc. Motion Picture* and *Television Engineers*, 83, 3, 189–191.

DELAMONT, S. (1973). *Academic Conformity Observed – Studies in the Classroom*. Unpublished PH. D. thesis, University of Edinburgh.

FLANDERS, N.A. (1970). *Analysing Teaching Behaviour*. New York: Addison Wesley.

HALLIDAY, M.A.K. (1969). Relevant models of language. *Educ. Rev.*, 1, 26–37.

HAMILTON, D.H. (1973). *At Classroom Level: Studies in the Learning Milieu*. Unpublished PH. D. thesis, University of Edinburgh.

HARRIS, M. (1968). *The Rise of Anthropological Theory*. London: Routledge and Kegan Paul.

MEDLEY, D.M., and MITZEL, H.E. (1598). A technique for measuring classroom behaviour. *J. educ. Psychol.*, 49, 86–92.

NASH, R. (1972). *Contexts of Learning in Schools*. Unpublished Ph. D. thesis, University of Edinburgh.

WALKER, R., and ADELMAN, C.L. (1972). *Towards a Sociography of Classrooms*. Final report to the SSRC, grants HR 996/1 and HR 1442/1, mimeographed (available from the National Lending Library).

WALKER, R., and ADELMAN, C.L. (1976). Strawberries, In Stubbs, M., and Delamont, S. (Eds.) *Exploration in Classroom Research*. London: Wiley (1976).

WITHALL, J. (1949). The development of a technique for the measurement of social-emotional climate in classrooms. *J. exper. Educ.*, 17, 347–361.

The Characteristics and Uses of Systematic Classroom Observation

D. McIntyre and G. Macleod

Overview

This paper is an attempt to examine the validity of the various criticisms which have been directed at systematic observation, and to consider, in the light of these criticisms, the conditions in which and the purposes for which systematic observation can be useful. By systematic observation procedures, we mean those procedures in which the observer, deliberately refraining from participation in classroom activities, analyzes aspects of these activities through the use of a predetermined set of categories or signs. This analysis may take place during the observation, or may be based on selective records such as audio and video recordings, or on transcripts of classroom discourse. In the first part of the paper, we shall attempt to identify and to categorize the criticisms which have been made, and to consider how far each of these criticisms is valid in its identification of necessary and distinctive characteristics of systematic observation procedures. In the light of these identified characteristics, we shall consider, in the second part of the paper, the extent to which systematic observation is or is not appropriate in pursuing certain kinds of classroom research questions.

Criticisms of Systematic Observation

One of the more puzzling features of British criticisms of systematic observation has been its tendency to focus predominantly on one particular system, that of Flanders (1970). Furthermore, much of this criticism has been curiously wrongheaded, consisting as it does of complaints that Flanders had not solved problems which he was not trying to solve. For example, Walker and Adelman (1975) use their 'strawberries' incident to show that Flanders' system does not capture 'just those local, immediate and personal meanings that are educationally most significant' (p. 74). In claiming to know what is 'educationally most significant', these writers appear to us to have decided *a priori* on the answers to questions which much classroom research is designed to explore; but it is surely obvious that if Flanders had been trying to study pupils' 'local, immediate and personal meanings', he would not have developed a system with only two categories for pupil talk. One of the things that Flanders' system *is* aimed at doing is identifying instances of pupil-initiated ideas in classroom talk, and 'strawberries, strawberries' clearly falls within that category. In this instance at least, Flanders' system does what he intended it to do perfectly adequately; and to criticize it as Walker and Adelman do is like criticizing a physicist for not doing biological research. More generally, it appears to us that Flanders' work has received more than its fair share of criticism. Our major concern, however, is not to defend his system, but simply to point out that this is only one system among many. Many of the aspects of classroom activity not considered with his system are recorded by others. There are many other systems which do not share the weaknesses or indeed in some cases the strengths, of this system. It is, of course, entirely appropriate that the limitations and weaknesses of specific systems should be pointed out; and those who use this approach have in fact been very active in pointing out the weaknesses in each other's systems. But it is important not to confuse this with more fundamental questions about the inherent weaknesses and limitations of systematic observation in general.

A criticism frequently made of Flanders' system, most notably by Delamont (1976a), and explicitly generalized to other systematic observation, is that the procedures used are based on certain ideological assumptions about teaching. Flanders' and several other related systems are ideologically based in the sense that they were designed in the hope of demonstrating the merits of 'indirect' or 'democratic' teaching. We should judge that theorizing and research based on this kind of commitment is not in general a wise research strategy, but we do not see anything inherently objectionable about it. Any research undertaking reflects implicit values in the sense that the researcher focuses attention on some things to the neglect of others, and it is in this sense only that most observation systems are ideologically based. But systematic observers have the distinctive merit that they make quite explicit the aspects of teaching on which they are focusing attention, and make any ideological commitment quite transparent. There is no reason to believe that those using other approaches do not have differential concerns and ideological commitments, but in their case it is impossible to judge how far these concerns and commitments have influenced their conclusions.

One common criticism of Flanders' system, however, does stem from a very obvious and fundamental characteristic of all systematic observation procedures: the categories in terms of which classroom behaviour is described are *predetermined*, and information irrelevant to these predetermined categories is not systematically recorded. Delamont and Hamilton (1976) are explicit in their criticism of this defining characteristic of systematic observation: 'The potential of interaction analysis to go beyond the categories is limited' (p. 9); and this, they rightly point out, means that analysis of data must be in terms of the concepts used in defining the categories. The value of systematic observation is therefore totally dependent on the descriptive and explanatory power of the concepts inherent in the system used. It is not, however, self-evident, as Delamont and Hamilton appear to suggest, that 'this should necessarily impede theoretical development' (p. 9). That must depend on a number of considerations to which we will return.

The use of predetermined categories has been criticized also on the grounds that one 'risks furnishing only a partial description' (Delamont and Hamilton, 1976, p. 9). Hargreaves (1972, p. 133), for example, complains that 'interaction analysts have been compelled by their method to ignore much of the elementary nature and structure of teacher – pupil interaction' and in losing the detail of the interaction, have failed to preserve its 'essential qualities'. Hargreaves, like Walker and Adelman is claiming that he knows before he starts what the essential qualities of interaction are; if those using systematic observation could make similar claims, they would have no need to justify the use of predetermined categories. Certainly, however, detail *is* lost and only a partial description is provided, but that is the case whoever the observer is and however he observes. The issue is *not* one of whether information is neglected, but rather one of how it is determined what information will be neglected. The competent systematic observer can be confident that he has decided what information he wants to collect and that he has not neglected any of this information. At the opposite extreme, one may collect information of a much more varied kind, noting whatever seems intuitively significant, but of course one neglects what seems unimportant and also what does not catch one's attention. The neglect of information as such is not a sustainable criticism of systematic observation.

One further criticism which is sometimes related to the pre-determined nature of systematic observation categories is that many systems are not suitable for all kinds of classroom context. A system devised to analyze lecturing, or one devised to categorize pupils' behaviour when working individually, tends to be unsuitable for the analysis of classroom discussions. As Walker and Adelman (1976) suggest, 'radical changes in the contexts of talk involve different qualities of communication, and these ultimately engage different identities in their participants' (p. 136). This criticism has been made, and has to be considered, at two quite different levels. At one level, it is perfectly clear that major differences in the social organization of classes and in the patterns of communication within them result in different kinds of phenomena and raise different kinds of question. Any researcher who did not recognize and take account of this, whatever methodology he adopted, would simply be incompetent. It is therefore reassuring, and far from a cause for complaint, that those using systematic observation have recognized the need for different observation systems for different kinds of classroom setting. But Walker and Adelman use the term 'context' in another sense, which leads to a more serious criticism of systematic observation. They say:

> In a class that has been together with the same teacher for a long time, each child can create a distinct identity which gives to teacher – pupil talk the quality of cryptic short-hand. The culture of the class becomes so strong, the meanings it assigns to particular items of talk so rich, that the talk itself becomes almost inaccessible to an outsider.
>
> (Walker and Adelman, 1976, p. 141)

In so far as such a state of affairs exists in a classroom, the possibilities of useful systematic observation – or indeed of any kind of observation – must be severely restricted: where talk is incomprehensible to the outsider, he cannot begin to analyze it. Any researcher would have to start by attempting to make himself less of an outsider, so that the meanings which were shared between teacher and pupils, but exclusive to them gradually became accessible to him. When he too came to share in their shared meanings, then he would have to decide whether or not it was appropriate to develop or to modify systematic observation procedures for use in this classroom.

We must confess that we have rarely been in classrooms which remotely resemble those described by Walker and Adelman. Yet we think the implied assertion cannot be denied: *to the extent that, and in those respects that, classroom activities involve shared meanings between teacher and pupils which depend upon the distinctive cultural and historical context of that classroom group, systematic observation is not an appropriate research technique.* Walker and Adelman clearly consider such distinctive shared meanings among teacher and pupils as phenomena of major significance for understanding classroom activities and therefore for the methodology of classroom study. We, on the other hand, are inclined to believe that such phenomena are relatively rare, and that when they do occur, the extent to which classroom communication is dependent on them is marginal. Fortunately, there seems no reason why observers should not be able to discover empirically the incidence of the use of such meanings in the contexts in which they are working: Walker and Adelman would seem to agree that recognition of the occurrence of effective communication which is not meaningful to the observer is quite possible.

In passing, it may be noted that it is necessary to distinguish such shared *meanings* between teacher and pupils from shared knowledge between them. In any classroom, teacher and pupils will share knowledge of past events within that classroom, including knowledge of what has been talked about, what projects or experiments have been done, and what films, curriculum materials or objects have been looked at. Where particular kinds of research questions are being investigated for which such shared knowledge is more generally relevant, for example questions concerned with how pupils' thinking on a particular theme develops in relation to the way the teacher presents that theme, only a very time-consuming research design involving continuous observation may be appropriate. But in general, it is only when shared knowledge is used to provide a distinctive *medium* for continuing communication that it raises problems for the observer.

A more general criticism of systematic observation is that, as Hargreaves (1972, p. 135) puts it, 'no account is taken of the meanings which participants give to their interactions'. This is certainly the case. Furthermore, systematic observation does not provide any evidence on the mental activities of participants. Delamont and Hamilton (1976) quote Smith and Geoffrey (1968, p. 96), who put this well:

> The way (the teacher) poses his problems, the kind of goals and sub-goals he is trying to reach, the alternatives he weighs . . . are aspects of teaching which are frequently lost to the behavioural oriented empiricist who focuses on what the teacher does to the exclusion of how he thinks about teaching.

Both these comments are making unquestionably valid assertions about the evidence which systematic observation provides. It may be necessary, however, to emphasize what is, and what is not, being validly asserted. First, systematic observation provides no direct evidence on the actions of participants which are not overt or on their perceptions of their own or others' actions; but it cannot be validly asserted that:

1 no justifiable inferences can be made about mental activities or perceptions from systematic observation data; or that
2 there *are* techniques for obtaining direct evidence about mental activities or perceptions; or that
3 systematic observation precludes the use of other techniques for obtaining indirect evidence about mental activities or perceptions.

The other thing which has to be emphasized is that it is to the meanings attached to events by individual participants that the observer does not have access, whereas communication is dependent on a shared system of meanings. When an observer describes such events as 'Smith directed Jones to sit down', or 'The conversation was about the conservation of energy', or 'Smith made a negative evaluative comment on Jones's performance', he *is* clearly talking about the meaning of the observed acts rather than describing meaningless behaviour. He is not, however, attempting to interpret the distinctive meaning attached to these acts by any one of the participants. Instead, he is making use of the system of conventional meanings which is implicit within the culture to which the teacher and the pupils and he himself belong. Because he is a member of the culture, not a stranger, the observer is able to categorize classroom events on the basis of the shared meanings within the culture. What he is unable to do is to take cognizance either of any meanings shared between the teacher and pupils as a result of aspects of their distinctive shared history which he has not yet understood, or of the varying connotations which individual participants attach to events.

The implications of this interpretation of what the observer is doing perhaps require some elaboration. When Smith looks at Jones and says 'Jones, why does the blue substance spread through the liquid?' (probably with a particular kind of voice inflection), and then silently looks at Jones (probably with a particular kind of facial expression), the observer can unambiguously categorize the event as 'Smith asks Jones a question seeking an explanation of diffusion in a liquid'. Now Smith might describe the event as 'giving Jones a chance to show he knows something', and Jones might describe the event as 'Smith trying to get at me'; but if either of them denied the validity of the observer's description, they would simply be wrong, because the observer would be describing at least part of what the behaviour which occurred means in English in Britain. No assumptions are made here about the effectiveness of classroom communication; but the assumption is made that except in the distinctive circumstances to which Walker and Adelman have drawn attention, communication is dependent on the system of conventional meanings available within the wider culture. More fundamentally, this interpretation implies that the systematic observer is concerned with an objective reality (or, if one prefers, a shared intersubjective reality) of classroom events. This is not to suggest that the subjective meanings of events to participants are not important, but only that these are not accessible to the observer and that there is an objective reality to classroom activity which does not depend on these meanings.

A different focus of criticism relates to systematic observers' description of classroom activities in terms of defined units of behaviour. One kind of criticism of this suggests that systematic observers impose 'arbitrary boundaries on continuous phenomena' (Delamont and Hamilton, 1976, p. 9); and a closely related criticism, made, for example, by Hargreaves (1972), is that links and chains of behaviour are lost. The suggestion that boundaries are arbitrary is certainly a valid complaint against some of the earliest observation procedures, which used a simple time unit. Most systems, however, such as those of Bellack *et al* (1966), Gump (1967), Gallagher (1970), and Smith and Meux (1962) use units which are based on their authors' study and conceptualization of classroom activity: whatever weaknesses they may have, their units are not arbitrary. The suggestion that the phenomena being studied are continuous (and therefore, implicitly, that *any* boundaries or analytic units are misleading) is difficult to understand;

presumably such critics are not suggesting that classroom activity does not consist of differentiable events, but rather that these events are related one to another: if not, it is difficult to know what they might mean. This leads, then, to the suggestion that links and chains of behaviour are lost. Clearly this is the case so far as aspects of behaviour which are not reflected in the predetermined categories are concerned. Equally clearly, however, it is far from the case for those aspects of behaviour which *are* reflected in the predetermined categories; and indeed, the systematic abstraction of these aspects of behaviour greatly facilitates the recognition of chains of inter-related events, and of recurrent patterns of such relationships.

Another criticism of systematic observation research has been that it is over-concerned with quantification and with seeking statistical general-izations. For Stenhouse (1975), this is a major complaint:

> In research terms . . . I believe (interaction analysis) is a cul-de-sac. And many of its weaknesses come from the attempt to provide quantitative data which will support generalizations, an attempt not of central importance to the teacher seeking an understanding of the unique as well as the generalizable elements in his own work (p. 148).

Stenhouse appears to take the curious view that supportable general-izations are relatively easy to attain, whereas valid statements about individ-ual classrooms present greater difficulties. However, he is quite correct in his view that the use of systematic observation procedures is geared to exploring and testing the generalizability of concepts and relationships through the quantification of aspects of classroom activity: there would be little point in spending the considerable effort which is necessary in order to devise clear and reliable ways of categorizing aspects of classroom activity if one were not then to make use of the resulting categories in counting and comparing.

To discover whether researchers who do not use systematic observation make use of quantification, we spent a few minutes – only a few minutes were required – turning over the pages of Stubbs and Delamont's (1976) book. The first quantitative statements which we found were as follows:

From Furlong (1976):

> 'A lot of Carol's classroom behaviour takes place in the context of an interaction set' (p. 28);

> 'Extreme behaviour like this is very rare' (p. 31);

> '. . . a fairly standard pattern of interaction emerged' (p. 36).

From Delamont (1976b):

> 'Miss Odyssey's interaction is generally less formal and less ritualized than Miss Iliad's' (p. 117)

> 'In a typical lesson, Mrs Cavendish would ask someone to volunteer . . .' (p. 126).

From Walker and Adelman (1976):

> '. . . quite a lot of the things the class found very funny, we did not "get" ' (p. 138).

> '. . . we often heard Jim Binham use phrases like . . .' (p. 140).

As one might expect, then, most observers base many of their conclusions about what happens in classrooms on quantification. What differentiates systematic observers from others is that their quantifications are precise, while other observers' quantifications are necessarily vague; and whereas systematic observers' generalizations *are* on a statistical basis, the basis of other observers' generalizations is far from clear.

A complaint which it is more difficult to come to terms with, because its emotive content seems to predominate over its descriptive meaning, is that systematic observation is mechanistic or that it implies a mechanistic conception of classroom activities. Against what is this complaint directed? Certainly the procedures involved in using systematic observation might be described as mechanical, if that is to mean that they are not creative: that is a necessary consequence of using predetermined categories. Also, there are of course those who view any commitment to systematic abstraction and to quantification as mechanistic, irrespective of the context: clearly systematic observation, when competently planned and implemented, lacks the concern for the particular, the spontaneity, and the intellectual confusion which some see as essential to humanity, and is in that sense mechanistic. One plausible interpretation of this kind of complaint which may have to be taken seriously is that the use of systematic observation implies an exclusive concern with overt behaviour, or with causal as opposed to teleological explanations, or with criteria of effectiveness as opposed to moral or aesthetic criteria. However, although the use of systematic observation may be compatible with these positions, none of these positions is implied by its use: the use of systematic observation does not in itself imply any distinctive concern or any theoretical position except for the assumption that within any culture actions have meanings which do not depend on the interpretations of individual participants.

Finally, systematic observation has been criticized on the grounds that assumptions are made about the lack of influence of the observer on the classroom activity. This is a criticism which is unquestionably valid and of considerable theoretical importance. Provided that sensible steps are taken to win the cooperation of teacher and pupils, however, and to accustom them to the observer's presence, and provided that it is recognized that the observer's presence is likely to reduce the incidence of acts which are perceived by participants to be nonconformist, we incline to the view that the influence of the observer's presence is not generally of major practical importance. Yet there is no way in which we could demonstrate that this is so, except by using procedures which would be technically very difficult and morally quite unacceptable.

This problem of ignorance of the observer's influence is, of course, one which is common to all observational approaches, except perhaps where the teacher is the observer and the kind of observation he is doing is such that he conceives of it as a part of his normal teaching activity. The participant observer either makes different assumptions about the influence of his presence, but is like the systematic observer in having no means for testing the validity of these assumptions, or else he may make no assumptions, but thus put himself in a position of finding out only about classrooms with observers in them.

Examination of criticisms which have been made of systematic observation has thus led us to the conclusions summarized in Table 1.

Table 1: Necessary and distinctive features of systematic observation

Characteristic	Necessary to systematic observation	Distinctive to systematic observation
1 Ideological bias	Yes	No
2 Value dependent on predetermined concepts	Yes	Yes
3 Partial description	Yes	No
4 Need to differentiate according to context	Yes	No
5 Inappropriate in so far as class and teacher have developed distinctive culture	Yes	Yes
6 Provides no direct evidence on individual participants' thinking or interpretations	Yes	No
7 Arbitrary units	No	
8 Neglect of relationship between events	No	
9 Quantification	Yes	No
10 Statistical basis for generalization	Yes	Yes
11 Implies behaviourist position	No	
12 Untested assumptions about observer's presence	Yes	No

Characteristics

From the criticisms made of it, we have thus been able to derive three
necessary and distinctive characteristics of systematic observation: its value
is totally dependent on the descriptive and explanatory value of the concepts
implicit in the system used; it is an inappropriate technique for use in any
classroom in which communication is dependent on a distinctive culture to
which the observer does not belong: and generalizations derived from
systematic observation are, in the first instance, statistical and based on
relatively precise quantitative data. In addition, we have suggested that
classroom observation is not in general the most useful available technique
to use in inferring how teachers or pupils think about what they are doing or
how they interpret events; and that the evidence which is collected by
systematic observation is about the 'objective reality' of the classroom, about
the meaning of classroom events in the culture to which the teacher, pupils
and observer belong.

Uses of Systematic Observation

Given that systematic observation has these characteristics, for what purposes if any is it useful? In view of the multiplicity of purposes for which
people study classrooms, we cannot hope to give an exhaustive answer to
this question.

Recognition of this multiplicity of purposes is important in discussion of
the methodology of classroom study, and it is our belief that it is a neglect of
this that has been responsible for much of the confusion and the heat which
has been generated in such discussion. For example, it appears obvious to us
that attempts to identify and compare teachers' and pupils' perceptions of
classroom situations are unlikely to be facilitated by the use of systematic
observation. On the other hand, it would be perverse not to use systematic
observation if one were attempting to discover to what extent certain specified innovations in teaching methods had been implemented. Decisions
about the data-gathering procedures appropriate for one of these purposes
carry no implications for the procedures appropriate for the other. Here,
however, we shall limit our discussion to the consideration of a few central
issues relating to two general questions which concern us: *Why do pupils
learn what they learn? Why do teachers teach as they do?*

The first thing to note about these questions is that they are ambiguous in
that one might be seeking in answer to them either purposive or causal
explanations. In general, either kind of explanation would be valuable, but
people with different theoretical standpoints will tend to emphasize one kind
or the other. We would note that the purposive version of the questions is

subsidiary to the causal version: one could answer a causal question of this type by saying that what distinguished those who learned something was that they wanted to learn it, and by then proceeding to identify their purposes in wanting to learn it. Usually, of course, an adequate causal explanation would have to include other factors such as the opportunity people had had to learn, whether they had attended to relevant stimuli, and the amount of practice they had had. Our point is simply that a purposive explanation of learning or teaching, while important, is by definition an arbitrarily limited kind of explanation, so that our understanding of teaching and learning will remain severely restricted unless we can establish causal as well as purposive explanations.

Considering the first of our questions, 'Why do pupils learn what they learn?', to discover what happens to pupils or what pupils do in classrooms, one might seek evidence about three kinds of thing: first, what pupils can report after having been in a classroom; second, their thought processes while in the classroom; and third, observable events during the course of classroom activities. We may assume that pupils can report, or in other ways reveal, *what* they have learned. Furthermore, some of the information which they have selected and assimilated will relate to the events which have occurred within the classroom and to their own mental activities in the classroom. We can find no reason to assume, however, that pupils' selection and retention of information corresponds closely with the characteristics of classroom events which influence their learning, or with the mental activities in which they have engaged while in the classroom. In other words, there is no reason to believe that pupils' reports on what happened will be a valid source of information about why and how they learn what they learn.

On the other hand, evidence about pupils' thought processes while in classrooms would be directly relevant to attempts to explain processes of classroom learning: our lack of adequate procedures for obtaining access to pupils', or indeed to teachers', thought processes during classroom interaction is the major barrier preventing progress in our understanding of classroom life. Even if one had such access, however, one would still be left with equally important questions about what *determines* a pupil's thought processes and in particular about how these are related to other classroom events. In addition, one might discover that much classroom learning could not be accounted for in terms of conscious processes. Thus analysis of the objective reality of classrooms must be an essential component in any rational strategy for explaining pupils' classroom learning. And, in the meantime, in the absence of evidence on pupils' thinking, the only possible way in which we can hope to increase our understanding is to seek direct relationships between characteristics of this objective reality and characteristics of what pupils learn.

Turning to our second question, 'Why do teachers teach as they do?', the connection between it and the first is clear: the only way in which a teacher can influence pupils' learning is through his overt activity in the classroom or by controlling other observable characteristics of the classroom environment. (Correspondingly, it is only through their overt activities that the pupils can influence the teacher.) Therefore, because what is of greatest importance about teachers as teachers is the influence they have on their pupils, when we ask 'Why do teachers teach as they do?', what we are primarily interested in explaining is teachers' overt activities in classrooms. Furthermore, there is a great deal of evidence to show that what teachers do in classrooms cannot be ascertained through extrapolations from teachers' accounts of their intentions or from their accounts of what they do. Taking one account from the many available, we reproduce Elliott's (1976) quotation of a teacher's reaction when confronted with aspects of the objective reality of his classroom:

> The playback of a class discussion was a shattering blow! I had no idea how much discussion was dominated by me, how rarely I allowed children to finish their comments, what leading questions I asked, and how much I gave away what I considered to be the 'right' answers (p. 62).

What we have so far shown is that attempts to explain teachers' classroom teaching or pupils' classroom learning must depend on analyses of the objective reality of classrooms. It does not, of course, follow from this that systematic observation procedures must be used. Whether or not this is the case will depend on considerations of how theoretical concepts and generalizations can best be generated and tested.

Since no-one concerned with the study of classrooms has been notably successful in generating and validating theoretical explanations, it would be foolhardy of us to attempt to specify how such advances will come. There are, however, various considerations which seem likely to be necessary but which most of us have tended to neglect.

First, we have nearly all of us been over-ambitious. Some of us, in attempting to work in terms of Grand Theory, have used concepts of such generality that no testable statements about classrooms emerge. Others, however, have still been seeking instant solutions to major problems of policy and so have failed to reflect adequately on the mediating processes whereby phenomena might be related. We are more likely to make progress if we take classrooms rather than general theories as our starting point, and if we seek relationships between events which impinge directly upon one another.

Secondly, in such study of directly related events, it is important to distinguish clearly between the different sets of events. Often these different sets of events are most appropriately studied by different procedures, for example by observation and by interviewing; but much of the potential value is lost if the information collected is collapsed to give one global picture in which gaps in each type of evidence are filled through inferences from the other type of evidence.

Thirdly, on the other hand, the different sets of events should be conceptualized in related terms. If we are seeking relationships between different things, we have to attend to those aspects of the different things which are most likely to connect them. One of the weaknesses of some systematic observation studies is that each set of events has been conceptualized in perfectly sensible ways for describing these events, but without the imposition of the further constraint that connections between the different sets should be sought in the initial conceptualization. Flanders' system provides a good example of those to which this criticism does not apply: teachers' actions and pupils' actions are categorized in conceptually related terms.

Fourthly, classroom research, like most educational research, has suffered from conceptual confusion. We cannot hope to make progress unless we spend much more effort on the clarification of the concepts we use and of the questions we ask.

Of the published research which we know, that which most clearly meets these four criteria is Elliott and Adelman's Ford Teaching Project (Elliott and Adelman, 1973); and we think it significant that this research produced some very interesting specific hypotheses about teaching and its effects. So too did Smith and Geoffrey's (1968) research, which also comes close to meeting our criteria. It may be noted that neither of these investigations used systematic observation. It is no criticism of these admirable studies, however, to note also that they did not go beyond the formulation of hypotheses. To test their hypotheses, they would have had to meet two further criteria. One of these is that corresponding to the need for conceptual clarity there is a need for operational clarity and precision. Conceptual definitions are rarely specific enough to allow the reliable recognition or categorization of particular events, and operational definitions which demonstrably correspond to the conceptual definitions are therefore also required. In the context of classroom observation, this means the use of systematic observation procedures, which are nothing more or less than articulated sets of operational definitions.

Systematic observation is required to provide the precision of categorization needed for testing hypotheses about classroom events. It also provides the other necessary condition, the precise quantification which makes statistical analyses possible. As was demonstrated earlier, theoretical generalization based on quantification is far from being the exclusive preserve of those who use systematic observation; only they, however, are able to quantify with sufficient precision to be able to test the validity of their generalizations.

Some very interesting studies have been reported in which systematic observation has not been used and yet from which the researchers concerned have drawn very firm conclusions. The study by Keddie (1971) of the stratification of classroom knowledge is a good example. Keddie's claims are important, but they cannot be claimed to have been substantiated by her

necessarily selective use of quotations. Assuming that her conceptual definitions were clear, it would not have been a major task for her also to construct
operational definitions and so to go on to provide precise quantitative data.
It might then have been very difficult to dismiss her conclusions, as one now
can, as the distorted interpretation of an observer highly committed to a
preconceived view of what happens in classrooms. In this way, potentially
important contributions to classroom research are largely wasted.

In general, there is a need in studying any aspect of classroom activity both
for flexible observation to generate useful perspectives and hypotheses and
for systematic observation to provide precise descriptions and to test
hypotheses. Furthermore both these phases, we have suggested, should normally involve the collection of other types of data to which the classroom
observations can be related. However, the variety of questions which can
and should be asked about classrooms makes any such generalizations dangerous. What we do think we have demonstrated is that the use of systematic
observation does not have many of the distinctive weaknesses with which it
has been charged, that it is an essential component in any strategy for
explaining what happens in classrooms, and that it complements rather than
opposes other techniques of classroom study.

References

BELLACK, A.A., KLIEBARD, H.M., HYMAN, R.T. and SMITH, F.L. (1966). *The
    Language of the Classroom*. New York: Teachers' College Press.
DELAMONT, S. (1976a). *Interaction in the Classroom*. London: Methuen.
DELAMONT, S. (1976b). 'Beyond Flanders' fields: the relationship of subject-matter
    and individuality to classroom style'. In: Stubbs, M. and Delamont, S. *Explora-
    tions in Classroom Observation*. London: Wiley.
DELAMONT, S. and HAMILTON, D. (1976). 'Classroom research: A critique and a
    new approach'. In: Stubbs, M. and Delamont, S., op. cit.
ELLIOTT, J. and ADELMAN, C. (1973). 'Reflecting where the action is: the design of
    the Ford Teaching Project', *Education for Teaching*, 92, 8–20.
ELLIOTT, J. (1976). 'Preparing teachers for classroom accountability', *Education for
    Teaching*, 100, 49–71.
FLANDERS, N.A. (1970). *Analyzing Classroom Behaviour*. Reading, Mass:
    Addison-Wesley.
FURLONG, V. (1976). 'Interaction sets in the classroom: towards a study of pupil
    knowledge'. In: Stubbs, M. and Delamont, S., op. cit.
GALLAGHER, J.J. (1970). 'Three studies of the classroom'. In: Gallagher, J.J.,.
    Nuthall, G.A. and Rosenshine, B. (Eds.) *Classroom Observation*. AERA
    Monograph Series on Curriculum Evaluation, Monograph No. 6. Chicago: Rand
    McNally.
GUMP, P.V. (1967). *The Classroom Behaviour Setting: Its Nature and Relation to
    Student Behavior*. Final Report, Contract No. OE-4-10-107, U.S. Bureau of
    Research, HEW.
HARGREAVES, D.H. (1972). *Interpersonal Relations and Education*. London:
    Routledge & Kegan Paul.

KEDDIE, N. (1971). 'Classroom knowledge'. In: Young, M.F.D. (Ed.) *Knowledge and Control*. London: Collier-Macmillan.

SMITH, L.M. and GEOFFREY, W. (1968). *The Complexities of an Urban Classroom*. New York: Holt, Rinehart and Winston.

SMITH, B.O. and MEUX, M.O. (1962). *A Study of the Logic of Teaching*. Urbana, Illinois: University of Illinois Press.

STENHOUSE, L. (1975). *An Introduction to Curriculum Research and Development*. London: Heinemann Educational.

STUBBS, M. and DELAMONT, S. (1976). *Explorations in Classroom Observation*. London: Wiley.

WALKER, R. and ADELMAN, C. (1975). 'Interaction analysis in informal classrooms: a critical comment on the Flanders system', *Br. J. Educ. Psychol.*, 45, 1.

WALKER, R. and ADELMAN, C. (1976). 'Strawberries'. In: Stubbs, M. and Delamont, S., op cit.

1.3

Revisiting Classroom Research: A Continuing Cautionary Tale

S. Delamont and D. Hamilton

> We took the challenge provided by our mentors to provide a mirror for educators. Our intent was to help educators look at themselves . . . to turn their attention to what *actually* goes on in schools rather than to be so singularly preoccupied with what *ought* to go on in them.
>
> (Wolcott, 1982, p. 7)

All classroom researchers share Wolcott's goal. In this paper we revisit a research area we surveyed together in 1972 and examine some of the routes taken towards Wolcott's goal in the last decade. In 1972 we were both research students in Liam Hudson's (1977) Centre for Research in the Educational Sciences at Edinburgh University, and participants in a series of small conferences on classroom research run at Lancaster. Responding to the prevailing orthodoxy we wrote a critical, even polemical, paper, making a strongly worded attack on the kind of classroom research which uses a prespecified coding schedule ('systematic' observation) and a determined plea for more attention to be paid to an alternative observational strategy, the ethnographic (also called participant observation or anthropological observation).

The article was accepted by a journal and appeared within twelve months (Hamilton and Delamont, 1974). It was also included as a 'position paper' in a collection of essays on classrooms (Delamont and Hamilton, 1976). Our arguments were by no means unique, as others were making similar points elsewhere (Coulthard, 1974; Walker and Adelman, 1975a). However we had, apparently, produced a benchmark, mentioned in everyone's literature reviews and either lauded or vilified in later debate. In ten years it has been reprinted at least eight times, and it has continued to be attacked by exponents of the 'systematic' observational tradition throughout the decade (e.g. McIntyre and MacLeod, 1978).

Such a *succes d'estime* is flattering, but looking back it also produces discomfiture in the authors. In some respects the paper is badly dated. Since 1972, although the basic arguments still retain their relevance, there has been a major change of emphasis in the American systematic observation research, and in Britain classroom studies have taken a path different from the one we foresaw. There has also been a rapid growth of ethnographic research in the USA and the UK in both pure academic projects and in the evaluation of innovations. It seems to be both necessary and desirable to prepare a new version of our argument which takes account of these changes. The basic position we adopted in the early 1970s is still the same, but it is hard to disentangle the argument from the specific empirical examples.

Accordingly in this paper we do three things: (1) examine the current state of play between the two traditions in classroom research; (2) present our reasons for preferring the ethnographic approach ourselves; and (3) look forward to the next decade of classroom studies. This article replaces the 1974 version, including as it does the same basic theoretical position and methodological arguments, in the context of recent empirical material.

Our position in 1974 was a cautious one. We argued for more attention to be paid to the then neglected ethnographic tradition, but also accepted that 'systematic' observation schedules had strengths. We concluded that researchers should be scrupulous in discovering the limits of whatever technique they adopted, and accepting those limitations explicitly. In 1984 we would wish to make the following general points about our position on classroom research.

Both of us are inclined towards the ethnographic approach to educational research, but not so fanatically or exclusively that we wish to dissuade other people using other methods. Part of our attachment to the ethnographic is a desire to treat educational research as an 'open-ended' endeavour, where premature closure is a dangerous possibility. Therefore we do not endorse views which treat research (i.e. ethnographic versus systematic observation; normative versus interpretive, etc.) as the equivalent of self-contained epistemological and theoretical paradigms. There is a tendency for educational researchers who advocate one 'method' or another to imply far too narrow and prematurely prescriptive views of what counts as legitimate enquiry.

Throughout this paper we draw a distinction between ethnographic and systematic classroom observation. However we wish to emphasize that any such distinction is not hard-and-fast. Differences between methods are often overplayed and the cleavage (complete in the minds of some researchers) is not absolute. We use the distinction to characterize the 'state of the art' and do not wish to endorse it.

Studying Classrooms in the 1970s

David H. Hargreaves (1980) has suggested that the 1970s were a 'notable decade' for classroom studies both because of the number of projects and the wide range of theoretical and methodological approaches. Hargreaves hoped that the 'three great traditions' of studying classrooms – systematic observation, ethnographic observation and sociolinguistic studies – would crossfertilize each other, and not waste time on squabbling from entrenched positions. Certainly the intellectual hostility between the various classroom researchers has lessened since we wrote in 1974. However, there is, at root, a real difference between the systematic observers and the ethnographers which cannot be glossed over. We address that difference, with empirical examples, and do not dwell upon Hargreaves's third approach: the sociolinguistic (but see Edwards, 1980). The underlying tension between the research done with a prespecified coding scheme and that done from an ethnographic perspective is the tension between positivism and inter-actionism which runs through all social science. It is a fundamental differ-ence of approach to the study of humans and human society, and it cannot be done away with by calling for interdisciplinary *rapprochements*. More than a century of social science research exists, based on distinct conceptions of humankind, and it cannot be wished away by the pious hopes of classroom observers. This is not the place to rehearse all the debates about positivism (see, for example, Davies, 1976, p. 16); about normative and interpretive paradigms (Cohen and Manion, 1981); or about sociologies of 'order' and 'control' (Dawe, 1970). But we do believe that the different traditions of classroom research which we discuss in this paper are merely one empirical example of two distinct kinds of social science methodology. Classroom research may well benefit from the approach advocated by Hargreaves (1980) but a desire to improve teaching (McIntyre, 1980) will not, in itself, overcome deep fissures between schools of social science. Bearing this *caveat* in mind, we outline some recent developments in classroom research on both sides of the Atlantic.

In the USA the early part of the 1970s saw the dominant approach to classroom observation as a systematic one. This was the group of prespecified coding schemes focusing on verbal behaviour and using it to measure/assess the empathy of the teacher and warmth of the atmosphere. These coding schemes came from a social-psychological tradition with its roots in the 1939–49 period (Amidon and Hough, 1967) and the best known example, Flanders' Interaction Analysis Categories (FIAC), dates from the late 1950s (Flanders, 1970). A directory of observational coding systems produced in the USA (as a researchers' 'pharmacopoeia') (Simon and Boyer, 1974) contained ninety-nine systems, 30 per cent of which were directly derived from FIAC. This domination was recorded in our paper, together with our concern about over-enthusiasm for such an approach. Even as we published our doubts about the field there was a change of direction in the USA (recorded by Rosenshine and Berliner, 1978). Rosenshine states that the emphasis on the socio-emotional climate of classrooms, and the 'warmth' of teachers which 'was a burning issue in the early 1970s . . . doesn't seem worth debating today'. In America attention shifted from the teacher and her speech towards the pupils and their behaviour. The systematic classroom research undertaken in the USA since 1974 has focused more closely on pupils' behaviour, especially their 'academic engaged time' (Denham and Lieberman, 1980). Flanders and his colleagues are no longer the dominant influence in the field (Borich and Madden, 1977). During the 1970s American classroom researchers also became much more interested in ethnographic procedures (e.g. Tikunoff and Ward, 1980; Spindler, 1982; Popkewitz and Tabachnick, 1981).

In Britain the pattern of research has been rather different. Although there have been a range of projects funded using prespecified coding schemes – and the investment in them has been much larger than that in 'pure' ethnography – most of the projects have used homegrown schedules. Inter-action analysis did not, as we had feared, sweep all before it. The British version of 'Mirrors' (Galton, 1978) looks different from its American foster parent. The large, and the influential, projects in the UK did not follow the Flanders' pattern in the second half of the 1970s. Hobbs and Kleinberg (1978), Bennett (1976), Rutter *et al.* (1979) and the ORACLE project (Galton, Simon and Croll, 1980) used principles very different from interaction analy-sis. Ethnographic studies have also proliferated in Britain since 1972 (Ham-mersley, 1980), although there are still many aspects of education in the UK for which such data are lacking.

In summary, the development of classroom studies since 1972 has been very different from the future we feared. Many of the changes are along the lines we hoped to see. However, we feel that there are valid points in our 1974 argument which we made specifically in relation to interaction analysis research, but have *general* application to the systematic observation sched-ules used since FIAC fell from favour.

The Continuing Critique of Systematic Observation

Our criticisms of the prespecified coding schedule as a research tool in the classroom are illustrated here with reference to two recent British systems: that of Boydell used in the ORACLE project (Galton, Simon and Croll, 1980) and that of Rutter and his colleagues (1979).

Our main criticisms of prespecified coding schedules are for their expo-nents strengths, and we, in making the following seven criticims, are not insensible that each of our flaws will be seen by others as a source of potency.

We set out our general points and then given particular illustrations of them from the two studies.

1 The aim of coding schemes using prespecified categories is to produce numerical and normative data. The findings are similar in kind to those produced by tests and questionnaires. Suitable for statistical treatment, the data produced tell the reader about 'average' or 'typical' classrooms, teachers and pupils.

2 Systematic observation schemes typically ignore the temporal and spatial context in which the data are collected. Thus although this is not explicit in the description of the schedules, most systems use data gathered during very short periods of observation (i.e. measured in minutes and single lessons rather than hours or days); and the observer is not expected to record information about the physical setting like that discussed by Hamilton (1976), Delamont (1976a, 1976b) or Bullivant (1978). For example, only ten of the ninety-nine systems in Simon and Boyer (1974) record any information about the physical environment at all. Divorced from their social and temporal (or historical) context in this way, the data collected may gloss over aspects relevant to their interpretation.

3 Prespecified coding systems are usually concerned only with overt, observable behaviour. They do not take directly into account the differing intentions that may lie behind such behaviour. Where intention is relevant to the observational category (as in Flanders's Category 2, 'Teacher praises or encourages') the observer has himself to impute the intention, making no attempt to discover the actor's actual or self-perceived intention. Thus by concentrating on surface features, interaction analysis runs the risk of neglecting underlying but possibly more meaningful features. A comprehensive understanding of classroom life may, for example, depend upon the translation of 'silent languages' (Smith and Geoffrey, 1968) or the uncovering of 'hidden curricula' (Snyder, 1971). The papers by Walker and Adelman (1976b) and Pollard (1980), and books by Hargreaves *et al.* (1975) and Swidler (1979) are examples of kinds of analysis which may be necessary to understand the underlying features of verbal interaction in the classroom.

4 Prespecified coding systems are expressly concerned with 'what can be categorized or measured' (Simon and Boyer, 1974, p. 4). They may, however, obscure, distort or ignore the qualitative features which they claim to investigate by using crude measurement techniques or having ill-defined boundaries between the categories.

5 Prespecified coding systems focus on 'small bits of action or behaviour rather than global concepts' (Simon and Boyer, 1974, p. 4). Thus, inevitably, they have a tendency to generate a superabundance of data

which, for the purposes of analysis, must be linked either to a complex set of descriptive concepts – customarily the original categories – or to a small number of global concepts built up from these categories (e.g. Flanders's 'direct/indirect ratio' built up from combinations of categories 1, 2, 3, 6, and 7). But since the categories may have been devised in the first place to reduce the global concepts to small bits of action or behaviour, the exercise may well be circular. The potential of these systems to go beyond the categories is limited. This circularity and lack of potential to generate fresh insights necessarily impedes theoretical development.

6 The systems utilize prespecified categories. If the category systems are intended to assist explanation, then the prespecification may render the explanations tautological. That is, category systems may assume the truth of what they claim to be explaining. For example, if a set of categories is based on the assumption that the teacher is in the same position as the leader of a T-group, any explanation of 'teaching' in other terms is not possible.

7 Finally, we feel that, by placing arbitrary (and little understood) boundaries on continuous phenomena category systems may create an initial bias from which it is extremely difficult to escape. Reality frozen in this way is not always easy to liberate from its static representation.

All these limitations inherent in interaction analysis systems are implicitly or explicitly acknowledged by their originators (e.g. Flanders, 1970, Chapter 2). However, they are not usually acknowledged by other researchers and soon slip from view even in the writings of the originators themselves. We believe that if such systems are to be used, these limitations must not be allowed to become implicit, but must be openly acknowledged all the time. The methods must not be seen as something they are not. To be valid as methods for studying the classroom, the techniques must be constantly scrutinized, not once accepted and then taken for granted. In 1972/3 we used the Flanders system to illustrate these points. However, they are general criticisms, equally applicable to the systems under scrutiny here.

Normative data are often interest-catching and attention-arousing, but they frequently raise more queries than they can solve. For example, Karweit (1981) reports a study of fifth-grade maths classes in which the amount of 'non-instructional time' varied from 3 per cent to 18 per cent of maths time. This is interesting, but in itself only tantalizing. We believe such findings are chiefly intriguing because they raise the issue of why teachers decide to do things so differently, and one strategy would be to ask participants for their accounts. Systematic observation precludes taking notice of such data.

In the first ORACLE book (Galton, Simon and Croll, 1980, p. 110) the authors, having spent two long chapters giving all the normative results obtained with two schedules disarmingly admit: 'most of the teachers differed in some respects from the typical profile.' They move on to separate six teaching styles which are the main topic of the project. Again the tantalizing question is *why* the teachers chose to act as they did. The ORACLE data cannot inform us about that.

In the interests of objectivity, many systematic research studies feel compelled to survey large numbers of classrooms. It is argued (correctly) that small samples may fail to provide statements relevant to the population at large. Such an approach (even if it can achieve true randomness) may, however, fail to treat as significant local perturbations or unusual effects. Indeed, despite their potential significance for the classroom or classrooms to which they apply, atypical results are seldom studied in detail. They are ironed out as 'blurred averages' and lost to discussion.

Perhaps the most infuriating normative finding comes from the Rutter (1979) study. The authors report (p. 112) a negative correlation between observed pupil behaviour and the head-teacher's emphasis on pastoral care reported in interviews. They offer various speculations about reasons for this, but there is nothing of the subtlety of the similar problem as examined by Metz (1978). Equally tantalizing is the Rutter team's finding (p. 118) that schools where lessons finished early had worse pupil behaviour than those which used up the whole lesson.

Lack of contextual data characterizes most research using coding schedules. Karweit (1981) discusses appropriate observational periods for 'the detection of time-on-task effects on achievement', and seriously suggests that five periods of ten minutes each can give a reliable estimate of the amount of engaged time. At another extreme Wolcott (1973) spent two full years observing one elementary school principal.

Galton and Simon (1980, pp. 190–1) report that the teaching styles they isolated using the Teacher Record were age-related. Older (and more experienced?) teachers adopted different classroom styles from younger (less experienced?) ones. This finding can only be understood if data are gathered on teacher careers and life histories of a kind eschewed by ORACLE. Similar criticisms about the lack of attention paid to context and meaning variables have been made about the Rutter (1979) research by at least three reviewers (Reynolds, 1980; Hargreaves, 1980; and Blackstone, 1980). The detailed study of 'progressive' Leicestershire primary schools by Ann and Harold Berlak (1981) shows the importance of observation in depth. They found that what, in a short period of observation, appeared to be unstructured classrooms were actually tightly controlled in ways not immediately visible to a visitor. The history of the class had to be built up in order to understand it.

Emphasis on Overt Behaviour

Our doubts about the undue emphasis on overt behaviour is echoed by
Harry Wolcott's (1981) comment on the systematic observers' efforts to
achieve inter-observer reliability:

> If I am directed to observe eye movement, gait, proximity etc., then we can talk
> about reliability, but when you so direct me, I become your observer, an
> extension of your senses or your system. With Flanders, I floundered, wonder-
> ing how a whole generation of 'trained' classroom observers could abide with
> so few categories for sorting everything that goes on in classrooms.
>
> (Wolcott, 1981)

The emphasis on overt behaviour is revealed as problematic in the American Beginning Teaching Evaluation Study (Denham and Lieberman, 1980)
and in the ORACLE project (Galton, Simon and Croll, 1980) when the
researchers studied pupils' academic engaged time. As the researchers admit,
observers have to 'guess', or 'impute', whether pupils are working, when, for
example, they stop writing and look out of the window. 'Thinking' is not
observable, yet is crucial to the observers' codings of pupils' work habits in
both studies. A parallel example, pointed out by Andrew Hargreaves (1980),
is the coding of pupil 'lateness' in the Rutter research. The Rutter team (1979,
p. 236) offer an unproblematic definition of a 'late' pupil, for the observer's
instruction states:

> The number of pupils in the class and the number who arrived after the start of
> the lesson is to be recorded.

Andrew Hargreaves points out that:

> 'being late' is subject to negotiation between teacher and pupil and dependent
> upon the criteria employed by the teacher, the reasons provided by the pupil
> and so forth.

The complexities and subtleties of such negotiations are examined in the
work of Stebbins (1975) and a comparison of the two sets of data reveals the
threadbare nature of the Rutter team's concept.

Crude Measurement Techniques

There is no doubt that observers can be trained to use complex coding
schedules with considerable reliability. However, some of the categorizations and distinctions which underlie such systems may do violence to classroom reality. In the Rutter research, teachers' actions were separated into
those 'on the topic' and those related to pupil behaviour. We accept observers
were able to do this, but argue that it is a pointless distinction in most schools.

Similarly the Rutter coding 'Personal' (the observer is told to 'score for specifically personal comments, which would usually indicate some background knowledge of, or interest in, the child, home, or activities') strikes us as a clumsy and crude categorization. The ORACLE project's Pupil Record includes a category 'RIS' which is 'not coded because the target is responding to internal stimuli' which we feel cannot but be arbitrary. In the BTES (Denham and Lieberman, 1980) learning is defined as a student getting a high number of correct responses on tests. The reader is told that 'If a student did not understand the task and made correct responses at about chance level, the situation was labelled low success rate' (p. 75). Defining successful and unsuccessful learning in such a way seems to us to be a violation of educational norms.

Circularity/Tautology/Reality-Freezing

Our three final points all deal with the way in which prespecified coding schemes are self-limiting. Boydell's Teacher Record makes a distinction between interaction with the whole class, with a small group, and with an individual. The ORACLE team (Galton, Simon and Croll, 1980, pp. 120–1) subsequently produced six teaching styles, three of which – individual monitors, class enquirers, and group instructors – are chiefly distinguished by the proportion of interaction they have with the three audience categories. Yet Group Instructors only spent 17.7 per cent of their time interacting with groups and 52.3 per cent with individuals.

The BTES and the Rutter works seem to us to be circular in the same way. Both studies assume that academic task involvement produces school achievement. That is, they take it for granted that what the school does affects the pupils. They set up the research with the assumption that the causal relationship runs in one direction, i.e. good teachers maximize pupils' learning time and hence their mastery, less effective staff lack this ability and pupils learn less. We do not know of any clear evidence that the reverse is not the case. Perhaps anti-school pupils prevent the teacher from engaging them? The research by Rutter and the BTES studies do not allow that argument to be examined. Research with prespecified coding schemes is governed by preordained descriptive categories (e.g. 'verbal', 'non-verbal', 'teacher', 'pupil') and does not allow and encourage the development of new categories. The ethnographic research can freely go beyond the *status quo* and develop new and potentially fertile descriptive languages, yet *Mirrors for Behaviour* (1974) failed to acknowledge that there are (or even can be) ' "metalanguages" for describing communication of various kinds' (p. 1) that are based on anything other than measurement or *a priori* categorization.

Two other criticisms of the systematic observation approach need to be made. We feel that all the systems used deny the observer the reflexivity needed to handle the role of classroom observer. It is naive to assume that there is no effect (Samph, 1976) from an observer's presence, but those using coding schemes either ignore the issue, or rely on coding it as a sufficient resolution. With one exception, all the systems in *Mirrors for Behaviour* make a rigid distinction between the observer and the observed. The former is considered a 'fly on the wall', detached from the classroom events. For example, in an observational study of English infant classrooms, Garner (1972) devotes no discussion to the impact of the observer. More particularly, his checklist makes no reference to infant behaviour directed towards the observer, though it is reasonable to assume that it did (or could) occur. This is remedied by Boydell's Pupil Record which has categories for pupils' interacting with the observer, although the books (Galton, Simon and Croll, 1980; Galton and Simon, 1980) have no reflexive discussion of the topic.

By maintaining a strict 'distance' from those being observed, interaction analysis may again promote an incomplete appraisal. As Louis Smith has pointed out, teaching must be viewed as an intellectual, cognitive process:

> The way (the teacher) poses his problems, the kinds of goals and sub-goals he is trying to reach, the alternatives he weighs . . . are aspects of teaching which are frequently lost to the behavioural oriented empiricist who focuses on what the teacher does, to the exclusion of how he thinks about teaching.
>
> (Smith and Geoffrey, 1968, p. 96)

In much of interaction analysis these aspects are rarely considered. They are labelled 'subjective' and placed beyond the bounds of the empirical world. This lack of reflexivity is part of the systematic observation tradition's claims to be objective. Its proponents argue that, compared to other forms of observation, their systems provide unambiguous data uncontaminated by observer 'bias'. However, the price paid for such 'objectivity' can be high. We believe that by rejecting as invalid, non-scientific or 'metaphysical' data such as the actor's ('subjective') accounts, or descriptive ('impressionistic') reports of classroom events, the prespecified coding approach risks furnishing only a partial description. Furthermore, in justifying the rejection of such data on operational rather than theoretical or even educational grounds, the systematic approach may divert attention from the initial problem towards more 'technocratic' concerns such as the search for 'objectivity' and 'reliability'. In the instructional handbook of the Flanders system, ten pages deal with observer reliability, but only two with how to understand classroom phenomena (see Flanders, 1966). In Galton and Simon (1980) an eighteen-page Appendix deals with replication, no space is made for participants' accounts.

These are our main reservations about the research tradition of observation of using prespecified coding schedules. Many of these objections centre on these systems' premature closure, a drawback we feel is avoided by the ethnographic alternative.

The Ethnographic Tradition

In 1972/3 it was necessary to explain to an educational audience in Britain what we meant by 'anthropological' observation, or ethnography. Even the latter term was relatively unfamiliar, whereas it is now well known enough to be used not only here but also as an entry in the new encyclopedia of educational research (Louis M. Smith, 1982) and in the series edited by Rist (*Studies in Ethnographic Perspectives on American Education*). Further reviews of British and American work can be found in Hammersley (1980), Borman (1981), Smith (1978, 1982) and Wilcox (1982). There are now many more texts of a methodological type (e.g. Hammersley and Atkinson, 1983). Indeed ethnography has grown in popularity and acceptability to the extent that one of the founding fathers Spindler (1982) could write:

> it is a rare research project today that does not have somewhere in the table of operations at least one ethnographer and somewhere in the research design some ethnographic procedures.

With the growth and proliferation of studies has come what Louis Smith (1982) calls 'zesty disarray' among different groups of ethnographers. We do not attempt to map or evaluate these here, instead we have summarized the 'common core' of ethnography.

Most of the earliest ethnographers were either anthropologists – who lived in alien cultures – or social scientists focusing on 'strange' ethnic groups in their own society. They suffered 'culture shock' and were forced to rethink their *own* preconceptions about everyday life by living among people who saw 'the same' phenomena differently or, indeed, did not even 'see' the same things at all. The most crucial difference between those using prespecified coding systems and ethnographers is that the former take for granted many aspects of school life, which the ethnographer struggles to make problematic. The ethnographer may not succeed in this aim, and the best admit this quite openly. For example, Wolcott (1981) says that it took a colleague from outside educational research:

> to jolt me into realizing that the kinds of data teachers gather 'on' and 'for' each other so admiringly reflect the dominant society and its educator subculture. 'At Task' measures particularly intrigued my friend. 'How incredible', he observed, 'that teachers would measure classroom effectiveness by whether pupils appear to be busy. How like teachers to confuse "busy-ness" and learning.'

The attempt to challenge one's own sense of familiarity in classrooms is usually made by the observer immersing himself/herself in the 'new culture'. Ethnographies involve the presence of an observer (or observers) for prolonged periods in a single or a small number of classrooms. During that time the observer not only observes, but also talks with participants; significantly, the ethnographer calls them informants, rather than subjects. Also, the anthropologist does not make such a strong category distinction between observer and observed as the interaction analyst does. Gussow and Vidich put the anthropological case most clearly:

> When the observers are physically present and physically approachable the concept of the observer as non-participant though sociologically correct is psychologically misleading.
>
> (Gussow, 1964, p. 240)

> Whether the field-worker is totally, partially or not at all disguised, the respondent forms an image of him and uses that image as a basis of response. Without such an image, the relationship between the field-worker and the respondent by definition does not exist.
>
> (Vidich, 1955, p. 35)

In addition to observing classroom life, the researcher may conduct formal interviews with the participants and ask them to complete questionnaires. Usually, to record his observations, the observer compiles field-notes or, more recently, field-recordings. Compared with the results produced by coding interaction with one of the published schedules the initial data gathered by the ethnographer are open-ended and *relatively* unstructured. The degree of openness varies between 'pure', 'exploratory' ethnographies (e.g. Bullivant, 1978) and 'applied', 'evaluation' ethnographies (e.g. Popkewitz *et al*., 1982).

The ethnographer uses a holistic framework. He accepts as given the complex scene he encounters and takes this totality as his data base. He makes no attempt to manipulate, control or eliminate variables. Of course, the ethnographer does not claim to account for every aspect of this totality in his analysis. He reduces the breadth of enquiry systematically to give more concentrated attention to the emerging issues. Starting with a wide angle of vision, he 'zooms' in and progressively focuses on those classroom features he considers to be most salient. Thus, ethnographic research clearly dissociates itself from the *a priori* reductionism inherent in the prespecified coding systems. In a very real sense, then, it operates with an open and 'unfinished' methodology.

It is often argued against anthropological studies that their results cannot be generalized to other settings. This criticism refers only to statistical generalization. To an anthropological researcher, the development of generally or universally applicable statements is quite a different task, one that is never achieved merely by carrying out a survey. Despite their diversity, individual classrooms share many characteristics. Through the detailed study of one particular context it is still possible to clarify relationships, pinpoint critical processes and identify common phenomena. Later, abstracted summaries and general concepts can be formulated, which may, upon further investigation, be found to be germane to a wider variety of settings. Case studies, therefore, are not necessarily restricted in scope. This issue has been addressed by Hamilton (1981) and Delamont and Atkinson (1981) and is not elaborated further here. However, we do feel that the kinds of generalizations produced from good ethnography are just as useful to both researchers and practitioners as those available from systematic observation. The prespecified coding systems, as we stated above, are often concerned with generating normative data, that is, in extrapolating from sample to population. It should be remembered, however, that statistical norms (e.g. the 'teacher-talk percentages' of Flanders, 1970) apply to the population *taken as a whole*, not to its individual members. They apply to individual settings only in probabilistic terms. And since settings are never equivalent, such statistical generalizations may not always be relevant or useful.

In our view the great strength of the ethnographic research is that it gets away from the simplistic behavioural emphasis of the prespecified coders.

We feel that much classroom description has been simply behavioural. It has tended to disregard the meaning(s) that behaviour entails. As already suggested, such an approach may miss important differences that underlie the behaviour. To the extent that classroom research claims to illuminate the processes associated with classroom life, it cannot afford to divorce what people do from their intentions. If it treats teachers and students merely as objects, it can only obtain a partial analysis, one that falls short of explanation in terms of the subjective processes that inform a teacher's or student's actions.

To inquire into subjectivity or relative truth is not, as is sometimes imagined, to accept solipsism or relativism. It can still be a central theme for empirical research, as Harré and Secord (1972, p. 101) point out,

> to treat people as if they were human beings it must still be possible to accept their commentaries upon their actions as authentic, though revisable, reports of phenomena, subject to empirical criticism.

This is related to the successful use of interaction analysis systems as teacher training rather than research tools (e.g. Wragg, 1974). As training instruments, they are used to give information back directly to the people being observed. Indeed, when audio-visual systems are employed, the observer and the observed can be one and the same person. Clearly, when interaction analysis is used in this way, the observer is more aware of the intentions and subjective processes involved and, at the same time, is sensitized to their temporal and social context. Thus, he or she has the necessary data to reach a more powerful understanding of the interaction. In this respect, interaction analysis as 'research' is fundamentally diffferent from interaction analysis as 'training'. In that it necessarily incorporates a phenomenological understanding as well as a behavioural description of the situation, its use in training is much closer to the ethnographic research model.

Classroom Research in the Future

In this final section we make a few points about the way we would like to see classroom studies develop.

1 There is still a danger that research will cease to consider the wider educational and social context of the classroom. To contrast 'classroom' with 'society' is to construct a false opposition. While it is possible, for research purposes, to regard the classroom as a social unit in its own right, it is only with considerable difficulty that it can be regarded as self-contained. An adequate classroom study must acknowledge and account for both the internal and external aspects of classroom life. In particular, classroom research should not be treated as a substitute for studies which look at the broader societal aspects of education. As Walker (1970, p. 143) has warned,

> any description of classroom activities that cannot be related to the social structure and culture of the society is a conservative description.

2 Development of audio-visual techniques has meant that much classroom research can work from recorded rather than 'live' data, that is, at one remove from the classroom. While this allows for *post hoc* analysis, it has the disadvantage that much of the (usually implicit) contextual data normally made available to the on-site observer may be lost. It is significant, we suggest, that at least some studies which have used visual and/or audio recordings still consciously supplement them with the physical presence of an independent observer (see Walker and Adelman, 1976; Erickson and Mohatt, 1982). In our view, while an elaborate technology can facilitate description of behaviour, it cannot furnish *explanations* for that behaviour. The methods themselves do not provide such a link, nor do they supplant the conceptual processes needed to generate explanations. In the past, classroom research – particularly the interaction analysis tradition – has poured forth an endless stream of comparative studies, hoping presumably that some conceptual clarity would mysteriously emerge. Technological sophistication is no substitute for conceptual vigour.

3 We recognize that, like all other research, every classroom study develops from certain premises, suppositions and interests held by the researcher. Typically, these reflect the ethos, especially the intellectual ethos, of his or her time. As we have noted, there is an insidious danger of an uncritical acceptance of techniques developed from different (and often forgotten) standpoints. As the history of mental testing amply illustrates, research methods and statistical techniques just as much as the theoretical constructs with which they are sustained, may bear the hallmarks, if not the scars, of earlier and possibly rejected assumptions. (See, for example, Smith and Hamilton, 1980.)

4 Research in classrooms, both using prespecified codings and using

ethnographic methods, would be improved if researchers read the literature more thoroughly, covering both existing empirical work and the literature on research methods. We concur with the position taken by Marten Shipman (1981), who argues that

> curriculum evaluators have not acknowledged with sufficient force that the wheel has already been invented . . . The mainstream research literature has come to be neglected . . . Those who launched the particular research perspective, and those who attacked them, did so from a knowledge of social science . . . many of those who practised evaluation (are) unaware of the long tradition on which they were drawing.

While Shipman writes about the evaluation of curriculum innovations the same points apply to studying classrooms. Classroom research is part of social science, and that means that there is a literature to be assimilated before, during, and after any particular research project.

5 There is one final issue on which we wish to dissociate ourselves from the prevailing pattern of educational research. This is the congenital and manic optimism with which much educational research is suffused. Absolute truth is heralded as lying just beyond the horizon. For example:

> A revolution in teaching is being fomented. If successful it will overthrow the hegemony of the centuries-old pattern whereby one teacher and 20–40 pupils engage for most kinds of instruction in a teacher-dominated discourse . . . If the revolution succeeds the teacher will spend much less time each day with groups of students in time-honoured ways . . . In short, a spectre is haunting research on teaching – the spectre of programmed instruction.
>
> (Gage and Unruh, 1967)

This optimism and its essentially nineteenth-century belief in rational man and the power of science (with its implicit denial of the historicity of truth) has been of considerable consequence, not least for classroom research. In a field where instant solutions are at a premium, this belief, surely, is unlikely to bear much fruit. Rather, it can often lead to premature closure (when an exploratory or heuristic stance would be more useful), to the presentation of cautionary notes dressed up as 'conclusions', and to the pursuit of short-term reliability at the expense of long-term validity. One sobering example here is the original publication by Neville Bennett (1976) of his findings on primary schools which were substantially modified when further analysis was carried out by Aitken, Bennett and Hesketh (1981). In summary, this belief can produce 'tunnel vision', a mental state where a clear view ahead is achieved at the expense of a fading appreciation of the past and an ignorance of what is taking place close by.

Since we first reviewed this research area several bandwagons have been and gone. At the time of writing, ethnography is booming in ways which disconcert such old hands as Spindler (1982) and Wolcott (1981, 1982). We sought in 1972, and are still seeking for a new, open-ended attitude towards research, in which eclectic combinations of research methods can be used and in which different problems can be tackled by different, and mutually appropriate, methods. Instead of looking for one solution to all problems, we suggest that more consideration be given to the nature of the specific problems being faced and, hence, to choosing a particular research strategy, appropriate for that problem.

Acknowledgements

The authors were financed by the SSRC, SCRE and the SED in the earlier phases of their careers when the preliminary research for this paper was conducted. The material for this revised version was gathered with the help of the Inter-Library Loan Service at University College, Cardiff.

Val Dobie, Sheila Pickard and Myrtle Robins typed this version of the paper and we are grateful to them for their speed and skill.

References

AITKEN, M., BENNETT, S.N. and HESKETH, J. (1981). 'Teaching styles and pupil progress: a re-analysis', *British Journal of Eduational Psychology*, 51, pp. 170–86.

AMIDON, E.J. and HOUGH, J.B. (eds.) (1967). *Interaction Analysis*. Reading, Mass., Addison-Wesley.

BENNETT, S.N. (1976). *Teaching Styles and Pupil Progress*. London, Open Books.

BERLAK, A.C. and BERLAK, H. (1981). *Dilemmas of Schooling*. London, Methuen.

BLACKSTONE, T. (1980). 'Review of M. Rutter *et al* (1979) *15 000 Hours*', *British Journal of Sociology of Eduation*, 1, No. 2, pp. 216–19.

BORICH, G.D. and MADDEN, S.K. (eds.) (1977). *Evaluating Classroom Instruction: a Sourcebook of Instruments*. Reading, Mass., Addison-Wesley.

BORMAN, K. (1981). 'Review of recent case studies on equity and schooling', in R.G. Corwin (ed.), *Research on Educational Organizations*, Greenwich, Conn., JAI Press.

BULLIVANT, B.M. (1978). *The Way of Tradition*. Victoria, Australian Council for Educational Research Press.

COHEN, L. and MANION, L. (1981). *Perspectives on Classrooms and Schools*. London, Holt Saunders.

COULTHARD, M. (1974). 'Approaches to the analysis of classroom interaction', *Edcuational Review*, 22, pp. 38–50.

DAVIES, B. (1976). *Social Control and Education*. London, Methuen.

DAWE, A. (1970). 'The two sociologies,' *British Journal of Sociology*, 21, No. 2, pp. 207–18.

DELAMONT, S. (1976a). 'Beyond Flanders fields', In Stubbs, M. and Delamont, S. (eds.), *Explorations in Classroom Observation*, Chichester, John Wiley.

DELAMONT, S. (1976b). *Interaction in the Classroom* (first ed., second ed., 1983). London, Methuen.

DELAMONT, S. and ATKINSON, P. (1980). The two traditions in educational ethnography: sociology and anthropology compared', *British Journal of Sociology of Education*, 1, No. 2, pp. 139–52.

DELAMONT, S. and HAMILTON, D. (1976). 'Classroom research: a cautionary tale?', In Stubbs, M. and Delamont, S. (eds.), *Explorations in Classroom Observation*, Chichester, John Wiley.

DENHAM, C. and LIEBERMAN, A. (eds.) (1980). *Time to Learn: a Review of the Beginning Teacher Evaluation Study*. Washington D.C., National Institute of Education (Department of Health, Education and Welfare).

ERICKSON, F. and MOHATT, G. (1982). 'Cultural organization of participant structure in two classrooms of Indian students': in Spindler G. (ed.), *Doing the Ethnography of Schooling*, New York, Holt, Rinehart & Winston.

FLANDERS, N.A. (1966). *Interaction Analysis in the Classroom: a Manual for Observers* (revised edition). Michigan, School of Education, The University.

FLANDERS, N.A. (1970). *Analysing Teaching Behaviour*. Reading, Mass;, Addison-Wesley.

GAGE, N.L. and UNRUH, W.H. (1967). 'Theoretical formulations for research on teaching', *Review of Educational Research* 37, pp. 358–70.

GALTON, M. (ed.) (1978). *British Mirrors: a Collection of Classroom Observation Instruments*. Leicester, School of Education, The University.

GALTON, M. and SIMON, B. (1980). *Progress and Performance in the Primary School*. London, Routledge & Kegan Paul.

GALTON, M., SIMON, B. and CROLL, P. (1980). *Inside the Primary Classroom*. London, Routledge & Kegan Paul.

GARNER, J. (1972). 'Some aspects of behaviour in infant school classrooms,' *Research in Education*, 7, pp. 28–47.

GUSSOW, Z. (1964). 'The observer – observed relationship as information about structures in small group research', *Psychiatry* 27, pp. 236–47.

HAMILTON, D. (1976). 'The advent of curriculum integration', in Stubbs, M. and Delamont, S. (eds.), *Explorations in Classroom Observation*, Chichester, John Wiley.

HAMILTON, D. (1981). 'Generalizations in the educational sciences: problems and purposes', in Popkewitz, T.S. and Tabachnick, B.R. (eds.), *The Study of Schooling*, New York, Praeger.

HAMILTON, D. and DELAMONT, S. (1974). 'Classroom research: a cautionary tale?' *Research in Education*, 11, pp. 1–15, (reprinted in Stubbs, M. and Delamont, S. (eds.), *Explorations in Classroom Observation*, Chichester, John Wiley).

HAMMERSLEY, M. (1980). 'Classroom ethnography', *Educational Analysis*, 2 No. 2, pp. 47–74.

HAMMERSLEY, M. and ATKINSON, P. (1983). *Ethnography: Principles in Practice*. London, Tavistock.

HARGREAVES, A. (1980). 'Review of M. Rutter *et al 15 000 Hours*', *British Journal of Sociology of Education*, 1, No. 2, pp. 211–16.

HARGREAVES, D. *et al* (1975). *Deviance in Classrooms*. London, Routledge & Kegan Paul.

HARRÉ, R. and SECORD, P.F. (1972). *The Explanation of Social Behaviour*. Oxford, Blackwell.

HOBBS, S. and KLEINBERG, S. (1978). 'Teaching: a behavioural influence approach', in McAleese, R. and Hamilton, D. (eds.), *Understanding Classroom Life*. Slough, National Foundation for Education Research.

HUDSON, L. (1977). 'Picking winners: a case study of the recruitment of research students', *New Universities Quarterly*, 32, No. 1, pp. 88–106.

KARWEIT, N. (1981). 'Time in school', in Corwin, R.G. (ed.), *Research on Educational Organizations*. Greenwich, Conn., JAI Press.

MCINTYRE, D. (1980). 'Systematic observation of classroom activities', *Education al Analysis*, 2, No. 2, pp. 3–30.

MCINTYRE, D. and MACLEOD, G. (1978). 'The characteristics and uses of systematic observation', in McAleese, R. and Hamilton, D. (eds.), *Understanding Classroom Life*. Slough, National Foundation for Educational Research.

METZ, M.H. (1978). *Classrooms and Corridors: the Crisis of Authority in Desegregated Secondary Schools*. Berkeley, Calif., University of California Press.

POLLARD, A. (1980). 'Teacher interests and changing situations of survival threat in primary school classrooms', in Woods, P. (ed.), *Teacher Strategies*. London, Croom Helm.

POPKEWITZ, T.S. and TABACHNICK, B.R. (eds.) (1981). *The Study of Schooling*. New York, Praeger.

REYNOLDS, D. (1980). 'Review of M. Rutter *et al* (1979) *15 000 Hours*', *British Journal of Sociology of Education*, 1, No 2, pp. 207–11.

ROSENSHINE, B. and BERLINER, D. (1978). 'Academic engaged time', *British Journal of Teacher Education*, 4, No. 1, pp. 3–16.

RUTTER, M. *et al* (1979). *15 000 Hours*. London, Open Books.

SAMPH, T. (1976). 'Observer effects on teachers' verbal classroom behaviour', *Journal of Education Psychology*, 68, No. 6, pp. 736–41, reprinted in Bennett, N. and McNamara, D. (eds.), (1979), *Focus on Teaching*, Harlow, Longman.

SHIPMAN, M. (1981). 'Parvenu evaluation', in Smetherham, D. (ed.), *Practising Evaluation*. Driffield, Yorks., Nafferton Books.

SIMON, A. and BOYER, G.E. (eds.) (1974). *Mirrors for Behaviour 3*. Philadelphia, Research for Better Schools Inc.

SMITH, J.V. and HAMILTON, D. (eds.) (1980). *The Meritocratic Intellect*. Aberdeen, The University Press.

SMITH, L.M. (1978). 'An evolving logic of participant observation: educational ethnography and other case studies', in Shulman, L. (ed.), *Review of Research in Education*, 6. Itasca, Ill. Peacock Press.

SMITH, L.M. (1982). 'Ethnography', in Mitzel, H. (ed.), *The Encyclopedia of Educational Research*, (5th ed.). New York and London, Macmillan (4 vols).

SMITH, L.M. and GEOFFREY, W. (1968). *Complexities of an Urban Classroom*. New York, Holt, Rinehart & Winston.

SNYDER, B. (1971). *The Hidden Curriculum*. New York, Knopf.

SPINDER, G.D. (ed.) (1982). *Doing the Ethnography of Schooling*. New York, Holt, Rinehart & Winston.

STEBBINS, R.A. (1975). *Teachers and Meanings*. Leiden, Brill E.J.

SWIDLER, A. (1979). *Organization without Authority*. Harvard, The University Press.

TIKUNOFF, W. and WARD, B.A. (1980). 'Conducting naturalistic research on teaching', *Education and Urban Society*, 12, No. 3 (May) pp. 263–90.

VIDICH, A.J. (1955). 'Participant observation and the collection and interpretation of data', *American Journal of Sociology*, 60, pp. 354–60.

WALKER, R. (1971). 'The social setting of the classroom: a review of observational studies and research', unpublished M. Phil. thesis, University of London.

WALKER, R. (1972). 'The sociology of education and life in school classrooms', *International Review of Education*, 18, pp. 32–43.

WALKER, R. and ADELMAN, C. (1975a). 'Interaction analysis in informal classrooms: a critical comment on the Flanders system', *British Journal of Educational Psychology*, 45, No. 1, pp. 73–6.

WALKER, R. and ADELMAN, C. (1975b). *A Guide to Classroom Observation*. London, Methuen.

WALKER, R. (1976). 'Strawberries', in Stubbs, M. and Delamont, S. (eds.), *Explorations in Classroom Observation*. Chichester, John Wiley.

WILCOX, K. (1982). 'Ethnography as a methodology and its application to the study of schooling: a review', in Spindler, G. (ed.), *Doing the Ethnography of Schooling*. New York; Holt, Rinehart & Winston.

WOLCOTT, H.F. (1967). *A Kwakiutl Village and School*. New York, Holt, Rinehart & Winston.

WOLCOTT, H.F. (1973). *The Man in the Principal's Office*. New York, Holt, Rinehart & Winston.

WOLCOTT, H.F. (1981). 'Confessions of a "trained" observer', in Popkewitz, T.S. and Tabachnick, B.R. (eds.), *The Study of Schooling*. New York, Praeger.

WOLCOTT, H.F. (1982). 'Mirrors, models and monitors: educator adaptations of the ethnographic innovation', in Spindler, G. (ed.), *Doing the Ethnography of Schooling*. New York, Holt, Rinehart & Winston.

WRAGG, E.C. (1974). *Teaching Teaching*. Newton Abbott, David and Charles.

Revisiting Hamilton and Delamont: A Cautionary Note on the Relationship Between 'Systematic Observation' and Ethnography

M. Hammersley

In 1974 David Hamilton and Sara Delamont published a paper about classroom research which compared the merits of systematic observation with those of ethnography (Hamilton and Delamont, 1974). While recognising the value of both research strategies, they were critical of systematic observation and sounded a warning about the possibility that one version of it, 'interaction analysis' (Flanders, 1970), might come to dominate educational research in Britain. Equally, they called for more ethnographic research in schools and classrooms on the grounds that this avoided many of the defects intrinsic to systematic observation. Their article has been reprinted many times and their arguments have been influential.

Last year a revised version of this paper appeared (Delamont and Hamilton, 1984). It updates their survey of British classroom research, noting that their predictions about the future of systematic observation have not been entirely borne out, repeating their criticism of research in this tradition, and welcoming the growth of ethnographic research. It is an interesting and useful article, but I want to comment here on what seems to me to be an unfortunate ambiguity in it concerning the relationship between systematic observation and ethnography.

At one point in the 1984 article the authors remark:

> Both of us are inclined towards the ethnographic approach to educational research, but not so fanatically or exclusively that we wish to dissuade other people using other methods. Part of our attachment to the ethnographic is a desire to treat educational research as an 'open-ended' endeavour, where

premature closure is a dangerous possibility. Therefore we do not endorse views which treat research (i.e. ethnographic versus systematic observation; normative versus interpretive, etc.) as the equivalent of self-contained epistemological and theoretical paradigms. There is a tendency for educational researchers who advocate one 'method' or another to imply far too narrow and prematurely prescriptive views of what counts as legitimate enquiry.

(Delamont and Hamilton, 1984, p. 5)

This is an important statement which one might hope would have some influence when so much current research on education seems to be paradigm bound. However, on the very next page of their article Hamilton and Delamont seem to adopt precisely the approach to the comparison of the two traditions which they began by rejecting:

The underlying tension between the research done with a prespecified coding scheme and that done from an ethnographic perspective is the tension between positivism and interactionism which runs through all social science. It is a fundamental difference of approach to the study of humans and human society, and it cannot be done away with by calling for inter-disciplinary rapprochements. More than a century of social science research exists, based on distinct conceptions of humankind, and it cannot be wished away by the pious hopes of classroom observers. This is not the place to rehearse all the debates about positivism . . .; about normative and interpretive paradigms . . .; or about sociologies of 'order' and 'control' . . . But we do believe that the different traditions of classroom research which we discuss in this paper are merely one empirical example of two distinct kinds of social science methodology.

(Delamont and Hamilton, 1984, p. 6)

There seems to be a direct contradiction here and, unfortunately, despite their own warnings against it, much of the rest of Delamont and Hamilton's article seems to assume that different forms of research exemplify self-contained epistemological paradigms.

In the central section of their article they list seven criticisms of systematic observation:

1 Systematic observation provides data only about 'average' or 'typical' classrooms, teachers and pupils.
2 It typically ignores the temporal and spatial context in which the data are collected.
3 It is usually only concerned with overt, observable behaviour and neglects 'possibly more meaningful features'.
4 Being concerned with what can be categorised or measured, it may distort, obscure or ignore qualitative features through crude measurement techniques or by using categories with ill-defined boundaries.
5 It focuses on small bits of action rather than global concepts. This leads to a lack of potential to generate fresh insights.

6 The pre-specification of categories determines what is discovered by the research.

7 Placing arbitrary boundaries on continuous phenomena obscures the flux of social interaction.

There is much truth in these criticisms. It is true that, typically, systematic observers do not collect data on the physical and temporal context of the behaviour they are observing, nor do they observe the behaviour of the actors in other settings than the classroom, or collect the actors' own accounts of their behaviour. Reliance on a single source of data is as unwise in this case as it is in others. Equally, a concern with specifying and counting observable indicators *can* lead to only those things being researched which are amenable to this kind of analysis.

However, these failings are not *necessary* features of systematic observation. In the 1974 article Hamilton and Delamont recognised this, but in the recent version these failings have become 'limitations inherent in interaction analysis' (p. 10). What Delamont and Hamilton are pointing to are defects in the current practice of systematic observation. They are right to suggest that these seriously threaten the validity of the findings produced, as some systematic observers have recognised themselves (McIntyre, 1980). However, it seems to me that there is nothing inherent in systematic observation, or for that matter in positivism, which would prevent the correction of these defects.

There is another feature of Delamont and Hamilton's account which reinforces the impression that, despite their disclaimers, they are recommending the rejection of one paradigm, systematic observation, in favour of another, ethnography. In neither version of the paper do they make any criticisms of current practice in ethnography (though Delamont has voiced a number of important criticisms elsewhere, Delamont, 1981). In the 1974 paper this was perhaps understandable, but given the growth in classroom ethnography over the last ten years some discussion of its weaknesses is surely called for. In particular, it ought to be pointed out that much ethnographic research runs into the same set of problems as systematic observation. We ethnographers also engage in classification of classroom events: as instances of 'interaction sets', 'survival strategies', 'material constraints', 'negotiation' etc. As a result we too run the risk that our classifications may 'obscure, distort or ignore the qualitative features which they claim to investigate', we too are freezing, and perhaps therefore reifying, continuous phenomena, and our categories may also 'assume the truth of what (we) claim to be explaining'. Such dangers are inherent in any kind of classification, they are only avoided by classifications which pick out similarities and differences which match the underlying structure of the world that is being studied.

Now while I would agree that an ethnographic orientation maximises the chances of developing new theoretical ideas and discovering new empirical facts, the *testing* of factual and theoretical claims is an equally important element of the process of inquiry. If ethnographers are to justify their claims about what happens in classrooms and why, they cannot avoid the measurement issues which have preoccupied systematic observers – notably the question of the typicality of the cases studied, and the relative frequency of different types of action. Yet it has to be said that ethnography, as currently practised, does not pursue effective testing of factual and theoretical claims. Too often the problems involved in linking concepts and data and the difficulty of assessing the force of rival explanations are simply ignored. While this may have some justification in exploratory research, all our research cannot be exploratory. And much ethnographic research which is labelled exploratory nevertheless announces its findings with full conviction and is taken by readers as having established certain facts and corroborated particular theories. Despite its very serious defects, research in the systematic observation tradition has at least addressed the problem of measurement. To lambast this research for its failings, while remaining silent about the problems of ethnography, will do nothing to improve the quality of classroom research.

In conclusion, then, I want to suggest that we follow Delamont and Hamilton's initial suggestion and renounce the temptation to treat systematic observation and ethnography as self-contained and mutually exclusive paradigms. To do otherwise distorts our understanding of both traditions and contributes to their ossification. It implies that there are just two alternative research strategies whereas in fact the process of decision-making in classroom research is far more complex. The appropriate analogy is not a fork in the road but a maze in which one is faced at every point with alternative routes. Moreover, the same dilemmas – between adopting sensitising and definitive concepts, between focusing on the typical or the atypical, between studying a small sample in depth or a large sample more superficially, etc. – face all researchers, whatever tradition they identify with. We will stand much more chance of finding effective solutions to the problems of classroom research if we recognise this and are prepared to learn from one another than if we simply bolster confidence in our own preferred strategies by castigating those who have made different choices. I can only echo Delamont and Hamilton's closing comments:

> We sought in 1972, and are still seeking for a new, open-ended attitude towards research, in which eclectic combinations of research methods can be used and in which different problems can be tackled by different, and mutually appropriate, methods. Instead of looking for one solution to all problems, we suggest that more consideration be given to the nature of the specific problems being faced and, hence, to choosing a particular research strategy, appropriate for that problem.

> (Delamont and Hamilton, 1984, pp. 23–24)

Acknowledgements

I am indebted to John Scarth for helpful comments on an earlier draft of this paper.

References

DELAMONT, S. (1981). 'All too familiar? A decade of classroom research', *Educational Analysis*, 3, 1, pp. 99–83.
DELAMONT, S. and HAMILTON, D. (1984). 'Revisiting classroom research: a continuing cautionary tale', in Delamont, S. (ed.), *Readings on Interaction in the Classroom*. London, Methuen.
FLANDERS, N. (1970). *Analysing Teaching Behaviour*. Reading, Massachusetts, Addison-Wesley.
HAMILTON, D. and DELAMONT, S. (1974). 'Classroom research: a cautionary tale', *Research in Education*, 11, pp. 1–15.
MCINTYRE, D. (1980). 'Systematic observation of classroom activities', *Educational Analysis*, 2, 2, pp. 3–30.

PART TWO
Studying Classroom Language

Language in Classroom Interaction: Theory and Data

V.J. Furlong and A.D. Edwards

Summary

The phenomena considered in this paper, in a variety of constituted forms, are aspects of verbal interaction in classrooms. We attempt to show that whether researchers approach classroom talk from the perspective of systematic observation, ethnography or sociolinguistics, their underlying theoretical assumptions determine the 'facts' that they record and the interpretations they are able to offer. By asking how researchers arrive at their abstract description of events, we try to place these different approaches to classroom interaction within a common framework, and to highlight their various strengths and weaknesses.

Introduction

How the social scientist constructs that abstract view of his 'world' which constitutes his theory has conventionally been seen as independent of the way he sets about testing it. The term 'methodology' can then be reserved for supposedly neutral and 'objective' techniques of investigation. This separation of 'theory' and 'method' is quite unrealistic. Whatever picture of social life the scientist presents is the outcome of selective observation and interpretation, because his theory determines not only how the 'data' are explained but also what are to count as data in the first place. Unless we can reconstruct the whole process 'through which the observer moves from his observations of the social world to his conceptual description of it, we are in no position to evaluate that description' (Phillipson, 1972, p. 79). By looking at the relationship between a researcher's theory and the data he gathers, we can understand more easily why such different accounts can be given of the 'same' phenomena. What are 'facts' from one perspective may be ignored from another.

In this review of approaches to classroom interaction, what is in question is not the 'objectivity' of the accounts but the researchers' awareness of their *selectivity* and the theoretical basis of that selectivity.

Systematic Observation: The View from the 'Outside'

Most of the time in classrooms, someone is talking. In the most common form of classroom research, a manageable record of what is said has seemed to depend on extracting the 'essential' qualities from an otherwise over-whelming stream of verbal behaviour. This has meant coding the talk according to some category system. Since the observer has to classify every-thing he hears into whatever number of categories his system provides, the actual words spoken are no longer recoverable. His instant judgments about the interactional significance of those words are what constitute his data.

The reliability of the main category systems is not in doubt – that is, suitably trained observers will usually agree with each other about what they heard. Their *validity* is only as 'good' as the theory (if any) behind them, because the researcher will 'hear' no more than his categories allow him to. These categories are not derived from his observations, but are imposed on them. They represent preconceived ideas about what is important in the classroom. Where do these ideas come from? 'Systematic' researchers rarely articulate their theoretical position in any detail, but their perspective can be described as positivist and behaviourist. 'Methodologically', they insist that they record what 'actually occurred', and see themselves as producing objec-tive data which can be analysed in 'normal' scientific ways (Amidon and Hunter, 1967, pp. 9–10; Medley and Mitzel, 1963). 'Theoretically', they tend to work from a simple model of stimulus (or initiation) and response. The teacher stimulates, and his pupils respond. Since it is the teacher's behaviour which is seen as explaining whatever patterns of verbal interaction are observed, feeding information back to him about his behaviour at certain critical 'decision-points' is intended to enable him to change (and improve) his teaching (Flanders, 1967; 1970, pp. 5–13).

If there is this 'gloss' of learning theory over the main category systems, their roots are no less firmly in early studies of group 'climate', and of 'authoritarian' and 'democratic' styles of group management. Particularly influential has been Bales' (1950) work on the 'task' and the 'socio-emotional' areas of group life, and his categorization of everything the members say as making a positive or negative contribution to one area or the other. This procedure has often been taken over in classroom research, with little explicit justification of its relevance. Thus Ober defines the teacher's main tasks as – 'to manipulate and control the content in ways that will facilitate learning to the ends determined by the learning objectives', and to 'create a positive socio-emotional climate in which the learner will feel comfortable and learning will be facilitated' (Ober, Bentley and Miller, 1971, p. 3). The teacher's ability to perform these functions is seen as dependent on skills which can be identified, described, and learned, and Ober's two observational systems are directed to these ends. They are said to allow 'any trained person who follows stated procedures to observe, record and analyze interactions with the assurance that others viewing the same situation would agree to a great extent with his recorded sequence of behaviours'. In other words, they would see the talk as performing the same socio emotional or task functions. What the quotation also makes clear is that reliance on *trained* observers brings the prospect of a pre-determined consensus. Events can be said to have 'occurred' in so far as trained observers will agree that they did so, their common frame of reference providing its own solutions to whatever problems of interpretation may arise. Complacent references to the 'accuracy' and 'correctness' of the record relate to *this* view from the 'outside' and not to how things may have appeared to participants in the interaction – or to observers working from a different theoretical vantage-point. Systematic observation fills a category system with precise and quantifiable data by working out its own presuppositions – by providing the data necessary to justify its existence and so constructing its own reality (Speier, 1973, p. 3).

Ethnographic Research

We can now see that these apparently 'objective' techniques for analyzing talk in classrooms impose a pattern on what they record which is derived from the theories of classroom instruction on which they are based. Because those theories dictate precisely what the researcher is looking for, it is not surprising that he finds it – and finds nothing else. An alternative to this restrictive procedure is provided by ethnographic research. Rather than studying large numbers of classrooms, as systematic observation usually demands, the ethnographer is likely to explore a single situation. As Hamilton and Delamont (1974) explain, 'Despite their diversity, individual classrooms share many characteristics. Through the detailed study of one particular context it is still possible to clarify relationships, pinpoint critical processes and identify common phenomena' (see also Walker, 1972;

Robinson, 1974). Ideally, ethnographic researchers reject completely the systematic observers' insistence on 'knowing precisely what to look for' (Ober *et al.*, 1971, p. 6). Quite deliberately, they adopt a 'catch-what-you-can' approach, making no attempt to control or ignore 'irrelevant' variables. If there is any categorization of the talk, it has to be done retrospectively – that is, in forms *derived* from the data. The record must therefore be sufficiently detailed to make possible the reconstruction of what happened (see e.g., Furlong, 1976). Indeed, the intention may be to present so full a description to the reader that he can 'experience a sense of event, presence and action' and also be able to check on the interpretation offered by the researcher (Kochman, 1972, p. xii).

This approach has the obvious appeal of an attempt to 'tell it like it is'. It also involves an irresolvable conflict. Although the ethnographer is committed to having as open a mind as possible during his period of observation, it is inevitable that he will begin his work with some preconceptions and some foreshadowed problems which will lead him to pay attention to certain incidents and ignore others. If he presents his observations as 'objective description', he is probably naively unaware of his own selectivity. On the other hand, if he follows a theory too closely, he will be accused of selecting observations to support his own point of view. The difficulty with observational work is therefore that of maintaining a balance between a 'guiding perspective' which allows the researcher to approach a classroom with no more than a focus and some general question in mind, and a set of preconceived ideas 'that dictate prior to the research "relevances" in concepts and hypotheses' (Glaser and Strauss, 1967, p. 33). The complex relationship between theory and data is not unravelled simply by producing richly detailed case studies. Theory will still dictate what questions are being asked, and what categories are likely to emerge in the analysis. It is essential, therefore, that the researcher makes explicit the theory that guided his observations and that provided the basis for his particular selective record of events. If he fails to do this, his account will seem more 'open' than it is, the observations being so impregnated with interpretation that they can support no other view of events than the one offered. This is precisely the criticism which Cicourel makes of Goffman's vivid portrayals of social interaction – for example, in *The Presentation of Self in Everyday Life* and *Behaviour in Public Places*. Goffman offers as description what is already heavily interpreted; it is 'prematurely coded . . . infused with substance that must be taken for granted, and subsumed under abstract categories without telling the reader how all of this was recognized and accomplished' (Cicourel, 1973, p. 24).

Susan Philips' (1972) very persuasive account of classroom interaction can be criticized in this way. In the context of an American Indian community, she contrasts the rules governing communicative performance in classrooms with those relating to other 'public' demonstrations of knowledge of skill.

She found that the Indian children talked more or less than their white contemporaries depending on the 'participant-structures' – the patterns of verbal interaction – established or permitted by their teachers. They appeared most at ease when working individually, or in small groups with no formalized allocation of speaker-roles, or where they could initiate contact with the teacher on a one-to-one basis. In more 'traditional' classrooms, where they were expected to listen to the teacher's exposition and answer questions on demand, they were reluctant to participate and became increasingly reticent as they grew older. Philips explains their silence by suggesting that there was a cultural discontinuity between the rules relating to learning situations in the Indian home and in the school, with the Indians rejecting the sharp separation of teacher-performer from pupil-audience. Convincing though her account seems, there is no discussion of how the data were gathered or organized. However useful the concept of participant-structures may be, we are given no idea of how Philips developed it – or indeed, of whether she went into her research with the concept already in her mind. She identifies four such structures. Are the various patterns recognized as such by the pupils? And might a more sensitive analysis have revealed more than four? The whole presentation is edited so as to support the argument.

This practice of fitting out an already formulated theory with supporting evidence is what Glaser and Strauss (1967, p. 5) call 'exampling'.

> A researcher can easily find examples for dreamed up, speculative or logically deduced theory after the idea has occurred. But since the idea has not been derived from the example, seldom can the example correct or change it (even if the author is willing) since the example was selectively chosen for its confirming power. Therefore one receives the image of a proof when there is none, and the theory obtains a richness of detail which it did not earn.

Mishler's (1972) work on classroom talk is a case in point, though it is more sociolinguistically than ethnographically oriented. He begins by explicitly criticizing category systems because they do not preserve the actual language that was used, and tries himself to retain those 'particular features of interactive speech' which are relevant to his 'general theoretical concerns with relationships amongst teaching, cognition and socialization' (pp. 268–9). His analysis of teachers' 'cognitive strategies', for example, is directed by three questions. He asks (a) how teachers focus their pupils' attention and (b) how they define and (c) evaluate the ensuing search for information. Brief extracts from three lessons are used to show how three teachers differ on these dimensions. But Mishler offers no reasons for having chosen these as the 'critical' aspects of cognitive stategy. For all the reader knows, he has simply 'dreamed them up', and then proceeded to find examples to fit them. The following quotation illustrates how he 'examples' a teacher's focusing of her pupils' attention:

At the same time as she has selected a specific feature of the situation for their attention, this teacher generalizes the issues involved, and moves the discussion from a concrete to a more abstract level. The shift from the particular concrete instance to the more general abstract class of events is accomplished by her use of the plural noun 'detectives' in her first sentence, and her use in her next statement of the indefinite article (p. 272).

Despite the apparent display of 'hard' evidence in the transcripts he includes, Mishler resembles the systematic researchers in the way he assigns teacher-statements to pre-ordained categories. The trick of classification may be done 'before your very eyes', but the result is the same. *Did* the use of a plural noun and an indefinite article 'accomplish' a shift in cognitive level? This is his understanding of what was done on a particular occasion, and we are invited to go along with it, but it is no more than a *post hoc* interpretation. Indeed, in its sociolinguistic orientation the study raises the general problem of how we recognize behavioural strategies in specific features of linguistic choice. It is to other sociolinguistic studies that we now turn.

Sociolinguistic Research: Language and Social Meaning

Systematic patterns of choice can often be revealed by including situational features in linguistic description. Rules of 'appropriate' usage constrain what can 'properly' be said, and speakers can use their knowledge of these rules to maintain or challenge a particular definition of the situation. 'Unmarked' usage is what is 'normal' *in the circumstances*. It so conforms to the participants' expectations as to be largely unnoticed, part of the taken-for-granted background to their interaction. 'Marked' usage breaks the rules, not haphazardly but in ways that have some special significance. It can therefore serve to re-define the situation. From this sociolinguistic perspective, language is studied as it is organized to serve social ends, and social relationships are studied in terms of how they are 'realized' linguistically (Hymes, 1971).

Such study is made easier where the situational constraints are relatively 'firm' and pervasive, and this is why classrooms have been seen as suitable for *basic* sociolinguistic research (Hymes, 1972; Sinclair and Coulthard, 1975; Edwards, 1976, pp. 157–65). In the 'traditional' classroom, the main communicative purpose is the transmission of knowledge from a teacher who knows to pupils who do not. Given this *relatively* overt and stable structure to the interaction, many 'potentially ambiguous utterances are likely to have one accepted meaning' (Sinclair and Coulthard, 1975, p. 6). For example, 'Is that someone talking in the back?' is likely to be interpreted as a command if the teacher says it, despite its interrogative form. And 'Would you please open your books at page 18' is unlikely to be taken as indicating that a refusal is possible, despite its tentative form. Such situated interpretations of what is meant depend on the participants' knowledge of what competent teacher and pupil interactions are like. This knowledge is also available to an observer experienced in the ways of classrooms, who can also make sense of what is said so far as it conforms to 'type'.

The approach outlined here is ambitiously followed in Gumperz and Herasimchuk's (1972) 'conversational analysis of social meaning'. Their aim is – 'to uncover the social assumptions which underlie the verbal communication process by focussing on actors' use of speech . . . to create and maintain a social situation' (p. 99). In the same way as a listener's grammatical knowledge enables him to establish the referential meaning of what he hears (i.e. who is doing what, and to whom), so his knowledge of what might be called a 'social grammar' (of social identities, social roles etc.) enables him to extend or perhaps modify his understanding of what was said in its particular context. In other words, what a speaker 'means' will often depend on who he is, when and where he is speaking, and on his relationship to the listener. In classrooms, the *role*-relationship of teacher and pupil is seen as providing a third 'level of interpretation' beyond those provided by lexis (the dictionary meaning of words) and syntax. An important part of the analysis is a detailed account of interaction in which a child acts as 'teacher', helping a younger pupil with his reading. Here the necessary pedagogic relationship had to be more obviously created. Where a 'real' teacher could rely heavily on the underlying social assumptions of her listeners, and on the 'ready made' clues to meaning contained in her relationship with them, the 'child-teacher' appeared to make far more use of facial expression, intonation and other communicative devices to 'create and maintain the situation'.

Instructive though this contrast is, it points to a danger that where the situation is a familiar one (as 'traditional' classrooms certainly are), the observer may fall back on his common-sense notions of what that situation is like to do much of his explanatory work for him. 'Context' becomes an unexplicated dumping-ground for what the participants too are supposed to know about that part of their social world. A recent analysis of classroom discourse is open to this criticism (Sinclair and Coulthard, 1975). The structure of the talk is described with very little reference to the 'pedagogical' (or social) structure, which is assumed to vary little from one teacher to another. Implicitly, the reader's experience of 'formal' classrooms is being relied on to do the filling-in. It could be argued that such classrooms were the wrong place to start building a framework for discourse analysis because they were *too* familiar, and this is certainly what an ethnomethodologist would argue. From his perspective, it is largely through the exchange of words that social realities are constructed, made 'visible' to participants, and come under their reflexive control. His concern with *how* interaction is initiated and sustained makes it inadmissible for the observer to find an unexplicated source of 'explanations' in the 'parts' which the participants are assumed to know in advance.

   This is not to deny, of course, that 'a setting supplies its participants with an interpretive basis as they routinely interact, a frame of understandings shared and enforced by them' (Speier, 1973, p. 34). Being interactionally 'competent' in a situation means being able to talk and interpret talk as others do, and to supply interpretive clarifications when confusions or misunderstandings arise. If he tries to show the nature of this 'competence' in *informal* classrooms, the observer will have far more obvious interpretive work to do because easy references to 'the' context are no longer possible.

   A supposed advantage of systematic observation-schedules is that they are broadly 'situation-proof' – that is, given the occurrence of something like class-teaching, the observer has no need of any prior acquaintance with that *particular* teacher or class. He can then go about the business of coding the talk without revealing the common-sense base from which he does so. It can be argued that sociolinguistic analyses have also been limited so far to situations in which communicative roles and purposes are so clearly defined that talk can be related to action in 'relatively predictable ways' (Walker and Adelman, 1972, pp. 27–8). When 'traditional' roles are abandoned, the observer's 'general knowledge' of classrooms will no longer be much use to him. In their own research in 'informal' classrooms, Walker and Adelman found it necessary to use film because much of the speech was impossible to understand without seeing what was going on at the time. This 'technical' problem was inseparable from

> . . . general questions about the kinds of information certain social situations both generate and require to exist, and about the minimum perceptions and transmissions of that information required to constitute and sustain identities with them . . . What we are working towards asking is what do you need to perceive, recollect and express in order to participate within certain settings?. . . (p. 19).

These questions could profitably be asked about 'formal' classrooms too, because they force on the researcher's attention the impossibility of using what is said as 'hard' data (i.e. as having fixed, determinate meanings), and the need to show how the situation is (and has been) talked into existence by the participants. By moving outside the deceptively 'firm' framework of 'normal' classroom interaction to analyze communication in small informal groups, Barnes has similarly been led to ask *how* pupils 'created' knowledge and simultaneously negotiated and maintained their relationships with each other through their verbal interaction (Barnes, 1976; Barnes and Todd, 1975). What he describes as 'exploratory talk' is seen as dependent on the degree of control over knowledge which pupils feel themselves to have, and also on their willingness to tolerate disagreements and avoid premature closures of discussion. The structure of the talk is seen as inseparable from the structure of social relationships within the group. Barnes' work therefore exemplifies what Blom and Gumperz (1972, p. 432) define as proper sociolinguistic analysis – 'Social and linguistic information are only comparable when studied within the same theoretical framework'.

Conclusion

Our objective in this paper has been to summarize the conceptual 'ground clearing' undertaken for our own research into the uses of language in informal classrooms. Its predominantly critical tone is therefore not that of spectators comfortably free from any risk of having to join in the game themselves. We have examined some of the main approaches to classroom interaction, recognizing that each of our compartments contains a greater diversity of contents than might have appeared in the summaries.

As we have seen, systematic observation has grown from a long line of research in group management. Flanders himself has acknowledged this heritage, but does not appear to appreciate the extent to which it has coloured his findings. His concern with 'direct', 'indirect' and 'flexible' teaching strategies reflects the opinions of many educationalists about what constitutes 'good' teaching, and this partly explains why systematic observation in general, and Flanders' schedules in particular, have been widely used in teacher training. The provision of rapid feed-back about how 'authoritarian' or 'child-centred' teachers are has an obvious and immediate 'relevance' denied to most educational research. But we question whether this approach can contribute to our *understanding* of classroom interaction. Systematic observation may seem to facilitate a 'scientific' approach to teacher behaviour, but it has done so in ways that show little social scientific sophistication and greatly underestimate the complexity and fluidity of classroom relationships. It is too easy and produces the dangerous illusions that we already 'understand' how classrooms work.

Ethnographic and sociolinguistic approaches (they are closely related) seem to us much more fruitful. Unfortunately, neither provides easy alternatives for classroom research. Some ethnographies can be criticized for having too little explicit theory, with the result that it is impossible to tell *why* the observer has chosen to report what he does. Other studies suffer from too *much* prior theorizing, with the observer simply having to select the right examples to fit his preconceived ideas. The 'right' balance is always a matter of compromise. Within the field of sociolinguistics, the problems are compounded by the need to be sensitive to sources of explanation in both linguistic *and* social spheres. We have suggested that both must be dealt with from within the same theoretical framework. One of the strengths of Barnes' recent work is that he does this. He also makes clear from the outset what concepts he will use to interpret the interaction he records. By including lengthy transcripts, he is able to make explicit what the interaction looks like from his particular perspective. This procedure can still be described as 'exampling'. Indeed, we doubt whether any real alternative exists. Without some guiding orientation, the observer's attention will 'scatter', and his account is likely to become either a desperate attempt to get everything in, or is a haphazard selection of the more dramatic items of behaviour. What damages research is not the absence of a truly 'open' mind at its outset, but the false presentation of classroom observations as 'objective' data constituting an independent test of the theory hidden within them. What observations will be selected as significant, and how they will be interpreted, will vary widely according to the researcher's perspective. Unless that perspective is made available for criticism and discussion, it is impossible to evaluate the usefulness of the research.

References

AMIDON, E. and HUNTER, E. (1967). *Improving Teaching: the Analysis of Classroom Interaction*. Holt, Rinehart & Winston.

BALES, R. (1950). *Interaction Process Analysis*. Reading, Mass.: Addison-Wesley.

BARNES, D. (1976) *From Communication to Curriculum*. Harmondsworth: Penguin Books.

BARNES, D. and TODD, F. (1975). *Frames: How to Understand Conversation*, SSRC Report. Leeds University Institute of Education. Published as *Communication and Learning in Small Groups*, London, Routledge & Kegan Paul (1977).

BLOM, J.P. and GUMPERZ, J. (1972). 'Social meaning in linguistic structures'. In: Gumperz, J. and Hymes, D. (eds.) *Directions in Sociolinguistics*. Holt, Rinehart & Winston.

CICOUREL, A. (1973). *Cognitive Sociology*. Harmondsworth: Penguin Books.

EDWARDS, A. (1976). *Language in Culture and Class*. London: Heinemann Educational.

FLANDERS. N. (1967). 'Interaction models of critical teaching behaviour'. In: Amidon, E. and Hough, J. (eds.), *Interaction Analysis*. Reading, Mass.: Addison-Wesley.

FLANDERS, N. (1970). *Analysing Teacher Behaviour*. Reading, Mass.: Addison-Wesley.

FURLONG, V. (1976). 'Interaction sets in the classroom: towards a study of pupil knowledge'. In: Stubbs, M. and Delamont, S. (eds.), *Explorations in Classroom Observation*. New York: Wiley.

GLASER, B. and STRAUSS, A. (1967). *The Discovery of Grounded Theory*. Chicago, Illinois: Aldine.

GUMPERZ, J. and HERASIMCHUK, E. (1972). 'The conversational analysis of social meaning: a study of classroom interaction'. In: Shuy, R. (Ed), *Sociolinguistics: Current Trends and Prospects*. Georgetown University Monograph Series on Language and Linguistics, Number 25.

HAMILTON, D. and DELAMONT, S. (1974). 'Classroom research: a cautionary tale', *Research in Educ.*, 11, 1–16.

HYMES, D. (1971). 'Sociolinguistics and the ethnography of speaking', In: Ardener, E. (Ed.), *Social Anthropology and Language*. London: Tavistock.

HYMES, D. (1972). Introduction to Cazden, C., John, V. and Hymes, D. (Eds.), *The

Functions of Language in the Classroom. New York: Teachers' College Press, Columbia University.

KOCHMAN, T. (1972). *Rappin' and Stylin' Out: Communication in Urban Black America*. Urbana. Illinois: University of Illinois Press.

MEDLEY, D. and MITZEL, H. (1963). 'The scientific study of teacher behaviour'. In: Bellack, A. (ed.), *Theory and Research in Teaching*. New York: Teachers' College Press, Columbia University.

MISHLER, E. (1972). 'Implications of teacher strategies for language and cognition'. In: Cazden, C. *et al.* (Eds.), *The Functions of Language in the Classroom*. New York: Teachers' College Press. Columbia University.

OBER, R., BENTLEY, E. and MILLER, E. (1971). *Systematic Observation of Teaching*. Englewood Cliffs, New Jersey: Prentice-Hall.

PHILIPS, S. (1972). 'Participant structures and communicative competence'. In: Cazden, C. *et al.* (Eds.), *Functions of Language in the Classroom*. New York: Teachers' College Press, Columbia University.

PHILLIPSON, M. (1972). 'Theory, methodology and conceptualization'. In: Filmer, P., Philipson, M., Silverman, D. and Walsh, D., *New Directions in Sociological Theory*. London: Collier-MacMillan.

ROBINSON, P. (1974). 'An ethnography of classrooms'. In: Eggleston, J. (Ed.), *Contemporary Research in the Sociology of Education*. London: Methuen.

SINCLAIR, J. and COULTHARD, M. (1975). *Towards an Analysis of Discourse*. London: Oxford University Press.

SPEIER, M. (1973). *How To Observe Face-to-Face Communication: A Sociological Introduction*. Pacific Palisades, California: Goodyear.

WALKER, R. (1972). 'The sociology of education and life in school classrooms', *Internat, Rev. Educ.* 18. 32–41.

WALKER, R. and ADELMAN, C. (1972). *Towards a Sociography of Classrooms*, SSRC Report. Centre for Science Education, Chelsea College of Science and Technology.

Scratching the Surface: Linguistic Data in Educational Research

M. Stubbs

Since the late 1960s, an increasing amount of educational research has been concerned with language in education, and in particular with language in the classroom. This article discusses some problems which arise when such studies attempt to use language as *evidence for educational statements*. It does not discuss any practical problems of collecting or analysing linguistic data; but considers problems involved in relating linguistic data to educational statements in a principled way. It suggests that many studies which do select aspects of language as data for educational statements have no principled basis for this selection, since they ignore the depth of organisation of the language itself. They often merely scratch the surface of the available linguistic data, restricting their attention to superficial characteristics of language in use.

We are, then, concerned with the question: How can language be used as data in educational research, in ways (to use J.R. Firth's phrase) that will avoid 'loose linguistic sociology without formal accuracy'? The argument in this article will be based on examples from educational research, but the argument could be made more general by substituting 'sociology' for 'education' throughout.

Although this paper will be entirely at a theoretical level, its argument has developed from empirical analysis of sound recordings of classroom language (Stubbs, 1975, 1976a) and other types of discourse (Stubbs, 1983; Stubbs 1986). In this data-based work, I often commit the sins of which I here accuse other researchers.

Language as Evidence

Language as a 'Marker' of Educational Processes

There is now a large volume of work which uses linguistic data as 'markers', 'indices', 'indicators' or 'evidence' for social-psychological statements which are of interest to educational theory and practice. Much of this work is concerned with studying classroom language: with recording, observing and analyzing teacher-pupil interaction and using the language as evidence about teaching and learning processes and outcomes.

Between the fieldwork and the published report some sequence of decisions such as the following inevitably takes place. Researchers return from the field with video recordings, audio recordings, notebooks or other data. From these recordings or notes, they *select* for quotation and discussion short *extracts* of, say, teacher-pupil dialogue. From these extracts, and probably more generally also within the corpus of data, they further *select* particular *features* of language which they regard as *evidence* for educational statements. However, precisely how such extracts do illustrate claims about the educational process is often not discussed. It is often simply assumed that particular details of what teachers and pupils say can be quoted, and can serve unproblematically as demonstrations of some educational process. Readers are expected to be able to recognise a particular teacher-pupil interchange or sequence of utterances as, for example, an instance of a 'closed teaching style', a 'democratic teacher', or a 'divergent pupil'. The fact that extracts of talk are quoted does, of course, mean that readers are free, to some extent, to form alternative interpretations. However, I want to question whether quoted utterances or surface features of language do provide evidence of anything non-linguistic.

Work of the type I have in mind includes many excellent individual studies which provide close, perceptive analyses of the ways in which language is used in schools and classrooms; and some generalisations have emerged about the relationships between 'language' and 'education'. But it is difficult to see in what way such studies are cumulative or even comparable. Certainly, they do not constitute a paradigm (Kuhn, 1962) tackling a well-articulated set of problems in well-defined ways, with agreed standards of solution and explanation, and drawing on a consensus of theory. As a whole, the studies lack coherence.

I am referring to studies of classroom language by researchers such as Adelman, Barnes, Cazden, Delamont, Flanders, Hammersley, Hawkins, Keddie, Mishler, Rosen, Sinclair, Stubbs, Torode, Walker and many others. I am not, of course, implying that these researchers think that they have much in common. But it is perhaps disappointing that such studies have very little in common beyond a loose notion that somehow 'language' is important in 'education'. I emphasise that individual researchers usually have well-defined notions, but overall there is nothing more than this loose consensus. The fact, for example, of studying language *in the classroom* provides no principled basis for relating such research. The fact that different pieces of research are carried out in similar physical settings can provide no rationale for them (Atkinson, 1975: 180, argues this point very clearly).

Unprincipled Selection of Data

The very tenuous and unprincipled relationship between the kinds of studies I have cited is evident from two things.

First, different studies claim to relate features of language to a very mixed collection of social-psychological concepts, including: the educability and cognitive orientation of pupils (Bernstein, 1971a); teaching strategies, for example 'open' versus 'closed' (Mishler, 1972); the teacher's role, for example democratic versus authoritarian (Flanders, 1970); methods of social control in the classroom (Hammersley, 1974; Torode, 1976); different types of classroom organisation (Walker and Adelman, 1976); pupils' and teachers' differing concepts of classroom knowledge (Keddie, 1971; Furlong, 1976). These are a few examples of rather different types of educational process for which language is used as evidence: the list could, of course, be extended.

Second, different studies select a wide range of not obviously related linguistic units, both formal and functional, as 'indicators' of these social-psychological and educational processes. These include: different teachers' use of pronouns (Mishler, 1972; Torode, 1976); the complexity of nominal group structure in children's language (Hawkins, 1969, 1977); the functions of teachers' questions and different types of question-answer exchanges (e.g. Barnes *et al.*, 1971; Mishler, 1972); functional categories of speech acts (Stubbs, 1976a); intonational and paralinguistic features (Gumperz and Herasimchuk, 1972); the overall structure of teaching 'cycles' (Bellack *et al.*, 1966). This list could also be extended.

It is not unfair to say that many researchers seem to feel justified in picking out, as evidence, any feature of language which appears intuitively to be interesting. Mishler (1972:297) is one of the few researchers to admit that he has been 'relatively eclectic in the types of linguistic units used in drawing inferences'. Less misleading terms than 'eclectic' might be *ad hoc* or *unprincipled*. Given how little we know about the communicative functions of different aspects of language, it would clearly be a mistake to *restrict* enquiry to any one particular type of linguistic feature, and I am certainly not proposing that. Walker and Adelman (1976) have demonstrated very clearly that utterances with educational significance may be found in unexpected places. However, this is only to admit that research is still proceeding along heuristic and therefore unprincipled lines, still searching for the socially significant features of language. This does not mean, however, that one is condemned to pick and choose linguistic items at random, unrelated to the organisation of the linguistic data as a whole. This would, in any case, merely lead to the unending task of looking for more and more particular features of language, unless these particulars are related to a coherent framework. I am, then, using the term 'unprincipled' to refer to studies in which surface features of language are picked out at random and not related to underlying linguistic statements and descriptions.

Two things might immediately strike the linguist about such research. First: linguistic items are selected, usually with no explicit justification, from several different levels of language – including lexis (i.e. individual words), syntax (i.e. grammatical structure), semantics (i.e. meaning), language function, and discourse (i.e. overall conversational structure). Second: these items, either as unique items or according to their linguistic class membership, are then often related directly to social-psychological categories, rather than being first *related to the linguistic and sociolinguistic systems and structures in which they are terms.*

For example, the fact that a teacher uses pronouns in a certain way has been said to be evidence of his style of social control (Torode, 1976) or of his pedagogical message (Mishler, 1972). And the fact that children use pronouns in a certain way has been said to be evidence of their intellectual orientation (Hawkins, 1969). It is not obvious, firstly, that the use of pronouns can be considered apart from other characteristics of the speaker's language. Nor, secondly, is it obvious that the use of pronouns relates *directly* to social and psychological processes.

These two related points amount to the criticism that such studies characteristically attempt to relate isolated linguistic variables to social-psychological categories, *as though the language had no organisation of its own.* This point is well made in an article by Coulthard and Ashby (1976). They argue, with reference to sociological studies of language, that 'sociological categories should not be used to classify stretches of speech as though [the speech] had no other organisation'. This means that these studies often attempt to relate concepts at quite incompatible levels of abstraction and generality. Isolated, surface features of language are taken as indicators of deep, general and highly abstract social-psychological categories.

One body of work which does explicitly discuss how to relate linguistic and sociological categories at an equal depth of generality is Bernstein's. His work is an attempt to state causal relationships between a theory of educational transmissions and pupils' social class, family type, cognitive orientation and use of language. He accuses other researchers of not having recognised the depth of abstraction of the problem (Bernstein, 1975:25). Unfortunately, the deep, underlying principles and categories which Bernstein proposes are entirely unrelated to any naturalistic linguistic data.

Bernstein has never made any statement which formulates precisely either how sociolinguistic codes or the concepts concerned with educational transmission (e.g. 'framing') are realised in language.

Atkinson (1985) provides an extremely useful and clear interpretation of Bernstein's work, in which he argues that linguists and others have simply failed to see the type of highly general and abstract social theory which Bernstein proposes. But it seems to me that Atkinson still does not tackle the problem of how Bernstein's theories can be tested in particular cases, to see whether they fit the empirical data. In fact, on his own admission, Atkinson does not discuss the large body of empirical studies done by Bernstein's research colleagues in London. Bernstein is clearly not interested merely in a theory of linguistic variation; he is not, as Atkinson points out, a sociolinguist *manqué*. Nevertheless, the relation between the broad structuralist social theory and the linguistic data remains unclear.

Reductionist Descriptions

Much important twentieth-century work in linguistics has been concerned with the complexity of surface and underlying systems and structures in language, and has consequently ignored the relations between language and its social contexts of use. (This is true at least of mainstream American linguistics in the Bloomfield to Chomsky tradition, but less true of British work from Firth to Halliday). However, recently much attention has been paid to the importance of relating language to its social contexts of use. Within linguistics, Hymes (1964) and Labov (1970) in particular have led the attack on the Chomskyan concept of a grammar which is independent of social context and on the concept of context-free grammatical competence. In addition, within sociology, much attention has been paid to the importance of studying social interaction in social contexts. The arguments here are well known: that a failure to study contexts reifies the object of study, by neglecting the interpretative procedures by which situated meanings are constructed, and by failing to treat as problematic the ways in which social order is successfully accomplished by members. The arguments usually amount to the criticism that context-free studies of language are reductionist: they reduce praxis to process; they reduce the study of meaningful behaviour to the study of ideal-typical structures, taking for granted how such structures are interpreted and used in context; and they refuse to study the essential meaningfulness of human behaviour, and how people make sense of social interaction.

I have also discussed elsewhere (Stubbs, 1975) how studies of classroom language are often decontextualised by being treated in strange isolation from other types of social interaction, such as casual conversation, doctor-patient consultations or committee meetings, which are organised by comparable sociolinguistic rules; and also in isolation from sociolinguistic findings about radically different kinds of classroom organisation in other cultures. Again, just the fact of collecting data in the physical setting of classrooms does not mean that the study will be an adequate account of language in context. Studies of classroom language will remain theoretically *ad hoc* unless they are related to general sociolinguistic principles of language behaviour and draw on observations of everyday life in other settings.

It is therefore no solution to reductionism to make loose references to context and to interpretative procedures *if this ignores the inherent structural and systemic complexity of language*. To proceed directly from isolated features of language to social-psychological categories is itself severely reductionist, for it ignores the partly autonomous, complex organisation of the language itself. Many levels of organisation are simply bypassed.

I use *systemic* in this paper in its technical linguistic sense, as the adjective corresponding to a linguistic *system*. A *system* is a closed set of choices or options in a language which are mutually defining. Thus, English has a number *system* comprising two *terms*, singular and plural. Old English had a three-term system, comprising singular, dual and plural. Clearly, plural means something different in two-term and three-term systems. Most linguistic systems are, of course, much more complex than this. Languages are then regarded as systems of systems. Systems may be identified at different *levels* of description. Linguistics traditionally uses the term *level* to refer to phonology, morphology, syntax and semantics, but usage here is variable (see Stubbs 1986 chapter 2).

Two Examples

To make these points clearer, I will discuss briefly two extreme and well-known examples of studies which pass directly from isolated, surface features of language, to social-psychological statements, whilst entirely ignoring the inherent linguistic organisation of the data.

Flanders' (1970) work on teacher-pupil interaction in classrooms is well-known and has been very influential. The basic research procedure involves coding teachers' and pupils' utterances, every three seconds, into a series of discrete categories in a pre-prepared category system. There are now a large number of articles which critcise Flanders, and similar research, for bypassing all the interpretative problems involved in 'coding' language data. A linguistic version of this criticism is that such a coding scheme necessarily ignores any inherent linguistic organisation which the talk itself has. Flanders' interaction analysis categories (FIAC) require utterances to be coded directly as pedagogical acts (e.g. lectures, praises). The codings of these acts are then taken as immediate evidence of 'indirect' or 'direct' teaching: the teacher's 'I/D ratio' being computed directly from the simple addition and division of utterances coded into different categories (Flanders 1970:102). This I/D ratio is then further taken, by implication, and with no further intervening argument, as evidence of a teacher's social role, e.g. 'democratic' or 'authoritarian'. This procedure thus takes us directly from utterances (the language data) to social role (a very high level social-psychological concept), with no intervening discussion of *how the language itself is organised*.

Specifically, the sequential organisation of the classroom dialogue is ignored. Flanders (1970:2) claims to study the 'chain of small events' in the classroom. But FIAC cannot be used to study the structure of classroom talk, because 'events' are defined arbitrarily as 'the shortest possible act that a trained observer can identify and record'. That is, the 'chain of events' has nothing to do with the autonomous organisation of the talk itself. This organisation is taken for granted in the observation. Briefly, we have to know where an event occurs in structure before we can know what kind of event it is.

A second study which passes directly from surface linguistic features to deep social-psychological categories is the well-known experiment by Bernstein's colleague Hawkins (1969) on how young middle class (MC) and working class (WC) children talked to a researcher about a series of cartoon pictures showing some boys kicking a ball through a window. Hawkins found that the WC children used more pronouns, whilst the MC children used more nouns and complex nominal groups in their narratives. Hawkins takes this finding about the complexity of the nominal group as direct evidence of different cognitive orientation in the two groups. His argument is that the MC children have more possibilities of elaborating and differentiating what they are talking about (since one cannot modify a pronoun with an adjective: one can say *good boys*, but not* *good they*).

An alternative interpretation is, of course, possible: the pronouns used by the WC children take account of the conversational context in which the language is used. The hearer can see the pictures and does not need to be told explicitly who *they* are and where they kick the ball. That is, the pronouns do not necessarily have any cognitive function: they might have a discourse function, that is, a *linguistic* function. The data could be explained with reference to factors in the conversational context: that is, they could be given a *sociolinguistic* explanation. They do not have to be accounted for in psychological terms. When Bernstein himself discusses the experiment (1971a:219) he relates the different language use to context, and not directly to intellectual potential.

More recently, Hawkins (1977) has written a book in which he himself provides a very considerable reworking and reinterpretation of the data in his 1969 article. In his book, Hawkins takes, like Bernstein, a much more cautious line, and admits that in his earlier work he has crucially ignored the social context and the functions of the language. But he may have weakened his claims so much that there remains nothing left to argue with. He has, for example, entirely dropped all references to cognitive ability, claiming now simply that WC and MC children talk differently in the interview situation (which, it is pointed out, is broadly similar to test situations in school). The point is that the working class child assumes a different relation between speech and situation, and therefore operates with different ways of reporting and constructing social reality (Atkinson 1985:121). Hawkins further claims (pp. 200 ff.) that the children talk differently because of speech differences in their home backgrounds. This would be interesting if it could be documented, but the only evidence presented (pp. 64, 202) is hypothetical interview data: mothers were asked how they *would* talk to their children in different situations.

There are, however, major points to be gained from the book. First, it emphasises the widely divergent interpretations which can be placed on data about social class variation in language-use. Second, it demonstrates that everything is vastly more complex than popularised accounts of an elaborated/restricted dichotomy suggest. Hawkins' analysis is careful and painstaking: what we are dealing with is differences in relative frequency of items which all the children use, and therefore with performance not competence (pp. 108, 186–7). The care which has gone into the linguistic analysis of the nominal group is considerable, and if readers get nothing else from the book, they ought at least to see the sophistication required of such analyses, and therefore the total inadequacy of impressionistic comments on WC and MC language. Finally, however, as a result of this detail, Hawkins' analysis could be interpreted as data against the codes-theory altogether, on the grounds that if no absolute and clear-cut differences exist between children's language, and if it is all a matter of relative frequencies in usage, and is all highly context-dependent, then there does not seem to be much support for the notion of two discrete underlying codes. At most we have (that characteristically Bernsteinian term) 'orientations' (pp. 183, 203 and elsewhere). (See also Stubbs, 1978).

Sociolinguistic Work on Language and Social Context

The question arises, then, of what kinds of relationship linguists have found between language and its social contexts of use. I will take some examples from Labov's work to illustrate the depth and complexity of these relationships.

In his original work on the social stratification of English in New York, Labov (1966) found strong correlations between speakers' social class and their use of phonological variables. (Labov, 1966, is now out of print, but most of the material has been revised and included in Labov, 1972.) For example, simplification of word-final consonant clusters (e.g. *tol'* for *told*) correlates more strongly with working class than middle class membership. Such linguistic variables therefore have predictive power: they are socially significant and can be interpreted as an index of social structure. Note two complications however.

First, Labov found a great range of absolute values of such phonological indices, but agreement in the pattern of variation. When he looked only at the speech of individual speakers he found oscillations, contradictions and alternations which were inexplicable. On the other hand, the language turned out to be highly determined when charted against the overall social variation between speakers. In other words, the language of a speech community turns out to be more regular and predictable than the speech of an individual. Thus the absolute use of an isolated linguistic variable tells us nothing: correlations are found only by looking at the relative frequency of use of linguistic variables across a speech community. What one finds is that, if speakers are rank-ordered both in terms of their use of selected linguistic variables and in terms of their social class, these rank-orders' coincide (apart from various 'cross-over phenomena' connected mainly with particular linguistic sensitivity in the lower middle class to features of language in the course of change).

Second, some linguistic variables are entirely ambiguous as indices either of the social class of speakers or of the formality of the conversational context. That is, some linguistic items serve both as demographic and as stylistic markers. One can therefore draw no inferences from a speaker's language about his social class, unless one also knows whether the social, conversational context was formal or informal. In Labov's words, one cannot tell a casual salesman from a careful pipefitter.

Labov distinguishes, in fact, between different types of linguistic item. An *indicator* correlates with some demographic characteristic of the speaker, say, social class; but does not vary in the speech of the individual. A *marker* is evidence of, say, social class, but also varies stylistically according to the formality of the situation. Empirically, both types of item are found.

In more recent work, Labov (1973) has studied the language of pre-adolescent Black gangs in New York. He has found the boys' language to be a sensitive *index* of how closely the boys are involved in the street culture. The language of core members of the gangs (discovered independently by socio-metric techniques) turns out to be different in describable ways from the language of peripheral members ('lames'). But the important point is that the language is not different on the surface, for example, in the use of particular words or isolated items. There is, in fact, no absolute difference between the language of the groups. That is, for any feature of Black English Vernacular which core members use, lames will also be found to use it. What is different is the whole system. Labov's finding is that the core members' language is more consistent in its use of the rules of Black English Vernacular. Thus, they might delete the copula in 100 per cent of cases (in sentences like: *He my brother*) where lames will follow the rules only some of the time. The *index* of membership of street culture is therefore provided only by the *overall consistency of the whole grammatical system*:

> . . . the consistency of certain grammatical rules is a fine-grained index of membership in the street culture.
>
> . . . It must be remembered that all of these boys appear to speak BE [Black English] vernacular at first hearing.
>
> . . . All groups use the same linguistic variables and the differences in the system are internal variations in the organisation of similar rules: differential weightings of variable constraints.

(Labov, 1973:81, 88)

Labov also points out the severe practical and theoretical problem that the core members of the sub-culture, whose language is most consistent, are precisely those who are most inaccessible to researchers. It is the lames, whose knowledge of the sub-culture is inadequate, who are most likely to be informants for educational researchers.

The main warning from such work is that, if language is to be used as evidence of social structure and processes, then the language must be examined *as a system*, not as isolated items. Relationships are found between linguistic *systems* and sociological categories. Therefore, the language data must be studied for its own linguistic, systemic organisation. In general, then, the relation between language and educational statements is much less direct and more abstract than many educational studies assume.

Sociolinguistic studies of the relationship between language and context also recognise the importance of speakers' attitudes and perceptions of language, as an intervening link in the chain between language forms and social processes. Much recent sociolinguistic work has concentrated not only on features of how language is used in context, but on the social values which speakers attach to language. (For American studies of language in education which emphasise this, see especially Cazden *et al.*, 1972.) Labov (1969) has suggested that a speech community is defined by speakers who hold the same linguistic attitudes and stereotypes. The phonological variables which are indices of a speaker's social class are often raised to the status of stereotyped and stigmatised features for speakers themselves. But there is a complex relation between speakers' perceptions of other speakers' speech and actual behaviour. Labov's general finding is that people perceive in categorical terms what is, in fact, variable speech behaviour. Thus, a speaker who simplifies word-final consonant clusters in some linguistic environments some of the time may be perceived as doing it all the time, if the frequency of consonant cluster simplification rises above a critical perceptual threshold.

There has been little work on the institutionalised attitudes to language

transmitted by Colleges of Education and schools. But what little there has
been suggests that schools and colleges often take highly prescriptive attitudes to pupils' language. (See Milroy and Milroy, 1974, for data on Belfast,
and Macaulay, 1977, for data on Glasgow).

I now move on to discussing one particular level of linguistic organisation
whose study cannot really be avoided by educational researchers.

Classroom Language as a Discourse System

Much classroom research is actually concerned with studying classroom
dialogue: in terms of teacher's questioning strategies, pupils' responses to
teachers' questions, the kinds of exploratory discussion amongst groups of
pupils working on tasks, and so on; if not immediately concerned with
studying the dialogue itself, much work nevertheless draws its data from
such sources. And much other work admits that it ought to be concerned
with teacher-pupil interaction, or that study of teacher-pupil interaction
would be required to provide empirical substance to theoretical points (see
Keddie, 1971:156, and many other examples).

The Organisation of Classroom Discourse

Most studies of the classroom are, then, inevitably concerned with how
teachers and pupils interact; that is, with aspects of teacher-pupil dialogue,
discussion, conversation or discourse. There are now many studies which
demonstrate in detail that discourse (multi-party conversation) is a complex
linguistic system: a highly patterned, rule-governed activity describable in
terms of several interrelated ranks of description. That is, *discourse has its
own organisation*. Major studies of how spoken interactive discourse 'works'
are by Sacks (e.g. 1972) and his colleagues in the USA, and by Sinclair and
his colleagues in Britain (Sinclair and Coulthard, 1975). This latter work is
on teacher-pupil discourse amongst other discourse types. Many quite specific proposals have now been made concerning how spoken discourse can
be analysed structurally and systemically, in terms of the linguistic 'mechanisms' which make it 'work'. Much work has been done for example on
minimal interactive units, at the rank of question-answer pairs. (Cf. Sinclair
and Coulthard, 1975, on exchanges; Sacks, 1972, on adjacency pairs;
Goffman, 1971 on interchanges.) Often classroom researchers (e.g. Barnes,
1969) have worked with an intuitive notion of such discourse units. Larger
discourse units are also discoverable. Schegloff and Sacks (1973) suggest
ways in which whole conversations are structured. The most specific suggestions have come from work in Birmingham (Sinclair and Coulthard,

1975) which proposes several hierarchically ordered ranks of structural units into which discourse can be analysed on formal grounds. The details of such analyses are not important here. What is important is that any attempt to relate isolated linguistic units to non-linguistic categories completely by-passes these levels of conversational organisation.

The general point is as follows. Language is a relatively autonomous system, or more accurately a system of systems. Within language, discourse or conversation constitutes a relatively autonomous level of linguistic organisation. That is, it is possible to formulate discourse structures (including two-place structures such as question-answer) and systems of choices (if A says x, then B will say $y1$ or $y2$, and will not say z). In other words, it is possible to begin to specify how conversation works. It is also possible to specify how different discourse types work, for example, how teacher-pupil dialogue typically differs from a doctor-patient consultation. Treating teacher-pupil interaction as a linguistic discourse system means studying the formally recognisable linguistic 'mechanisms' by which the talk is organised and made coherent. That is, studying, amongst other things, how topics are introduced, sustained and closed, or how one speaker's talk is related to another's. Many formally identifiable markers of discourse cohesion have now been identified, including lexical repetition, parallelism of syntax and intonation, anaphora, ellipsis, and sentence continuations. (Halliday and Hasan, 1976, is a very detailed discussion of these topics.)

If language data are selected from observations or recordings of classroom language, these data are necessarily abstracted from their context in discourse structure. Any principled study of such data must therefore take account of their own organisation.

The Transmission of Educational Knowledge

There is another powerful reason why educational researchers should be interested in such linguistic organisation. In ignoring it they are in fact ignoring a vast resource, much deeper and richer than surface linguistic items. Studying teacher-pupil interaction as a linguistic discourse system can provide educationally interesting insights which are not available to studies which bypass this organisation. One example is as follows.

Much recent educational research has been concerned with the sociology of knowledge: with how educational knowledge is socially defined, selected and made available to pupils. Much of this work raises 'predominantly conceptual issues' (Young 1971:2) and provides no detailed specification of how knowledge is actually transmitted from teachers to pupils. There is much theorising, but few case studies. (Case studies based discursively on classroom interaction include Keddie, 1971; Furlong, 1976.) Studies in this area can usefully be done at different levels: one can study, for example, how the curriculum defines knowledge (e.g. Hamilton, 1976). However, description of how teacher-pupil discourse is sequentially organised could also provide much information for the educationalist interested in how teachers control the knowledge which is presented to pupils. By studying discourse sequencing, one can study in empirical detail: how teachers select bits of knowledge to present to pupils; how they break up topics and order their presentation; how these discrete items of knowledge are linked, how distinct topics are introduced and terminated, how pupils' responses to questions are evaluated; how pupils are made to reformulate their contributions; how bits of knowledge are paced and allowed to emerge when the teacher considers it appropriate. I cannot see how such topics could be studied, other than in an *ad hoc* way, by looking at isolated utterances or features of language. But by studying the overall structure of the teacher-pupil interaction as a discourse system, these topics are inevitably studied.

Studying teacher-pupil talk as a discourse system would, for example, provide one way of studying how classroom knowledge is 'framed' (Bernstein, 1971b). Only by studying how teachers control the classroom discourse itself can one then study how this also controls the transmission of educational knowledge. Only preliminary studies have so far been done on how the concept of framing may be grounded in sound recordings of classroom language (Stubbs 1983: ch 7; Walker and Adelman, 1972, 1976).

Such topics of study are simply not available to researchers who treat language at the level of isolated surface features, ignoring its abstract, underlying, sequential and hierarchical organisation.

Pots and Kettles

It often happens that educationalists, and sociologists in general, accuse linguists of ignoring the contexts in which language is used. 'Contexts' here generally mean social and cultural contexts. Such accusations are often true. (The fact that they are also no news to linguists, who are quite aware of the idealisations they make, and have strong reasons for making them, is often ignored by critics, but this is another matter which does not concern us here.) But in this paper, I am accusing educationalists, in their turn, of ignoring contexts. By 'contexts', *I* mean levels of linguistic organisation in the data: one such level is discourse sequence.

I am not claiming that, by taking account of linguistic organisation, everything can be explained. This would clearly be factually wrong. Reference to the social context is often necessary in order to account for how language is used.

Nor am I arguing that the social functions of language ought to be related explicitly to the linguistic forms that realise them: the problem of the relationship between language forms and functions is a quite separate issue, which I have only mentioned in passing in this article. It is well known, in academic debate as in everyday life, that we often think people are saying what we expect them to say. When linguists talk about language, they are often heard as insisting that educational and social researchers pay more attention to language forms. But this is only one concern of linguists, and it has not been my concern in this article.

What I am arguing is that it is often tempting to proceed directly from language to social context, bypassing levels of organisation in the middle. As a principle, and even if it does not always work, one ought to try and account for linguistic data on its own terms before turning to sociolinguistic, sociological or psychological explanations. The argument is not that one ought to study language as a system *instead of* studying the social context; but that one ought to study language as a system *before* trying to relate it to the social context. Linguists and educationalists both accuse each other of being reductionist.

Conclusion

I have discussed some theoretical problems in relating linguistic data to social-psychological statements in a principled way. There are various ways of thinking about these problems.

First, it is the problem of how researchers can place some control on their intuitions. What is to stop researchers picking out isolated linguistic items or classes of items and taking these as 'evidence' of democratic social control, closed learning sequences, or whatever? Second, it is the problem of idealisation. Descriptions of phenomena have to simplify and idealise: otherwise they would merely reproduce the features of the original under study, rather than make hypotheses about what it is significant to describe. Third, therefore, it is the problem of how to avoid reductionist statements. Clearly, descriptions of language which ignore its social context of use and social meanings are severely reductionist and unlikely to be of any interest to the educationalist. But in concentrating on the use of language in context, one must not ignore the complexity of the language system itself, by reducing the linguistic data to a string of isolated features.

As a whole, studies of language in education have attempted to relate a mixed collection of surface linguistic features to a mixed collection of deep social-psychological categories. This is a prima facie indication that such studies are unprincipled in that they treat the linguistic data as a mere resource, as though it had no organisation of its own. I suggest finally that classroom researchers are inevitably concerned with using teacher-pupil dialogue as a source of data, and that they should therefore be concerned with how the dialogue works: that is, with teacher-pupil discourse as a linguistic system in its own right. To ignore teacher-pupil talk as a discourse system is, in any case, to throw out the baby with the bathwater, and to ignore a much richer source of data than isolated and surface linguistic items.

I find it difficult to see what direct relationship there could possibly be between isolated, surface features of language and learning and teaching strategies. For example, the cognitive complexity of an argument will never be computed merely by calculating the number of subordinate clauses it contains, the mean length of its sentences, the complexity of its noun groups, or the rarity of its adjectives. Nor can a teaching style ever be defined merely in terms of the number of closed questions the teacher asks or the number of pupil initiations. The relationship between language and educational processes is much less direct than this, and seems to depend crucially on a notion of the organisation of the language as a *system* of communication. This is a much deeper, more powerful and more interesting concept of language. At present, many educational studies are only scratching the surface of the language data which they use.

Acknowledgements

This chapter is a revised version of an article first published in Clem Adelman (ed). *Uttering, Muttering*, London, Grant Mc Intyre, 1981, pp. 114–33.

References

ATKINSON, P. (1975). 'In cold blood: bedside teaching in a medical school', in Chanan, G. & Delamont, S. (eds.), *Frontiers of Classroom Research*, National Foundation for Educational Research.
ATKINSON, P. (1985). *Language, Structure and Reproduction: an introduction to the sociology of Basil Bernstein*, Methuen.
BARNES, D., BRITTON, J. and ROSEN, H. (1971). *Language, the Learner and the School*, Penguin, revised edition.
BARNES, D. and TODD, F. (1977). *Communication and Learning in Small Groups*, Routledge and Kegan Paul.
BELLACK, A. *et al.* (1966). *The Language of the Classroom*, New York, Teachers College Press.
BERNSTEIN, B. (1971a, 1975). *Class, Codes and Control*, vols 1 and 3, Routledge and Kegan Paul.
BERNSTEIN, B. (1971b). 'On the classification and framing of educational knowledge', in Young (ed.), 1971, and in Bernstein, 1971a and 1975.
CAZDEN, C., JOHN, V. and HYMES, D. (eds.) (1972). *Functions of Language in the Classroom*, New York, Teachers College Press.
COULTHARD, R.M. and ASHBY, M.C. (1976). 'A linguistic analysis of doctor-

patient interviews', in Wadsworth, M. and Robinson, D. (eds.), *Studies in Every-day Medical Life*, Martin Robertson.

DAVIES, A. (ed.) (1971). *Language and Learning in Early Childhood*, Heinemann.

FLANDERS, N. (1970). *Analysing Teaching Behaviour*, Addison-Wesley.

FURLONG, V. (1976). 'Interaction sets in the classroom', in Stubbs and Delamont (eds.), 1976.

GOFFMAN, E. (1971). *Relations in Public*, Allen Lane.

GUMPERZ, J.J. and HERASIMCHUK, E. (1972). 'The conversational analysis of social meaning', in Shuy, R. (ed.), *Sociolinguistics: Current Trends and Prospects*, Georgetown Monographs on Language and Linguistics.

HALLIDAY, M.A.K. (1961). 'Categories of the theory of grammar,' *Word*, 17, 3.

HALLIDAY, M.A.K. and HASAN, R. (1976). *Cohesion in English*, Longman.

HAMILTON, D. (1976). 'The advent of curriculum integration: paradigm lost or paradigm regained', in Stubbs and Delamont (eds.), 1976.

HAMMERSLEY, M. (1974). 'The organisation of pupil participation', *Sociological Review*, August 1974.

HAWKINS, P. (1969). 'Social class, the nominal group and reference', *Language and Speech*, 12, 2.

HAWKINS, P. (1977). *Social Class, the Nominal Group and Verbal Strategies*, Routledge and Kegan Paul.

HYMES, D. (1964). 'Directions in (ethno) linguistic theory', *American Anthropologist*, 66, 3, 2.

KEDDIE, N. (1971). 'Classroom knowledge', in Young (ed.), 1971.

KUHN, T.S.(1962), *The Structure of Scientific Revolutions*, University of Chicago Press.

LABOV, W. (1966). *The Social Stratification of English in New York City*, Washington.

LABOV, W. (1969). 'The logic of non-standard English' in N. Keddie (ed.), *Tinker, Tailor*, Penguin, 1974.

LABOV, W. (1970). 'The study of language in its social context', *Studium Generale*, 23, 1; revised version in Labov, 1972.

LABOV, W. (1972). *Sociolinguistic Patterns*, University of Pennsylvania Press.

LABOV, W. (1973). 'The linguistic consequences of being a lame', *Language in Society*, 2.1

MACAULAY, R.K.S. (1977). *Social Class and Education*, Edinburgh University Press.

MILROY, J. and MILROY, L. (1974). 'A sociolinguistic project in Belfast', Mimeo.

MISHLER, E. (1972). 'Implications of teacher-strategies for language and cognition', in Cazden *et al.* (eds.), 1972.

SACKS, H. (1972). 'On the analysability of stories by children', in Gumperz, J.J. and Hymes, D. (eds.), *Directions in Sociolinguistics*, Holt, Rinehart and Winston.

SCHEGLOFF, E. and SACKS, H. (1973). 'Opening up closings', *Semiotica* 8, 4.

SINCLAIR, J. MCH. and COULTHARD, R.M. (1975). *Towards an Analysis of Discourse*, Oxford University Press.

STUBBS, M. (1975). 'Teaching and talking: a sociolinguistic approach to classroom interaction', in Chanan, G. and Delamont, S. (eds.), *Frontiers of Classroom Research*, National Foundation for Education Research.

STUBBS, M. (1976a). 'Keeping in touch: some functions of teacher-talk', in Stubbs and Delamont (eds.), 1976.

STUBBS, M. (1976b). *Language, Schools and Classrooms*, Methuen.

STUBBS, M. (1978). 'Review of Hawkins' *Social Class, the Nominal Group and Verbal Strategies*', *British Journal of Educational Studies*, 26, 2.

STUBBS, M. (1983). *Discourse Analysis*, Basil Blackwell.

STUBBS, M. (1986). *Educational Linguistics*, Basil Blackwell.

STUBBS, M. and DELAMONT, S. (eds.) (1976). *Explorations in Classroom Observation*, Wiley.

TORODE, B. (1976). 'Teachers' talk and classroom discipline' in Stubbs and Delamont (eds.), 1976.

WALKER, R. and ADELMAN, C. (1972). *Towards a Sociography of the Classroom*, Report to SSRC, Mimeo, HR/1442/1.

WALKER, R. and ADELMAN, C. (1975). *A Guide to Classroom Observation*, Methuen.

WALKER, R. and ADELMAN, C. (1976). 'Strawberries' in Stubbs and Delamont (eds.), 1976.

YOUNG, M.F.D. (ed.) (1971). *Knowledge and Control*, Collier-Macmillan.

Talking and Teaching: Reflective Comments on In-Classroom Activities

W. Sharrock and R. Anderson

Introduction and Conclusions

One complaint which is often made against sociologists is that they tell you what you already know. There is substance to such a complaint, though it might be a little more precisely worded to indicate that they tell you what they know as though they were telling you something that was news. Telling people things they already known is not always a redundant pursuit, for there are times when it is important (and difficult) to keep attention focused upon the well-known, for that can all too easily be left out of account when abstract or theoretical thinking is being done.

What we have to say here, if there is any truth to it, will be no great news to teachers who will be wholly familiar with the kinds of things we pay attention to, but we will be trying to show the importance of taking note of these things in any proposed sociological rendition of life-in-the-classroom. Though what we have to say is said in response to and in continuance of the internecine disputes over the nature of sociology itself, we will contrive to suppress or simplify technical sociological issues and will make the argument as accessible as we can to the working teacher.[. . .]

Whilst the introduction of the audio and video recorder has proven a significant step forward in social research, we should not confuse ends and means; we should bear in mind that whilst the question of what we are to look at is by no means a trivial one, it is a little less important than the question of how we are to look at whatever we do look at. Indeed, there are critical ways in which the decision as to how we are to look at things determines what we shall be seeing when we look.

It is perhaps an unusually early moment at which to give our conclusions, but we will nonetheless offer them now, using the remainder of the chapter to get back to them.

We will endorse the view that what goes on in classrooms is (often, in large part) talking and that, therefore, to understand teaching we must look at talking. There are senses in which an understanding of teaching would be entirely coincident with an understanding of the organization of talking, but to see how teaching and talking do relate, it is always important to be clear about what is understood to be 'the organization of talking'. There are ways of representing the organization of talking which will represent the things that go on in classrooms well enough, but which will in other respects comprehensively miss the point of the activities so represented.

Sources of Trouble, Sources of Order

There are tendencies inherent in (at least certain modes of) sociological reasoning which lead researchers to pay attention to almost everything that goes on in a social setting except the relevant business of the setting. Though there is a wide variety of sociological specialisms, including the 'sociology of education' along with 'the sociology of science', 'the sociology of work', the sociology of medicine' and so on, it might be more accurate if they were to be renamed to characterize more faithfully their actual content. Hence, the sociology of medicine could more accurately be called 'the sociology of almost everything about health provision exlcuding the nature of medical "treatment" ' and, in a matching fashion, the 'sociology of science' could be called 'the sociology of almost everything about science, except the work of making scientific investigations and discoveries'.

This point is no longer quite so true as it was a very few years ago, for some people, under the pressure of views like our own and from other considerations, are recognizing the importance of taking serious and central note of the need to look at the actual business in which the parties to the setting are actively engaged.

Acknowledging such a need and fulfilling it are, alas, two quite different things and it is easy enough to slip over into doing something very different even when we set out to fulfil it. To fulfil it here, we shall be doing no more than recommending that attention be paid to in-classroom talk as involving the oral exposition and inculcation of a subject. In plainer words, regard classroom talk as matter of talking through a subject in such a way that it can be learned.

As we have pointed out, to say that teaching involves talking will be no news to teachers, but as we also remarked, in thinking theoretically about a familiar activity it is only too possible to exclude obvious and vitally relevant matters from consideration.

We do not, then, say that teachers are unaware of the oral nature of much of their practice, but we do advise them that they will not find it easy to take account of it in applying sociology to their own classrooms and they will not find many (if any) resources in sociology for enabling them to do so. In talking of the need to develop ways of seeing what goes on in classrooms, for example, talking history, talking sociology, talking biology, then we are talking about the need to do something which will have to be underrtaken almost from scratch.

There are, we said, inherent tendencies in sociology which militate against the treatment of the 'substance' or 'business' of social activities. Some sociologists will even differentiate explicitly between 'form' and 'content' and elect to attend to form rather than content! Of these inherent tendencies, we think there are two main and related ones, namely generality and abstraction.

Here we touch upon what are, within sociology, very deep issues indeed. It is simply taken for granted that sociology is or is to become a generalizing discipline. Though there is much discussion as to what that means and amounts to, in practice its current implication is for people to tend to case their descriptions in very generalized terms. Having studied a classroom, a few classrooms, even a substantial number of classrooms, the researcher feels required to cast his report in terms of comments about '*the* language of teaching' (Edwards and Furlong, 1975), or '*the* work context of teaching' (Denscombe, 1980), or '*the* organization of pupil participation' (Hammersley, 1974). Thus the operative aim of much research is to see instances of the activity under scrutiny as being typical or representative of the whole category that they instance. Consequently, a classroom comes to stand in for *the* classroom.

Our objection to this approach is not at all the usual one, namely, that a few instances studied in some detail are not a sufficient basis for generalization to the type or category. No – because this usual and standard criticism requires the assumption that the aim of generalizing is the right one and that the issue for discussion concerns means of obtaining it. For us, ends come into question. For the presumption of the need for generalizing involves the desire to talk about classrooms-in-general before we can seriously claim to have understood what goes on in any one of them.

We do not accept the stock reply that to understand a classroom *is* to understand it in general terms, i.e. to see it as the product of the same factors or forces which produce order and organization not in one, but in the generality of classrooms. We do not think that this is the right way at all and would say that generalization is a matter of understanding the relationship between instances, and to do so requires an understanding of the instances themselves. We need do no more to counter the stock reply than resort simply to pointing to the consequences of a premature wish for generality. The desire to generalize has the inevitable consequence of directing the attention of researchers to the organization of classrooms only insofar as they resemble one other. It creates an interest in those elements of classroom organization that are the same from classroom to classroom, regardless of the diversity of things that might otherwise be seen to be going on in them.

The employment of abstraction is the problematic accompaniment of the urge to generalize. The argument goes that science must abstract, that we all do abstract and that we cannot avoid doing so. Accordingly, to understand the organization of classrooms we must abstract, we must leave out of account what is being taught. Whether the pupils are being taught music or chemistry or English or history, we must look at the general dynamics of the organization of classrooms as collective and co-ordinated occasions; or at the formal properties of teacher-pupil relations and the power asymmetries that obtain; or at the sequencing of question-answer alternations in talk.

We suggest, however, that whilst abstraction may be an inevitable feature of scientific work, it is a strategic one, whereas the question of what we can leave out is pivotal. And what we can leave out depends upon what we are trying to do. We think that we are looking for something rather different from those sociologists who may seem in many respects to occupy something like the same position as us. We are interested in the question of how actions are done, how activities are organizsed or, more accurately, how they organize themselves. We are not interested in seeing what standard of typical patterns the same sorts of activities 'fall into', but on the contrary want to see how activities are accomplished without caring whether they do or do not show the same forms of arrangement as other activities.

Consequently, we are not looking for those sorts of patterns which become visible only through comparing many different occasions or undergoing a sophisticated sociological training. We want to attend to those matters which are visible in the midst of the activity which manifests them. We attend to such matters because we want to emphasize those things which are practically indispensable to the staging of an occasion as that occasion.

Thus our emphasis shifts away from questions about the way one occasion resembles others of the same sort in favour of questions which ask about the way a specific occasion is put together. In short, we move to questions about the occasion's specificity, about the way 'this one' is put together. We recognize that such a characterization of our approach seems repetitive and could be thoroughly opaque so we will shortly attempt a more lucid formulation of these contentions by providing illustrations for them.

From this point of view, the 'business' of occasions is not something which can be abstracted out. On the contrary, its treatment becomes something which is analytically inescapable. From our point of view, the practical organization of the classroom is inextricable from its 'subject matter'.

For some sociological analysts, it is wholly legitimate to disregard the question of how teachers and pupils talk history or biology or whatever. If their interest is in questions like the share-out of talk in the classroom between teacher and pupils, or the sorts of distribution of types of utterances (interrogative, imperative, etc.) amongst different types of parties to a classroom, then it does not really matter about the content of the talk. If, however, such investigations are intended to contribute to understanding the operation of social life and settings, then the selection of such topics leaves quite unclarified the nature of the relationship between the patterns of distribution which they reveal and the workaday business of taking 4x through the administrative reforms of King John in period 3 on Tuesday.

From our standpoint, we cannot afford to abstract out such matters for it is precisely the issue of what is to be said/talked about which is the issue for practical organization.

For those who must conduct classes, the question of what is to be talked about and how, word by word, it is to be talked about is the very stuff of the work. The working teacher cannot dispense with the content of the talk and utter a sequence of interrogatives and imperatives. To continue with the example from history, he must ask for the names of kings, the dates of battles, the summary content of court rolls, the enumerated content of legislation and so forth. What can be mere detail for the sociologist interested in distributional aspects of talk cannot be so treated by the speakers and hearers in the setting, for they must 'enact' that 'mere detail', they must produce it in and as the business that they do.

A cautionary point – we are not saying that the parties to classroom activity cannot dismiss things as mere detail, for assuredly they can and do. If they do so, however, then it is incumbent upon us not to take this dismissal as a standard of our own judgement of what does and does not deserve attention. Instead, we must treat it as the occasion for considering, for example, the way in which exposition of a subject can involve dispensing with details on that occasion.

Contrastive Orientations to Phasing

Let us try to clarify the character of our argument by exemplifying the contrast we are trying to make through the consideration of how 'phasing' in a lesson, seminar, or lecture might be treated. Though the points we are making can be applied equally to the organization of the lesson, seminar, or lecture, the problems and practices we shall choose to illustrate our comments will tend to relate most specifically to the environment which is most familiar to us, that of higher education.

We must take our argument most carefully at this point because we can seem to be producing a glowing contradiction, i.e., criticizing generalized accounts of teaching on the one hand, but providing an equally generalized, even over-generalized, version on the other. Let us make it quite clear, then, that the following remarks make no kind of pretensions to being, or even preparing to be, some generalized, systematic account of how teaching is organized. They are addressed to some issues of principle which bear upon research methodology and they are generalized remarks only in this sense. At no point is any mention of 'teaching' to be taken to imply that the kind of practice we are talking about is a standard or widespread one. We are talking purely of some things than can and do happen in the world of teaching, things that must be allowed for in any putatively general account of that activity. Thus, comments on 'teaching' are not presented as the products of careful study of instances of that phenomenon but as suggestions as to how we might begin the inspection of such instances.

We are taking it that the elemental problem is to understand not what patterns activities fall into, but how they are 'put together' into whatever patterns they might make: it is the assembling, not the final shape of the assembly, that is of interest. This contrast applies to the treatment of phasing.

It is clear enough that activities in classrooms often have an episodic character, that the kinds of activities being engaged in over time differ quite considerably and that progress through them is made by 'finishing' with one kind and 'initiating' another. Thus, we can see that the typical class moves from arriving-and-settling-in at the beginning through to clearing-up-and-preparing-to-leave at the end.

What are we to make of this episodic character to events? One thing that can be and has been (Hargreaves *et al*, 1975) made of it is an effort to identify a standard and ordered sequence of phases for the typical classroom and an associated set of procedures for moving from one stage to the next. Of course, we know only too well that in actual classrooms the episodic arrangements are endlessly voiced, that the duration, constituent activities, character and interrelationship of discernible episodes are all greatly diversified. If we wish to achieve an identification of generally followed phases without necessitating an inordinate amount of detailed study of an enormous range of classroom activities, then the way to do so is to make the stages simple and very abstract, to characterise them in such general terms that they will readily be applicable to any classroom. For example, we can readily identify broad stages like 'entry', 'settling in' 'down to business', 'finishing up', 'leaving'. In the same way, we can identify practices for moving from one phase to the next. These practices too can be done, for example, abstractly and generally, e.g. by using 'changing place and position' and 'making announcements of phase transition'. Such broad categories would encompass the multitudinous range of doings from 'sit down' through 'I want all of you to come over here' and 'get your books out' to 'now its story time' or 'you can go now'.

It is not *too* difficult, then, in a rough way to contrive an order of phases to a lesson, but how does it contribute to our understanding of the way activities are organized, or done? By studying diverse classroom activities, we can contrive categorizations which are sufficiently abstract to classify the activities in them all. By comparing and contrasting aspects of these different locations one with another, we can build up a composite picture of them all, but by doing so we beg the question of how they achieve the order that we find them to have. How came this order-of-phases? Is it the product of some 'logic of social interaction' or what? How do the phases we as sociological analysts identify relate to those that the participants can discriminate? How do they 'follow through' this order-of-phases? Do they (somehow) simply fall into it or fall in with it, or do they aim to produce it? And if they aim to produce it, how do they ensure its accomplishment? These questions are surely compellingly relevant to any claim to understand how ordinary in-classroom activities work. Indeed, before setting out to identify general properties of classroom activity, we need to have given a lot of thought to what we are doing it for.

In the analytical mentality of the researcher, one of the things that an effort to discriminate phases and episodes requires is their precise definition, the identification of exact points of transition. The approach requires an orientation to activities in a way designed to pick out and bound as sharply as possible the discriminable episodes. Yet, we note that one thing which is widely noticeable about classroom activity is that the parties to it are engaged not in discriminating episodes (as a cognitive or perceptual matter), but in segregating them (as an organizational or managerial matter). Therefore, the extent to which the researcher can identify distinct phases will depend upon the extent to which the parties have kept them separate. It is easy to talk about the ordered phases of 'settling in' and 'getting down to business', but casual observation shows that the extent to which 'settling in' takes place before 'getting down to business' depends on the extent to which people insist on getting settled in first. Thus, a start can be deferred whilst waiting for all parties to arrive and until everyone present has subsided into silence. Equally well, a start can be made even as people are arriving and settling in or starts and restarts can be made in response to the appearance of late arrivals. Sometimes, indeed, a start can be made and then abandoned in favour of some other item of business. The extent to which episodes are ordered, and segregated, then, can depend upon the extent to which someone insists that they be so shaped. Thus the teacher can insist, 'no start until you are all ready.'

Similarly, it is possible for parties to orient to and achieve imperceptible transitions between episodes, to move things from one phase to another in such a way that the realization that a transition has been made will occur only retrospectively, being noticed only when in the midst of the new phase. The visibility of the organization of in-classroom activity in its course is something that is deeply implicated with their organization. It is a practically relevant matter for teaching and lecturing whether people should be clearly aware that they are stopping doing one thing and starting to do another, different one, or whether they should be started off doing one thing and led into doing something quite different without being aware what is happening to them.

We are not, however, suggesting that phases 'just happen', that classroom activities 'turn out' to have an episodic structure. On the contrary, they turn out to have such a structure because it has been projected from the outset.

Although what goes on in the classroom does have a moment-to-moment organization, it is not organized on that basis alone, for the moment-to-moment organization represents (can represent) the realization of a prior design, the fulfilment of an intended succession of phases. For some parties to the occasion, then, the future development of the occasion will have been anticipated. It will not, however, have been idly anticipated in the sense that it was expected and it did happen. Rather, it will have been actively anticipated in the sense that it will have been projected and action taken to bring it about as projected.

The projection of an anticipated course of development implies, for understanding what is going on at any point in time, attention being paid to the way in which present activities possess the potential for future development. We have to attend to the way in which the arrangement of matters now is being undertaken in order to provide for the possibility that later (in fifteen minutes, say, or 'after we have finished what we are doing now') the parties will be 'in position' to make the projected transition from this episode to that. Thus, present activities can be examined as 'preparation' or 'groundwork' for the achievement of a required transition: just what do we have to do now to ensure, for example, that there will be time to clear away before the bell goes and the next class comes in? Just how do we make a start so that we not only visibly 'get down to business' in such a way that first remarks will identify the topic being initiated, but also ensure that the mode of address to this topic will produce coherent subsequent talk that will lead into the next topic as its natural successor? For example, it is possible that as a lecture begins, and specific remarks are made, the lecturer has no idea how specifically the transitions will be made. Instead the talk is genuinely improvized, and, having begun, ways will be found to bring about the promised organization. Indeed, laying things out at the beginning, by giving a promised arrangement, is a way of keeping the business to an anticipated course. To write things up on the board in anticipation of doing them is a way of ensuring that they will get done. To list things to be talked of is a way of reminding ourselves later, when we have talked on some of them, which other intended objects of discussion we have promised. In fact, promising is a way of construing future possibilities of development by setting up commitments to do the promised activity.

An important aspect of phasing is pacing. We would certainly not want to be taken as arguing that those who project a course of development for a class have a definite and precisely timed preconception of the course to be taken. Matters can be more or less definitely anticipated and subsequent development can be tied more or less firmly to a strict scheduling. The pacing of phasing may follow a strict schedule so that the approach of the scheduled termination of a phase may also terminate that activity without regard for its stage of completion. Alternatively, an activity may be brought to a 'natural' closure by means of the expeditious and truncated treatment of matters outstanding. Adherence to the schedule can be given priority, but need not be. Nor need any strict scheduling be attached to a projected arrangement in the first place. We can pace ourselves so that matters will be treated, however long that proves to take. Therefore, the completion of a task in hand will be guaranteed, though all will have to wait to see how long that will take, to see what will have to be said to comprise exhaustive talk adequate-for-our-purposes to some topic. Thus, announcements of projected phasings can take the form of contingency plans of the sort, 'I'll try to finish talking about that this week but if not I'll carry over into the next class. On the other hand, if I do get to the end then I'll start on . . . .'.

Providing the Organization

In the previous section, we have been trying in part to make a contrast between (1) the idea that it is the researcher's job to find an organization in activities which is standard and related to the requirements of sociological theory, and (2) the idea that we might look to find the organization that is, so to speak, put there to be found.

The organization in (2) is not put there to be found by sociologists; it is the organization that is put there to be found by participants in the activity being organized. It is the organization that is put there to be found by the students, colleagues, administrators and all those who have legitimate interests in and rights to know 'what goes on in classrooms'. In fact, so far we have been taking it for granted that talk in classrooms can be seen as carrying out the tasks of teachers and students or pupils and we have been leading up to the point that it is someone's task to give the occasion organization.

Returning to the main theme, then, we can say that the task of giving an organization to events in a classroom often falls to the teacher though it need not necessarily do so. How the class is to be run, what it is to do, who is to do what – these are matters which can be collectively decided, and negotiating a division of labour in organizing the occasion (or the course) can be one feature of the occasion (or course) itself. Further, the word 'negotiate' has been somewhat abused in recent years in sociology in the form of a generalized conception of social order as negotiation, but in the arrangement of some classes it can and does find quite liberal application. For the arrangements of a class can be made in the form of a deal of the sort, 'if you'll do this, then I'll do that', and 'if you'll do this I won't do what I could, i.e. if you'll talk up I won't set assignments for you to do.'

Of course, the task of giving the occasion organization does usually fall to the teacher and the work involved is not achieved simply through the making of talk in the classroom alone, but through the production of artefacts such as the provision of course outlines, organized reading lists, essay lists and the adoption of a textbook's organization as the model for the course to follow. In these ways, parties to the classroom activities can be informed about the purpose and content of the course, the topics to be treated and their sequential or phased order of treatment.

Again, we do not want to be understood to be proposing that it is invariably the case that the teacher decides these matters. We are well aware that the negotiation of a division of labour for a course can involve such matters as electing a theme and deciding an order of topics. Even where teachers retain control of the course organization, they can attempt to 'farm out' the work of discovering thematic unity, developing arguments or cumulating information in course activity. For example, the provision of required readings as a basis for the organization of classes can give students the task of making out the connections between texts and between topics. Tussles can and do take place over the discoverability of projected course contents, with students complaining that they cannot see the plan, direction, unity, development or payoff in the things they are presently doing. Thus teachers often have 'time out' from projected organizational arrangements in order to review and debate these very arrangements with a view to proposing and accomplishing some reconstruction of them.

Such observations of classroom organization are sometimes criticized on the grounds that we cannot understand what goes on in a classroom without reference to the 'context' within which activities are set. Often, this argument is about whether we need to 'relate' what goes on in the classroom to the organization of the school as an organization, or to the organization of the society as a whole, especially its history and class structure.

It is all too easy to exchange views about the importance of 'context' without ever achieving any sort of clarity as to what is to be counted as relevant for inclusion in 'context'. Here, we cannot pursue the very complicated question of the role of 'context' very far save in one of its most cogent aspects, namely, the question of whether in understanding in-classroom activities we can do so without reference to 'a wider social setting'. One argument about the importance of 'context' supposes that there is a determinate, all-inclusive context, that of the society as a whole, and that no action or activity can be understood unless it is set against this 'context'.

In sociology, there is much controversy about this. One issue, which many people think is the most important, concerns scale. Roughly, sociologists are divided between those who look at societies as a whole and those who look at face-to-face transactions. Still others seek a compromise and try to show that the way to resolve controversy (if it can be resolved) is to treat both approaches as complementary. Without denying the legitimacy of looking at life in the classroom with all the accompanying fine details of conduct, these concilliators suggest that we need to understand how the classroom 'fits into' the society as a whole.

We have already suggested that the key methodological question is never only 'what do we look at?', but always and importantly is also 'how are we to look?'. Clearly, then, in our view, scale cannot be the significant question. Here we disagree with most students of in-classroom activities who are likely to share the assumption that the consideration of scale is crucial. In their view, such a consideration does reflect a real difference in what is done, because they tend to see their contribution to the sociology of education as that of turning attention away from the study of 'the education system as a whole' and towards the examination of 'what really goes on in classrooms'.

We do not see any point in taking militant positions *vis-à-vis* the issue of whether we should or should not confine our attention to what goes on in the classroom, especially since we are trying to raise questions as to what (from a sociological point of view) does 'go on' in classrooms. Further, we do not see all answers as cumulative and interconnected and the question as to whether we can or cannot understand what goes on in the classroom without reference to the 'wider social context' seems only to raise other questions: what aspects of life in the classroom do we seek to understand? Do we require reference to 'external' considerations to understand them?

As we have already noted, questions about the organization of actions are often begged and never more evidently so than in sociologists' discussions about the relationship between in-classroom activities and the 'wider environment'. For their arguments presuppose that they have a clear understanding of how activities actually do relate together and that they do understand the way in which local events such as classroom activities build up into that most complex system of activity, the society as a whole. We do not simply doubt, but go so far as to deny, that such an understanding has been attained. The argument is that our task is precisely that of understanding how one action relates to another, how one activity relates to another.

In the first instance, this task does not query the relationship between two specific actions, A and B, but raises the question of the kinds of relationships that are to be looked for. Thus, many think of the kind of relationship between activities to be looked at in causal terms, i.e. does one action bring about another? Others like the idea that actions can be looked at as part of a strategy to see what kind of calculated connection action A may have to B as a way of achieving a goal. On our part, we are trying to suggest yet another way of looking for connections, namely that actions are to be looked at as constituents of courses of action, to see how they relate to each other in carrying out the courses of action they make up. This way of making our point may be too abstract and some exemplification will be useful.

In a classroom it may be that there is something which can be pointed to as 'the business' of that class, i.e. what it has been organized to do. For example, in a lecture it is the case that, sometimes, the lecture 'makes one point' and that what the lecture has to say is said briefly, in so many words, at a late point in the lecture's course. Nonetheless, a great deal of talking may be done in that lecture prior to the making of that point. How does that talking relate to the making of the lecturer's point? It can, of course, relate in a great many ways, but it could be, for example, that the previous talk provides 'scene setting' for the making of that point, laying the groundwork for the business of that class by giving the students background to the point to be made, by giving them technical information to let them understand the point when it is made, by providing context for the point to be made so that its significance will be seen when it is made, by 'setting up' the argument so that the point will come as a surprising conclusion and so forth. The work of the lecture may, then, be preparatory to, elucidatory of, facilitating progress toward and explicating the sense and significance of its own conclusion. We are suggesting, then, that it is in terms of their 'organizational contribution' that we can look at the diverse activities in the classroom, to see – as we illustrate with the example of the lecture – what role they play in getting the work of the classroom done.

Understood in such terms, what is 'going on' in the classroom consists in its business-like organization and a bare transcription of the talk, however faithfully it might depict every sound made in the classroom, would not, for those involved in the classroom, count as an adequate record of what was said and done. A page of student notes, however sparse, listing 'main points made' might be, for them, a better, more relevant, more useful record, identifying not 'what was said' but, instead, 'what the lecturer was getting at with what was said . . .'.

For students to show that they understand what took place it would not do for them to produce a good record of the talk in a lecture for they are required to attend to that talk not as specific utterances but as the presentation of a subject matter. Consequently, they are required to see what is said as, for example, exhibiting a subject's principles, steps in a developing argument. They are required to see in the talk things that will never be explicitly said, to identify hints, allusions and elliptical references, to see the connection between what is said here and now and what has been said in previous meetings of the same course or in different courses than this. That they understand what was said is not shown by reciting the words that were used; they show they follow the sense and course of remarks by reformulating them, by saying things in their own words, by seeing what is said as something that can equivalently be said in quite other words. For teachers, reading

ing student assignments and examinations is a way of finding out what has been 'going on' in the classroom, how the things that were being said were being understood, what arguments, themes, conclusions, etc. were being extracted from the talk, etc. It is not usual for such readings to yield surprises.

The Oral Exposition of a Subject

Throughout, we have been trying to return attention to the 'official business' of the classroom, to play up the extent to which talk of and thought about events in the classroom are inextricably involved with what ought to be going on in classrooms.

It has often come to be conceived as a mark of sociological artfulness to show that what goes on in any social setting is almost anything except its official business. Just as in courtrooms the waiting, rather than the trial, can be seen to take up the time and effort, so in classrooms the struggle-for-control rather than the teaching can be seen to be what is important. We do not wish to deny this importance. After all, it is a matter which will be the material for common room/staff room gossip and speculation for any teaching organization. At the same time, however, we would wish to give recognition to the fact that the struggle-for-control is usually undertaken in the service of getting some teaching done and that keeping control and getting through the requisite subject matter are tasks which can be done concurrently.

We are suggesting that there is no need to suppose, because teaching is sometimes a struggle-for-control, that it is generally so. Therefore, we need not see all that goes on in any classroom as instrumental in maintaining control and need not think of all occasions where someone is not overtly maintaining control as being ones in which they must, therefore, covertly be doing so. Rather, we should ask: when does control arise as a problem for teachers? And when it does, how then is it resolved?

We would rather see this question asked because it does not then tempt us to exercise ingenuity in contriving ways of seeing how talk about the imagery in *Othello* is 'really' an exercise in social control. We want to propose that it been seen instead as talk which is really an exercise in identifying the imagery in *Othello*. Of course, we know that the 'official business' of the classroom does not occupy all the time, and does not always take place in class. Knowing these things does not mean, however, that the analysis of that 'official business' when it is done should be slighted.

Although, a lot of the time, the talk in the economics class is not of marginal utility or other recognizably relevant matters, a lot of the time it *is* about such matters. As a discipline, we sociologists are a long way from

understanding how lists, anecdotes, diagrams, sketches, equations, assertions, interrogations, allusions to writings, monologues, demonstrations,
picture shows with commentaries, discussion of handouts, walking the
streets and talking about what is seen – how these comprise 'teaching sociology' or 'chemistry' or 'economics' or whatever. Drawing pictures, making
lists, reading out quotations, putting things in numerical form, summarizing
arguments, these sorts of things are the practices of our society and we do not
think that anyone can yet claim to understand how such practices work
(other than in a practical sense). Nor does anyone know how, heteroge-
neously combined, they can serve to comprise 'a basic course in statistics',
'advanced chromodynamics' or 'an introduction to physics for those without
maths' and in the course provide, for example, a 'rigorous and systematic
exposition of principles', 'a guide for beginners' or 'a basis for independent
practice'.

Some More Conclusions

We always find it cheering to end with the recognition that as yet we, as
analysts, understand very little about the things we study. After all, this
recognition means that more or less everything remains to be done. At the
same time, we stress that *members* routinely accomplish their everyday
business without undue problems. We hope that we have fulfilled our promise of making some inroads into the study of this taken-for-granted accomplishment in classrooms. That is to say, into the practical management of
'doing teaching'.

References

DENSCOMBE, N. (1980). 'The work context of teaching', *British Journal of the
     Sociology of Education*, vol. 1, No. 3, pp. 279–290.
EDWARDS, A.D. and FURLONG, A.V. (1975). *The Language of Teaching*.
     Heinemann.
HAMMERSLEY, M. (1974). 'The organization of pupil participation', *Sociological
     Review*, 22, No. 3, pp. 355–68.
HAMMERSLEY, M. (1976). 'The mobilization of pupil attention', in Hammersley,
     M. and Woods, P., (eds.), *The Process of Schooling*. Routledge and Kegan Paul.
HAMMERSLEY, M. (1977). 'School learning: the cultural resources required to
     answer a teacher's questions', in Woods, P. and Hammersley, M., (eds.), *School
     Experience*. St. Martin's Press.
HARGREAVES, D., HESTER, S.K. and MELLOR, F.J. (1975). *Deviance in
     Classrooms*. Routledge and Kegan Paul.

Putting Competence into Action: Some Sociological Notes on a Model of Classroom Interaction

M. Hammersley

The study of classroom interaction has a quite surprisingly long history, and one of its distinctive features is a baffling array of approaches with different purposes, foci and terminologies. Despite this diversity, however, much of the most recent work in the field shares a fundamental idea which contrasts with the older 'classroom observation' tradition.[1] Crudely put, it is non-behaviourist: it has not sought to restrict itself to the description and explanation of 'observable behaviour'. Rather, the central aim has been to discover the assumptions, rules, strategies, etc. which underlie and produce classroom interaction. Nevertheless, within the boundaries of that common theme, there are still some major differences of approach and it is on one of these that I want to focus on here.

Now, of course, the nature of the approach one adopts depends on one's purposes, and in the case of classroom interaction we are faced with several different disciplines as well as different schools of thought within those disciplines. My criticisms in this paper are not meant to suggest that there is only one set of proper purposes, or that classroom interaction is the 'territory' of one discipline. However, I do think that we should work towards the situation where the purposes, theories and findings of neighbouring disciplines are at least compatible and preferably complementary. It is certainly true that much sociology ignores linguistics, indeed much sociology ignores language, and that is a target for justifiable criticism. However, in this paper I want to point to some sociologically troubling aspects of some recent work in linguistics, sociolinguistics and the philosophy of language,[2] though I shall focus specifically on some recent work in the first discipline. I want to try to show that this work, while in many respects instructive, predicates a kind of sociological theory which is unsatisfactory in a number of different ways.[3]

I want to contrast what I shall call competence and action models of social interaction.[4] In the competence approach, particular instances or recurring patterns of human activity are treated as competent displays of culture membership, and the discovery of the rules or procedures by which that activity was, or could have been, produced is taken as the exclusive goal. I would count the following as examples of such an approach: 'the ethnography of speaking',[5] speech act analysis,[6] conversational analysis,[7] and discourse analysis.[8]

Action theory, on the other hand, while similarly anti-behaviourist, treats patterns of activity as the product of interaction between groups with different concerns and interests, who define situations in distinctive ways and develop strategies for furthering those interests, often by means of negotiation and bargaining with one another. In relation to any particular action, the action theorist asks what intentions and motives underlie it and how these relate to the actor's perspective or definition of the situation. Examples of an action approach can be found in interactionist ethnography,[9] transactional anthropology,[10] and social phenomenology.[11] Some work seems uneasily to span the divide between the competence and action approaches, that of Goffman being the most obvious example.[12]

At the risk of disclosing something of what is to come, I could say, baldly, that competence theories are concerned with explaining social order, action theories with detecting and accounting for patterns of social control.[13] However, for me this indicates the deficiencies of both, rather than the superiority of one over the other.

My argument is that, as an overall framework, the action approach is the more promising. However, this framework is underdeveloped, in part, I think, because of a kind of empiricism whereby more emphasis has been placed on investigating the content of perspectives and strategies employed by particular groups of actors in particular settings than on developing the underlying theory. The result has been that the concepts which are central to the action model, 'perspective' and 'strategy', have an inadequate and usually implicit theoretical context which takes the form of a vague pluralism in which different groups simply have different interests and different views of, and strategies for dealing with, the world.

There are two implications of this implicit theory relevant here. The first is that definitions of the situation tend to be treated as though they are produced out of nothing. This ignores both the cultural resources which are used to produce them and the fact that perspectives often become institutionalised. The second relevant feature of this implicit theory is that it fails to recognise the problem of mutual understanding which arises if different groups have different perspectives. Unlike Mead the founder of interactionism, latter-day interactionists have not tended to address the question of how communication and the co-ordination of action are possible.[14] Those working within competence approaches, on the other hand, have addressed both these problems and made some progress in dealing with them. I am not suggesting, therefore, that work done by those operating within a competence framework is simply mistaken and should be discarded, but rather that it must be recast into an action-based approach, a process which will transform the latter.

Having briefly sketched what I regard as the deficiencies of the action model, I want to turn now to the failings of the competence approach. To illustrate my arguments I shall focus on the work of Sinclair and Coulthard (1975), since this is the best-developed treatment of classroom interaction employing a competence approach.[15] However, I think my arguments apply equally to the other variants of competence theory.[16]

What I want to suggest is that the competence model amounts to a kind of cognitive functionalism sharing similar virtues and vices to normative functionalism.[17] The virtues are a disciplined search for systematic interrelation between the apparently unconnected, a concern with describing whole systems, and a willingness to seek explanations for the 'obvious'. Its vices are a reification of patterns of interaction as they exist at one socio-historical location into universal structures fulfilling universal functions;[18] an assumption of widespread consensus about rules and a neglect of the complex patterning of interests involved in social interaction; and an inability to explain change except as the result of the impact of external events. In this paper I shall try to show that these criticisms are also applicable to the competence model of classroom interaction.

Where normative functionalism, at least in its Parsonian form, is concerned with the norms and values that must be internalised by members of a society if that society is to function, those researchers working within the competence framework set out to specify the rules or procedures that underlie the competent performance of various kinds of social activity. In both cases the nature of the product – a properly functioning society and the performance of a particular activity – are treated as consensually defined and/or as analytically identifiable. Thus, in their introduction, Sinclair and Coulthard explain their choice of classroom interaction as a focus in terms of its characteristic structure:

> we decided it would be . . . productive to begin . . . with a more simple type of spoken discourse, one which has much more overt structure than 'desultory' conversation, where one participant has acknowledged responsibility for the direction of the discourse, for deciding who shall speak when, and for introducing and ending topics.
>
> (1975, p. 6)

Here we have the distribution of conversational rights as it typically occurs in the classroom proposed as a feature of a type of discourse. With this reformulation an element of necessity is added. Certain features of classroom interaction are 'fixed' as constitutive of that discourse type. Furthermore, these features seem to be thought of as in some sense functional:

> Verbal interaction inside the classroom differs markedly from desultory conversation in that its main purpose is to instruct and inform and this difference is reflected in the structure of the discourse. In conversation, topic changes are unpredictable and uncontrollable, for as Sacks has shown, a speaker can even talk 'on topic' without talking on the topic intended by the previous speaker. Inside the classroom it is one of the functions of the teacher to choose the topic, decide how it will be subdivided into smaller units and cope with digressions and misunderstandings.
>
> (Coulthard, 1977, p. 101)

One of the implications of the treatment of these features of classroom interaction as constitutive of a type of discourse is that any deviation from this pattern is conceived as resulting in meaninglessness:

> It is deviant to withhold feedback continually, and we have a tape of one lesson where a teacher, new to a class, and trying to suggest to them that there aren't always right answers, does withhold feedback and eventually reduces the children to silence – they cannot see the point of his questions.
>
> (Sinclair and Coulthard, 1975, p. 51)

An implication of this is that there are no rational grounds for deviance, it is the product of whim:

> This category (teacher direct) covers all exchanges designed to get the pupil to do but not say something. Because of the nature of the classroom, the Response is a compulsory element of structure. This is not to suggest that children always do what they are told, but it does imply that the teacher has a right to expect the pupil to do so. Just as anyone can produce an ungrammatical sentence when he feels like it, so a pupil can break the rules of discourse.
>
> (Sinclair and Coulthard, 1975, p. 50)

Yet we have evidence that pupils often have different conceptions of how one should behave in the classroom from teachers, and this, in part, is because they have different patterns of interest.[19] And even if we did not have such evidence it would be cavalier to dismiss pupil deviance in this way. Now I don't want to deny that, in many senses, classroom interaction is a collaborative product, with teachers and pupils operating on the basis of similar working definitions of 'proper classroom behaviour'. I am not suggesting that the classroom is inevitably, or even typically, a setting in which there is an implacable conflict of interests between teachers and pupils: the relationship between the parties is much more subtle and complex; indeed, it is a mistake to assume that there are only two parties to classroom interaction and that these parties are stable.[20] However, conflicts do arise and these cannot be accounted for by the competence model except in terms of inappropriateness and irrationality.

But not only does this approach not provide us with any room for a satisfactory explanation of deviance, it also involves an implicit and quite inadequate account of conformity: participants conform because any other behaviour is 'inappropriate'. And yet, in many lessons, much teacher talk is expended in getting pupils to conform to the rules and even to respond to directives. Thus there arise what one might call disciplinary digressions, which can amount to anything from a look to a half-hour lecture. Furthermore, these often involve promises and threats of various kinds, which indicates that teachers recognise the possibility of rational alternative lines of pupil action even if rhetorically they often deny such a possibility.

In the same way, presenting the teacher's behaviour in terms of following the rules of discourse is unsatisfactory. We must investigate why these rules seem appropriate and, in part, the explanation is likely to be that such patterns seem to teachers to facilitate their goals; though sometimes they may not, as in the example quoted above of the teacher who seeks to avoid giving feedback.

As a result of its failure to deal with motivation, the competence approach is unable to account for the possibility of change in patterns of classroom interaction, or even for the processes of socio-historical development which have produced those patterns which currently exist. The rules of discourse are presented as static and somehow given. Furthermore, the status of the rules documented by Sinclair and Coulthard is unclear: is the evidence for their existence statistical regularity or is it that these are oriented-to features of interaction? If the former, the problem arises that statistical regularities are not always normative. If the latter, the authors certainly do not provide evidence that all the rules are oriented to, and even where they do provide such evidence they appeal to their own and their readers' knowledge of classrooms rather than establishing that these particular participants orient to them.

Now I think I can anticipate two kinds of response to these arguments. The first is that competence theorists do, of course, recognise the breaking of rules for strategic purposes. Thus, immediately prior to the extract from page 51 quoted earlier, Sinclair and Coulthard comment: 'So important is feedback that if it does not occur we feel confident in saying that the teacher has deliberately withheld it for some strategic purpose' (p. 51). The second response is that the competence model is being criticised for not doing something which it was never intended to do. According to this argument, its goal is the specification of the rules which define classroom actions and thereby make it possible for teachers and pupils to understand one another's actions. It is not intended to be a full account of what is actually done by teachers and pupils.

I want to reply to both these points simultaneously. It is perfectly possible for a competence theorist to recognise the strategic breaking of rules, so long as that strategy is not intended to modify, and does not result in modification of, those rules. But once this is admitted as a possibility, rules are no longer a sufficient basis for the explanation of action, nor can a useful distinction be drawn between rule-related and strategic considerations as bases for action. This is, I suspect, why Sinclair and Coulthard, after making the comment quoted above about the teacher's strategic withholding of feedback, then go on to say that, if this is done continually, the pupils are reduced to silence.

What I am arguing, then, is that the distinction between discourse rules, on the one hand, and the strategies employed by teachers (and presumably also pupils), on the other, is not viable. Sinclair and Coulthard do not provide us with any strong grounds for accepting a distinction between discourse and pedagogy. They base this distinction on the notion of 'linguistic patterning': thus 'a year's work' has no linguistic structure, whereas 'a lesson' does (1975, p. 20). But we are not told what 'linguistic patterning' is, or what the other forms of patterning are from which it is being distinguished. From what little is said about the pedagogic level it is quite unclear how the patterning there is similar to and different from that at the other levels. Indeed, the meaning of the term 'linguistic' is obscure. Sometimes it seems to mean speech, as when they talk about 'linguistic introductions' (p. 19) and linguistic and non-linguistic responses in distinguishing between elicitations and directives. Now this interpretation of 'linguistic' does not necessarily rule out linguistic order beyond the level of the lesson, though one would have to study the talk of the parties to lessons separately, given their frequent dispersion before and after such occasions. And, indeed, this would allow us to deal with the important issue of topical coherence between lessons. However, it would rule out what the authors call 'reacts' since these are neither verbal nor 'non-verbal surrogates' for the verbal. Despite their inclusion of reacts, however, by the very nature of their data, and perhaps because of their disciplinary affiliations, the authors generally tend to restrict themselves to 'the linguistic' in this sense.[21]

This definition of 'linguistic' as 'the verbal' leads to a number of problems, one of which concerns the distinction between directives and elicitations. Elicitations are defined as requiring verbal responses, directives non-verbal responses. Here, it seems to me, the authors take what for for them is an important consideration – the verbal/non-verbal contrast – to be a central feature of the orientations of participants. I think they are mistaken, and offer the following examples to suggest this:

    (a) T: Now, who can tell me where Israel is? Go on then Jackson. (Pupil walks out to the front of the classroom and points to a place on the map drawn on the board.)

    (b) T: Do you think that's clever?
        P: No.

     T: No what?
     P: No sir.

While the teacher's utterance in (a) would presumably be classified by Sinclair and Coulthard as a directive, I suggest that it has more in common with elicitations. Conversely, 'No what?' seems best described as a directive even though it requires a verbal response. I suggest that the verbal/non-verbal distinction is not a satisfactory basis for distinguishing between directives and elicitations.[22]

There is, however, another way in which 'linguistic patterning' can be interpreted. It may be taken to mean the application of the notion of structure developed at the level of grammar to the analysis of social interaction. The goal here is the specification of rules of choice and chain. While linguistic patterning in grammatical terms is based on form, at the level of discourse it is to be based on function. Here again, though, we are faced with problems of interpretation: what kind of function is this and how are we to identify functions? The authors seem to identify function with teacher intention: 'Grammar is concerned with the *formal* properties of an item, discourse with the *functional* properties, with what the speaker is using the item for' (1975, pp. 27–8; original emphasis). Yet, clearly, only some kinds of teacher intention are to be included; much of what the teacher does in the classroom is left to the pedagogical level, but the basis for this allocation is not made explicit. So, for example, why is teacher direct – pupil react included while pupil deviance – teacher direct is excluded? In both cases the connection is complex because decision making, and not just rule following, is involved, though this is perhaps most obvious in the case of the latter connection.[23]

One final methodological point. Sinclair and Coulthard, quite rightly in my view, ground their functions in actor intentions, though there are times when they seem a little ambivalent about this, for example when they talk of 'discourse value'. However, the nature of the evidence at their disposal – transcripts – is an inadequate base for the identification of intentions, and the authors seem to place considerable tacit reliance on their knowledge of why teachers typically do what they do without testing it. An example occurs where they discuss 'starters':

> Starters are acts of which the function is to provide information about, or direct attention or thought towards, an area in order to make a correct response to the initiation more likely, even though this function is often only impromptu, when the teacher realizes that the intended elicitation was not adequate. What he has said can, however, serve as a starter to get the children thinking in the right area, and then the more explicit elicitation has more chance of success.

> 1 T: *What about this one? This I think is a super one.* Isobel, can you think what it means?
>   (Sinclair and Coulthard, 1975, pp. 34–5; original emphasis)

While this is quite a plausible interpretation, it is not the only one. I think one could equally argue that here we have an attempt to mobilise pupil participation *per se*, and there are, no doubt, other candidate descriptions. Which is correct has to be tested, but it may not be possible to do this relying on transcripts alone.

Conversational analysts, of course, would criticise the authors for attempting to ascribe intentions and motives in the first place (as would many sociological structuralists and functionalists). My point is a less severe one: simply that I believe the identification of intention and motive is more difficult than the authors seem to take it to be and that the use of other data sources, such as participant observation and interviewing, is necessary. All data sources are imperfect, but in different ways, and that means that, through their combination, we may be able to counter the major validity threats.[24]

In conclusion, let me repeat what I said at the start. I am not suggesting that the work of Sinclair and Coulthard be discarded as worthless. It is a very useful analysis, pointing to a number of important features of classroom interaction and indicating some of the requirements, hitherto ignored, which such analyses must meet. But it seems to me to restrict its focus to a sub-set of classroom interactional phenomena which is not a viable object of study. Furthermore, and for associated reasons, it conceptualises classroom interaction in terms of the following of constitutive rules, a conceptualisation which opens it up to the standard, and I think effective, criticisms which can be directed against normative functionalism. To escape such criticisms it is necessary to abandon the distinction between discourse and pedagogy and to treat classroom interaction as composed of interrelated actions which are the product not just of rule following, but also of decision making. What any particular action is, what its function is, should be assessed, in the first place, on the basis of some investigation of the patterns of intention and motivation which produced it, and this requires the use of a wider range of methods than just the analysis of transcripts of classroom talk.[25] This is not to deny that much classroom interaction is heavily institutionalised, and thus does amount to rule following. The point is, however, that these rules have become established through strategic thinking and actions and, at any point, may be suspended, modified or transformed as a result of strategic considerations. Only an action approach can take account of these features of classroom rules. However, as I remarked earlier, for it to become in any reasonable sense adequate, action theory requires considerable development, and this process of development must draw on the work already done within the competence framework.

Notes

1 For an outline and discussion of this tradition see Hamilton and Delamont (1974). For a more detailed account see Walker (1971).
2 They would not trouble all sociologists, of course, but only those committed to what, in this paper, I call action theory.
3 Incidentally, I recognise the perilous nature of this enterprise. It is very easy to misunderstand work in other disciplines – for example, because one is unaware of some crucial qualification which underlies all work in a discipline, or because one fails to allow for differences in purpose between disciplines. I trust my criticisms will be taken in the tentative, constructive spirit in which they are intended.
4 These are convenience labels and may be misleading from the point of view of linguistics where the contrast to competence is performance. I am rather uncertain about the relationship between this distinction and the one I am proposing here. As I see it at the moment, the action approach would argue that the competence – performance distinction can only be made for particular points in the development of a sequence of social interaction, since performance is continually modifying competence in marginal respects, and sometimes in major ways.
5 Hymes (1977).
6 Austin (1962) and Searle (1965).
7 Sudnow (1972); Turner (1974); Schenkein (1978). Conversational analysis is a difficult case. While in terms of ethno-methodological principles it escapes most of the problems I shall document here – though at enormous cost – in practice conversational analysts often seem to deviate from these principles in ways which leave their work open to my criticisms.
8 Sinclair and Coulthard (1975) and Coulthard (1977).
9 For examples concerned with classrooms, see Berlak *et al.* (1975), Woods (1977), A. Hargreaves (1979) and Hammersley (1974 and 1976).
10 There is no work in this tradition on classrooms, but see Kapferer (1976).
11 Berger and Luckmann (1967) and Schutz and Luckmann (1974). Hargreaves, Hester and Mellor (1975) represents an approach to classroom interaction which spans the interactionist and phenomenological approaches and also shows traces of a competence approach.
12 Gonos (1977) argues that Goffman's work has been misunderstood, that it is not interactionist but structuralist (i.e. not an action but a competence theory). However, this is rather unfair on Goffman's commentators since there seem to be elements of both approaches in his work (compare *The Presentation of Self* with *Frame Analysis*, for example), though I think it is probably correct to say that structuralism of a kind is dominant at least in his later work.
13 For the distinction between 'order' and 'control' theories see Dawe (1970).
14 This criticism is much less true of the phenomenologists but this approach has resulted in very little empirical work. For an expansion of these criticims, see Hammersley (1978).
15 The only other work at a similar level of development is that of Mehan (1979).
16 With, as I remarked earlier, the partial exception of conversational analysis which, when it does avoid these problems, does so only at an exorbitant cost: that of restricting the focus of research to 'possible methods' for producing accounts of social phenomena.
17 I am using 'functionalism' here in its sociological, not its psychological or linguistic, sense. That there should be such a similarity is not altogether surprising in the case of Sinclair and Coulthard's work, if one remembers the links between Malinowski, one of the founders of functionalist anthropology, and Firth; and,

perhaps more significantly, between Durkheim and Saussure.

18 There are versions of functionalism which seek to avoid this problem, such as that of Merton (1957), but in my view their strategies for doing this undermine the functionalist scheme.

19 For example, D.H. Hargreaves (1967) and Lacey (1970).

20 Furlong (1976).

21 Incidentally, this tendency also appears in speech act analysis where what are in fact elements of social acts become designated as *speech* acts.

22 Having made this criticism, I suppose I ought to provide an alternative basis for distinguishing directives from elicitations. My current view is that directives demand compliance to a rule implied, or spelt out, in the utterance, where compliance is assumed to be within the capabilities of the target actor; and failure to comply, at least in the absence of a disclaimer (Hewitt and Stokes, 1975) or remedial action (Goffman, 1972; Lyman and Scott, 1970), will be read as unwillingness and/or deviance. An elicitation, on the other hand, requires the production of a sign (not necessarily verbal) which fills in a frame implied or present in the utterance (see Schutz, 1962, for the concept of sign as used here). Ability to provide this is not necessarily assumed and failure to provide an 'appropriate' answer is not necessarily treated as deviance, though ignorance can sometimes be treated as indicating incompetence or stupidity. There is a complicating factor, however: elicitations always presuppose a directive, and refusal to answer the questions will be treated as deviance.

23 It is, of course, possible to identify further patterns which seem to fit this notion of linguistic patterning: for example, one can distinguish between teacher questions designed solely to test attention or demonstrate the inattention of pupils, and those which are concerned with testing learning or knowledge. This is not in itself a criticism – this is the kind of distinction which can be picked up with increased delicacy. See Hammersley (1976).

24 This is the notion of triangulation which originated with Webb, Campbell, Schwartz and Sechrest (1966). For an account of the role of triangulation within ethnographic research, see Hammersely (1979).

25 I stress *in the first place* because I do believe it is possible to talk of unintended functions.

References

AUSTIN, J.L. (1962). *How to do Things with Words*. London: Oxford University Press.

BERGER, P. and LUCKMAN, T. (1967). *The Social Construction of Reality*. Harmondsworth: Penguin.

BERLACK, A. *et al.* (1975). 'Teaching and Learning in English Primary Schools'. *School Review*, 83, 2, pp. 215–43.

COULTHARD, M. (1977). *An Introduction to Discourse Analysis*. London: Longman.

DAWE, A. (1970). 'The Two Sociologies'. *British Journal of Sociology*, 21, 2, pp. 207–18.

FURLONG, V. (1976). 'Interaction Sets in the Classroom: Towards a Study of Pupil Knowledge'. In M. Stubbs and S. Delamont (eds.), *Explorations in Classroom Observation*. New York: Wiley.

GOFFMAN, E. (1971). *The Presentation of Self in Everyday Life*. Harmondsworth: Penguin.

GOFFMAN, E. (1972). *Relations in Public*. Harmondsworth: Penguin.
GOFFMAN, E. (1975). *Frame Analysis*. Harmondsworth: Penguin.
GONOS, G. (1977). 'Situation versus Frame'. *American Sociological Review*, 42, 6, pp. 854–67.
HAMILTON, D. and DELAMONT, S. (1974). 'Classroom Research: A Cautionary Tale'. *Research in Education*, 11, pp. 1–15.
HAMMERSLEY, M. (1974). 'The Organisation of Pupil Participation'. *Sociological Review*, 22, 3, pp. 355–68.
HAMMERSLEY, M. (1976). 'The Mobilization of Pupil Attention'. In M. Hammersley and P.E. Woods (eds.), *The Process of Schooling*. London: Routledge & Kegan Paul.
HAMMERSLEY, M. (1978). 'What is a Strategy?' Unpublished paper.
HAMMERSLEY, M. (1979). *Data Collection in Ethnographic Research*. Open University Course DE304, Research Methods in Education and Social Science. Milton Keynes: Open University Press.
HARGREAVES, A. (1979). 'Strategies, Decisions and Control: An Analysis of Interaction in a Middle School Classroom'. In J. Eggleston (ed.), *Teacher Decision-Making in the Classroom*. London: Routledge & Kegan Paul.
HARGREAVES, D.H. (1967). *Social Relations in a Secondary School*. London: Routledge & Kegan Paul.
HARGREAVES, D.H., HESTER, S. and MELLOR, F. (1975). *Deviance in Classrooms*. London: Routledge & Kegan Paul.
HEWITT, J.P. and STOKES, R. (1975). 'Disclaimers'. *American Sociological Review*, 40, pp. 1–11.
HYMES, D. (1977). *Foundations in Sociolinguistics*. London: Tavistock.
KAPFERER, B. (1976). *Transaction and Meaning*. Philadelphia: Institute for the Study of Human Issues.
LACEY, C. (1970). *Hightown Grammar*. Manchester: Manchester University Press.
LYMAN, S.M. and SCOTT, M.B. (1970). *A Sociology of the Absurd*. New York: Appleton Century Crofts.
MEHAN, H. (1979). *Learning Lessons*. Harvard University Press.
MERTON, R.K. (1957). 'Manifest and Latent Functions'. In R.K. Merton (ed.), *Social Theory and Social Structure*. New York: Free Press.
SCHENKEIN, J. (1978). *Studies in the Organisation of Conversational Interaction*. New York: Academic Press.
SCHUTZ, A. (1962). 'Symbol, Reality and Society'. In *A. Schutz: Collected Papers*, vol. 1. The Hague: Nijhoff.
SCHUTZ, A. and LUCKMAN, T. (1974). *The Structures of the Life-World*. London: Heinemann.
SEARLE, J. (1965). 'What is a Speech Act'. In M. Black (ed.), *Philosophy in America*. London: Allen and Unwin.
SINCLAIR, J.MCH. and COULTHARD, R.M. (1975). *Towards an Analysis of Discourse; The English Used by Teachers and Pupils*. London: Oxford University Press.
SUDNOW, D. (1972). *Studies in Social Interaction*. New York: Free Press.
TURNER, R. (1974). *Ethnomethodology*. Harmondsworth: Penguin.
WALKER, R. (1971). 'The Social Setting of the Classroom: A Review of Observational Studies and Research'. Unpublished M. Phil. thesis, University of London.
WEBB, E.J., CAMPBELL, D.T., SCHWARTZ, R. and SECHREST, L. (1966). *Unobtrusive Measures*. Chicago: Rand McNally.
WOODS, P.E. (1977). 'Teaching for Survival'. In P.E. Woods and M. Hammersley (eds.), *School Experience*. London: Croom Helm.

PART THREE
Macro and Micro Analysis

Ethnography: The Holistic Approach to Understanding Schooling

F.W. Lutz

Introduction

This chapter sets forth a particular definition of ethnography and argues for its worth in educational research. In doing so, I may appear to be too hard on other research methods and educational researchers who utilize them. I apologize if the following conveys such an impression. I, myself, have utilized various research methods in pursuit of answers to research questions. I quarrel not with the methods of other researchers, but with the occasional contention that ethnography is not empirical. True, it is not statistical, but nothing could be more empirical. Additionally, and more importantly for our purpose in this chapter, I believe that applying the term *ethnography* to a broad range of studies which utilize some number of ethnographic methods or techniques but do not conform to the rules of ethnography (either in data collection or analysis), and also do not result in an ethnography, is counterproductive to ethnography as a methodology and the educational research which ethnography could produce.

Ethnography and ethnographic methods have become increasingly in vogue among educational researchers during the last decade. That trend seems likely to continue into the next decade. In general, I believe this to be a promising situation for educational research. Yet one can note two commensurate and somewhat related and disturbing cross currents. As educators twist the tool to fit their data (rather than shape their understanding of the data with the tool), ethnography, in particular, and sometimes ethnographic methods, are often modified and occasionally bastardized. As this happens, ethnographers in anthropology have a defensible platform from which to voice their disciplinary bias that none but anthropologists should engage in ethnography. The expression of that bias is merely the second disturbing crosscurrent detracting from the productive use of ethnography in education. The first is the production of poor research and ethnography by people in education who, untrained in ethnography, claim to engage in it.

Of course, there are degrees of quality in ethnographies which, as often as not, exist in the eyes of the reviewer. In addition, there are legitimate uses of ethnographic methods short of ethnography. It seems best to disregard the first question of honest differences of opinion about the quality of an honest-to-goodness ethnography. Although quality is always a matter of concern, the second question is the one of importance to the thesis presented here. This thesis involves the difference between ethnography and ethnographic methods. *Ethnography*, as will be expanded upon more fully later in this chapter, is, according to Geertz (1973), first and foremost a 'thick description.' As such, it involves many techniques or methods which can be described as ethnographic, including, but not limited to, participant observation, interview, mapping and charting, interaction analysis, study of historical records and current public documents, use of demographic data, etc. But ethnography centers on the participant observation of a society or culture through a complete cycle of events that regularly occur as that society interacts with its environment. The principle data document is the researcher-participant's diary. Ethnography is a holistic, thick description of the interactive processes involving the discovery of important and recurring variables in the society as they relate to one another, under specified conditions, and as they affect or produce certain results and outcomes in the society. It is not a case study, which narrowly focuses on a single issue, or a field survey that seeks previously specified data, or a brief encounter (for a few hours each day for a year, or 12 hours a day for a few months) with some group. Those types of research are ethnographic but *not ethnography!* They may be good research but, when they are passed off as ethnography, they are poor ethnography and poor research.

Ethnography vs. Micro-Ethnography

Having rejected research using a *selected* and limited sample of ethnographic methods as ethnography – including those limited to various types of formats for scoring and recording the interaction of small groups – I shall turn to the question of the scope of ethnography. Is the study of primmary or small groups ethnography, particularly when those studies have severely limited boundaries for data collection which prohibit extrusion of data collection into the larger environment?

The notion of 'Face-to-Face Analysis of Social Interaction' tends, in my view, to define the object of research as dyadic or at least small-group situation, and to relate the methods of data collection and conceptual analysis to the general purview of sociology and social psychology as distinct from anthropology. Even taken in its broadest sense, the phrase tends to limit the observations, data analysis, and theoretical framework to a type often termed *micro-ethnography*, as contrasted with the broader notion of ethnography as usually applied in the field of social or cultural anthropology. Such a tendency is, unfortunately, consistent with the type of ethnography or ethnographic work most often encountered in education. It applies to the study of small groups, often to a larger group, such as a whole class, and occasionally to single schools. This limitation tends to exclude studies of educational issues and questions in a broader and at least as important context – that of the school district-community, cultural perspective. I suggest that the narrow focus, while generating some important knowledge, fails to shed light on the more complex issues that account for much of what goes on (or doesn't go on) in schooling.

In an instructive and very insightful article, T.M.S. Evens (1977) speaks eloquently and analytically of the theoretical problems inherent in a single and narrow reliance on either transactionalism or structural functionalism. He does an excellent job of pointing out the methodological inconsistencies in each method. A brief quotation from his conclusion will serve our purpose; and I can then move on to some application of his conclusion to my own concerns about how anthropology and ethnography are applied to research in education. Evens concludes:

> Like the process whereby individuals interact in pursuit of their own separate concerns, the program whereby they mind and construct their collective interest is both heteronomous and autonomous. Barth (for example see Frederick Barth's 'Analytic Dimensions in the Comparison of Social Organizations,' *American Anthropologists*: 74, 207–220) is right; incorporation (the process of the individual acting in the interest of the group as opposed to his own single self-interest) is in a sense transactional; but in a sense it is not – it is metatransaction. It at once deviates from and transcends transaction (p. 593).

Thus, Evens suggests that there is *transaction*, the process of individuals in pursuit of their separate concerns; and *metatransaction*, the process of incorporation or people in pursuit of collective interest. As the two conditions overlap in time and space, specifying which process one is observing is a problem of focus.

The question of focus is always arbitrary – for the photographer, the biologist, or the social scientist. What brings one thing into clearly observable focus distorts another thing. To focus the camera lens on the butterfly on one's nose distorts the face; to focus on the face distorts the horizon in the background; to focus on the horizon distorts both the face and the butterfly. The same is as true in the social sciences as it is in photography. The social scientist has a right to be arbitrary. But one should not call the picture of a perfectly good butterfly a picture of a horizon.

To focus on transaction is to distort incorporation. To focus on face-to-face interaction is certainly not to do ethnography; in fact, it is likely to prohibit it. As Evens points out, transaction fails to account for a great deal of human behavior. That a great deal of important learning occurs beyond the one-to-one, face-to-face transactional process of teacher and student is at least one of the basic arguments for schooling, or learning in the group situation called *public schooling*. It can be argued that ethnography, as defined here, is the best research method to study such other and important schooling phenomena.

The narrower the focus of a study of schooling processes, the more likely important, perhaps necessary, variables are to be unseen and unaccounted for. Not only are statistical studies guilty of this narrow focus, but micro-ethnography also tends to be too limiting when taken as individual studies. How can the behaviors of the urban teacher (Smith and Geoffrey, 1968) be understood without reference to *The Man in the Principal's Office* (Wolcott, 1973)? Or the principal's behavior be understood except in the broader context of the central office, school board, and community described by Iannoccone and Lutz (1970)? Such understanding is certainly not likely to be developed by the observation of face-to-face interaction alone or understanding through the application of transactional analysis alone. Such understanding requires a broader, holistic approach rooted in the cultural context in which school districts are constituted, school boards are elected, superintendents are hired and fired, schools are built and staffed, and in which teachers and pupils go about the business of schooling.

Ramsey (1978) has pointed to a situation that has tended to limit the focus of ethnography in education. She suggests that the experience and training of the anthropologists in education on the one hand, and the educator-anthropologists on the other, affect the values and norms and therefore the perceptions of the researcher. As one result, the classroom or the individual school is most likely to be the focus of anthropological research in education. Strangely, the anthropologist who chooses education as the society to be studied is often less familiar with, and less informed about, that society than his/her fellow anthropologist, studying an exotic culture, is about that culture. The anthropologist studying education is often unaware of the types of bureaucratic control exercised by federal agencies, state education departments, local boards and central office staff, as well as the influence of individual school administrators and teacher organizations. Far from being free of bias, however, such researchers enter the field with beliefs about public schooling developed through twelve years of personal participation and perhaps as many more years as parent and/or taxpayer, as a more or less disinterested (nonresearch) participant observer (Lortie, 1975). For such a person the research focus is most likely to be the classroom or a school where 'everyone knows' education takes place.

Educator-anthropologists who may know better (often coming out of some educator role – most probably teacher) find the classroom and/or the school their natural focus and entry into that participant-observer role. Such a person has had the same exposure to 'preprofessional' data as the anthropologist; in addition, these ethnographers are well steeped in the 'perspectives' developed in teacher education institutions and the 'best practice' ideologies of the working profession in the classroom. For both anthropologist in education and educator-anthropologist, the classroom and/or the single school is the most likely focus of research dictated by their biases and their ease of entry and data accessibility.

The Quest for Meaning

Whether one engages in micro- or macro-ethnography, one should be engaged in the search for meaning! The first step in this search is the development of as complete as possible a body of data that describes the phenomenon being studied. That is ethnography! According to Geertz (1973), ethnography is 'thick description.' From this thick description, the anthropologist attempts to build a model of the important and recurring variables and the relationships among these variables, that describes and accounts for the phenomenon. The anthropologist develops from the ethnography an operational model (from the data of events *observed* by the researcher) and a representational model (from the data gathered from 'native' informants about the 'native' *interpretation* and meaning of what happened). These models are combined by anthropologists, using general anthropological theory, into an explanatory model that conceptually explains and predicts behavior within the culture under specified conditions (Caws, 1974).

This, I believe, is the essence of theory building, an aspect of research frequently neglected in the usual psychostatistical research conducted in education. Too often we test meaningless or weak hypotheses with very powerful statistics, based on very large samples, almost always selected more on the basis of convenience than by a randomized procedure from the population which we intend to generalize. Important to my thesis here is that the more we limit our ethnographic focus, the more likely we are systematically to limit our ability to *discover* some extremely important variable affecting the phenomenon which originates outside our narrow focus. Thus, seriously to limit the focus of ethnography in education is to compound a problem of psychostatistical research in education – the very problem that such research should alleviate. Are there important and recurring conceptual variables that emanate outside the face-to-face, pupil-teacher transaction – or even the classroom or school interaction – that affect such often researched topics as classroom discipline, pupil achievement (learning), or curriculum structure? Can we ever understand, predict, affect, or control these educational processes unless we discover that these relationships exist?

The Holistic Approach

In order to counter the problems just suggested, educational research should engage in macro-ethnography. I refer to research that seeks explanation within a broad cultural content, regardless of where the focus begins, and couches that explanation in an even broader cross-cultural approach. Wolcott (1975) identifies what he considers to be appropriate criteria for making judgements about ethnographic research in schools. Although I take exception to certain aspects of his 'criteria', the article is extremely helpful in guiding decisions about such research. I would like to identify four 'ingredients' that I believe to be important if one is to pursue the holistic ethnography approach recommended here. These are:

(a) Use of a researcher trained to do ethnography (I do not necessarily mean an anthropologist as opposed to an educator-anthropologist)
(b) Entry into the educational system which permits the pursuit of data vertically as well as horizontally throughh the cultural system
(c) A cross-cultural perspective of the research
(d) Ability of the ethnographers to develop 'thick description' and bring anthropological models and theory to bear on that ethnography.

Regarding these four ingredients, some amplification may be helpful.

Trained Ethnographer

It should be unnecessary to point out that ethnography cannot be done by any bright person who happens to be a participant in a society. Too often (particularly in doctoral research or school district evaluation) we have allowed anyone who can see and hear and write a sentence to do 'descriptive research,' and some call that ethnography. Every person who can change a tire is not a mechanic; a person who can repair a faucet is not necessarily a plumber; anyone who can drive a nail is not a carpenter; all who can do a chi square are not statisticians; nor does it follow that everyone who can write a paragraph describing an encounter between a teacher and a parent is an ethnographer.

Who then is an ethnographer? It is easiest and most reliable to define an ethnographer as a person who *has published* one or more ethnographies – just as a novelist is a person who has published one or more novels. Based on such a definition, a person could be employed based on proven ability. The person's work and the criticism of that work can be reviewed and the decision can be made based on previous accomplishment. This is likely to be expensive if one seeks proven excellence.

Another method would seek persons whose education and background have been systematically designed so as to produce ethnographers. Such persons should be able to demonstrate in some fashion that they have been trained in ethnographic methods, particularly participant-observer field methods. They should possess in-depth knowledge and understanding of anthropological theory and models. They should be able to supply some unpublished examples of the application of these theories and models and some type of ethnographic work in which they have engaged. Examples of these may be unpublished papers, master's and/or doctoral theses. Although the run-of-the-mill anthropologist may be more likely to be a good ethnographer than the run-of-the-mill teacher, the risk of getting a poor ethnographer based on a degree alone still exists. I would not bet on a horse unless I saw its record of past performances under track conditions similar to those of the race day. As noted earlier, some anthropologists will hold certain biases about educational cultures that will distort their data and make their conclusions as useless or harmful as the nonanthropologically trained educator's.

Entry and Access

Lots of things are descriptive. A whole class of statistics is 'descriptive,' an essay can be 'descriptive,' a map or picture is 'descriptive;' a case study is 'descriptive,' and ethnography, in its particularly holistic 'thick' sense, is 'descriptive.' Because of this situation, I have come to despair of the use of the term *descriptive research*, for it masks so many kinds and so wide a quality of research. Ethnography is a very special kind of description – a thick description – requiring special skills and a well-defined method.

Essential to 'thick description' is that the data that may be collected by the researcher should not be limited by personal bias, theoretical framework, or the setting. I have already spoken about some of the limitations that can be due to the personal bias of the researcher. Some discussion of the limitation that may be set by an *a priori*, firmly believed, and rigid theoretical framework will be discussed later. Here I would like to discuss the nature of the research setting and entry into the field as that can restrict data collection and the quality of the ethnography and the research.

It is undoubtedly necessary for every ethnographer to establish some type of 'contract' with the society to be studied. Such a 'contract' may include: specifications about what records may and may not be examined; where the ethnographer may or may not go, when, and under what circumstances; which meetings may be attended and which are closed; how long the researcher will stay in the field; who (if anyone) has access to the field notes, and even who has the right to review and/or approve the ethnography and its analysis prior to publication, or under what circumstances they may or may not be published at all.

Although some agreement about the research conditions and their possible effect on the society being studied is, of course, necessary, a good general rule of thumb is that the more restrictions placed on the researcher, the more likely they are to adversely affect the research and its usefulness. For me the bottom line is this: I would never engage in ethnography (or other types of research) if I were required to amend my findings or their analysis to suit *anyone else*. I might take the risk of not being allowed to publish but never of being forced to publish (under my name or not) findings that I felt were incorrect or misleading – this includes the exclusion of important relationships because they were embarrassing to the society being studied.

Here is the crux of the matter. An ethnographer studies real, living and dynamic people and societies. What is found can help or hurt certain people and relationships. These people will recognize this fact before, during, and after the field research, and they will try to influence the researcher to 'understand' their possition, behavior, and point of view. In fact this propensity of the 'natives' to want the researcher to understand their position is always an effective key to the researcher's ability to obtain certain data. Of course, the ethnographer wants to know and therefore seeks the 'native' interpretation of events and meaning of events – this is called the *representational* model of the society. But the researcher must be free also to seek the *operational* model (the view of events and meaning as seen by the 'unbiased' researcher) and then to combine this with the representational model into a final explanatory model based on the anthropologist's understanding of the representational and empirical models. Anything that restricts the ethnographer's liberty to complete access to data seriously restricts the research and its usefulness.

There is absolutely no use in instituting a research project to discover if, in the final analysis, one is prohibited from discovering.

Depending on the situation, there are techniques for safeguarding individuals and/or organizations from harm without prohibiting the development of good ethnography and its findings. If the research is more nearly *pure* research – that is, concerned only with conceptual relationships and not initiated in order to effect any change at the specific organization level – the following can be recommended: All names and places can be coded. Only the type of organization or society and its characteristics survive such coding. No one should be able to identify the specific organization or society or any of its individuals under these circumstances. My own ethnography of the Robertsdale School District (Iannoccone and Lutz, 1970) is such an ethnography. I think it is impossible for anyone to identify the school district or the individuals concerned. Yet, I have had dozens of people tell me that the events and situations described in Robertsdale are just like those in their own district. We were interested in relevant and conceptual variables that could help explain governance in local school districts and we were apparently somewhat successful in that effort *without* identifying the specific persons or place.

But what if that research had been commissioned and subsidized by the Robertsdale School Board? What if the major purpose of the research had been an evaluation? I think there are two answers that can be lived with. For me the more acceptable is to develop a 'contract' providing for two products. The first is the evaluation for the school district. It is produced through the free and open access necessary to all ethnography. It may well produce some findings that the client did not wish to discover – but there they are. The school district is free to accept and use these findings or to reject them as 'untrue' and protect its status quo. The second part of this same contract would allow the ethnographer to develop the coded type of ethnography from the same data and after some specified time (usually one to three years) to publish a Robertsdale type of ethnography which leaves the particular person and place unnamed, unharmed, and unchanged.

Another type of contract is possible which would prohibit *any* publication (other than 'in-house') unless approved by designated persons within the society. I would not be pleased with this type of 'contract,' but I could accept it, under certain circumstances, as long as I was free to seek data and include it and its analysis in the in-house report. Under no circumstances can I imagine myself permitting in-house 'editing' of the data and interpretations except as that editing and interpretation were considered data for the final report. When the researcher is not free to seek data and write the final report, the research-evaluation is best called *whitewash* and not evaluation-research.

Cross-Cultural Perspective of the Research

In the preceding section, I mentioned that the search for important and recurring variables in an ethnography must go beyond the narrow focus of a classroom or school. This expansion beyond the culture of a single classroom or school I shall refer to here as *cross-cultural perspective*.

Three types of cross-cultural perspective may be identified. The first deals with the perspective of the researcher and will be dealt with under 'anthropological theory.' Of the two types of cross-cultural perspectives related to the research, the first concerns a single educational phenomenon as it is observed, described, and explained in *more than one* culture. This is important research but not exactly what I have in mind here. For the present, I am concerned with research limited to a single national culture. The second type involves the notion that a classroom may be observed as a cultural system, the school observed as a cultural system, and the school district and the larger society may each be observed as cultural systems – all within a single national culture. As we move from each subcultural system to the broader system, the actors in each system often hold alternative roles across the arbitrary cultural boundaries requiring separate behaviors, and such roles may be governed by different, often conflicting sets of expectations, norms, and values. Any specific observed behavior or representational meaning may be affected by or be affecting any other. Behavior in a classroom cannot be understood apart from the influences of smaller peer groups, the larger school, and the total school district-community. It is this particular cross-cultural perspective that I wish to examine here.

One can see how conditions that restrict data collection, mentioned in the previous section, must affect the researcher's ability to bring a holistic cross-cultural perspective to the ethnography. When viewed as a separate entity, the potlatch of the Kwakiutl Indians of the northwestern United States seemed to many anthropologists irrational and destructive to the culture. Later, more holistic ethnographies viewed the potlatch as a rational, integral, and necessary part of Kwakiutl culture.

The foregoing may serve to 'illustrate' the cross-cultural approach I have in mind. If the potlatch is viewed as a cultural phenomenon, separate and by itself, its meaning and rationality is lost. If one views the classroom as a culture, separate and by itself, it is likely that much of the meaning and rationality of the behavior observed will be lost. The more the researcher is limited in opportunities for data collection, the thinner the description; the thinner the description, the poorer the ethnography – all things being equal. Therefore, it is argued that the narrower ethnographic approach to the study of education is less satisfactory to the holistic cross-cultural approach.

Anthropological Theory

A third meaning of the term *cross-cultural approach* is sometimes used. This refers to the perspective the researcher brings to the research rather than the perspective of the research itself. In this reference, we refer to an understanding of the ethnographic literature describing other cultures. To this I would add a broad knowledge of anthropological models, concepts, and theory. This combination, which I refer to as *anthropological theory*, is the fourth ingredient required to do good ethnography in education.

Some have argued for purely descriptive ethnography, without the use of theory to guide data collection or to provide meaning or understanding of the data collected. I acknowledge the fear of allowing preconceived 'theoretical' notions to bias and distort the ethnography (the data), but I am at least as concerned about the random collection of data (unguided by any concept), the covert or unspoken bias that any social scientist must bring to his/her observations, and the dangerous discovery of something left unexplained.

It seems to me to be a terrible waste of time merely to wander around collecting things without any concepts to guide what one collects and, of necessity, avoids collecting. Imagine someone, totally without concepts, wandering about empirically attempting to understand the world by collecting, in some fashion, everything he comes upon and not knowing any system to classify those specimens. The notion boggles the mind. Everyone – layman and social scientist alike – must have, or must invent, some system to categorize the data observed.

This necessity leads directly to the second concern. If we must operate with some conceptual notions, the failure to be explicit about them is as self-deceiving and at least as likely to distort the ethnography as is the explicit statement of that conceptual framework.

Finally, disregarding the first two problems of attempting ethnography totally without concepts or without specifying them, the problem of discovery of something without at least an attempt to understand its meaning and relationship to other existing knowledge is at best not very useful and, at worst, very dangerous. Imagine someone empirically experimenting with the elements carbon, hydrogen, oxygen, and nitrogen without understanding the theoretical properties of $C_3H_5(NO_3)$, nitroglycerin. The same potential exists in the social sciences. At one level we may foment revolution; at another we merely replicate Columbus's error when he failed to understand that he had discovered a 'new world.' At the very least, knowledge alone is a lower-order activity, in the cognitive domain, than is understanding and synthesis.

Often models developed from less complex societies can provide useful, fresh, and creative views of our more complex organizations. Wolcott, (1977), used Hoebel's (1972) definition of moiety to examine the adopting (or lack of adoption) of an innovative practice in school districts. His ability to use this model makes the research more generalizable. This ability to draw from a broader range of anthropological models and theories, in order to make sense of the data and to understand them, I refer to as the *fourth ingredient*.

In its narrow sense, and as defined up to this point, ethnography is thick description alone. But I would suggest that, if limited to this narrow definition, ethnography falls short of its research potential. As description alone it is knowledge alone, a body of data without analysis. It is the cognitive domain of knowledge without understanding or synthesis. It cannot be generalized beyond the specific case. It is a useful picture of some culture or society, at some moment in time. It preserves something that may otherwise be lost. In that sense it is useful and may even be fascinating and interesting. But it is useless in helping others explain or predict complex human behavior in organizations.

Geertz (1973) has said, 'Any chronic failure of one's explanatory apparatus . . . tends to lead to a deep disquiet . . .' (p. 100). Further he states, 'Cultural analysis is (or should be) guessing at the meanings, assessing the guesses, and drawing explanatory conclusions from the better guesses – not discovering the continent of meaning and mapping out its bodyless landscape' (p. 20). Finally and concisely he says, '. . . it is not worth it, as Thoreau said, 'to go round the world to count the cats in Zanzibar' (p. 16).

Thus, ethnography is thick description, but that thick description is not sufficient for what is proposed here, for it leaves us without prediction or explanation. Through research, meaning and understanding can (or should) be brought to human experience in complex organizations. As Harris (1975) points out:

> The manifest inability of our overspecialized scientific establishment to say anything coherent about the causes of life styles does not arise from any intrinsic lawlessness of life-style phenomena. Rather, I think it is the result of bestowing premium rewards on specialists who never threaten a fact with a theory (p. viii).

It is this threatening of facts with a theory that is the fourth essential element of good ethnography. If a fact cannot be accounted for by a theory, then either it is not a fact, or if you are sure it is a fact, the theory is insufficient and must be modified. Confronted with this dilemma, the ethnographer returns to the field for additional observations, informant data, to consult some written record, or recheck a diagram. If additional observations as well as informant information and other data sources consistently reaffirm the fact, the ethnographer carefully gathers data about the conditions and related variables surrounding the fact. This information is then used to modify or restate the theory, making it a better theory. Through this process Columbus would have understood that he had discovered a 'new world,' and not a westward route to the East. This is the process of good ethnography and through that process, I believe, what presently passes for educational theory can be improved.

Summary

I have tried to demonstrate that there is a critical need in educational research to broaden our perspectives not only beyond the usual psychostatistical research but also beyond the narrow focus of face-to-face interaction and micro-ethnography. In doing so, ethnography in schools must go beyond the usual scope of the classroom or the individual school, explaining educational processes in the broader context of the school district and the culture. Further, the concepts of face-to-face interaction and transaction are not sufficient to accomplish this goal. Four essentials in accomplishing this research goal have been suggested: (a) a trained ethnographer as researcher; (b) thick description as ethnography, used as the data base; (c) a cross-cultural approach to data collection; (d) the use of anthropological theory in analysis. By engaging in such research we are very likely to develop more meaningful hypotheses about educational processes and more humanistic educational theory.

References

CAWS, P. Operational, representational and explanatory models. *American Anthropologist*, 1974, 76-(1), 1–10.

EVENS, T.M.S. The predication of the individual in anthropological interactionism. *American Anthropologist*, 1977, 79-(3), 579–597.

GEERTZ, C. *The interpretation of cultures*. New York: Random, 1973.

HARRIS, M. *Cows, pigs, wars and witches*. New York: Random, 1974.

HOEBEL, E.A. *Anthropology: the study of man* (4th ed.). New York: McGraw-Hill, 1972.

IANNOCCONE, L., and LUTZ, F.W. *Politics, power and policy: the governing of local school districts*. Columbus, Ohio: Charles E. Merrill, 1970.

LEX, B. Voodoo death: new thoughts on an old explanation. *American Anthropologist*, 1974, 76-(4), 818–823.

LORTIE, D.C. *School teacher*. Chicago: University of Chicago Press, 1975.

LUTZ, F.W., and RAMSEY, M.A. The Voodoo killer in modern society. *Personnel*, May–June 1976, 30–38.

RAMSEY, M.A. Cultures and conflict in local school disricts. In F.W. Lutz & L. Iannaconne (Eds.), *Public participation in local school districts*. Lexington, Mass: Lexington Books, 1978.

SMITH, L.M., and GEOFFREY, W. *The complexities of the urban classroom*. New York: Holt, Rinehart & Winston, 1968.

WOLCOTT, H.F. *The man in the principal's office*. New York: Holt, Rinehart & Winston, 1973.

WOLCOTT, H.F. Criteria for an ethnographic approach to research in schools. *Human Organizations*, Summer, 1975, 34-(2), 111–127.

WOLCOTT, H.F. *Teachers vs. technocrats*. Eugene, Ore: Center for Educational Policy and Management, 1977.

Self-Contained Ethnography or a Science of Phenomenal Forms and Inner Relations

R. Sharp

Summary: This article develops a critique of ethnography in educational research. It is argued that ethnography concerns the study of the phenomenal forms of everyday life. Beyond these phenomenal forms are inner relations, causal processes, and generative mechanisms which are often invisible to the actors. A science of social totalities, deriving from Marx, is advocated which can elaborate the relationship between phenomenal forms, the world of appearances, and deeper social structural causal mechanisms. This science cannot be generated by ethnography alone but only through historical and comparative analyses of modes of production in history. The argument is illustrated by an imaginary ethnographic study of a typical 'fascist' school in Germany and by a discussion of developments taking place in schooling systems in the contemporary world.

A theory of reproduction is required which locates the analysis of capitalist schooling systems in a broader theory of the reproduction of all the economic, political, and ideological requirements for capitalist accumulation and the role of the state in this process. Ethnography carried out in schools informed by such a theory has a political rationale. It can lay the foundations for a critique of the world of appearances in everyday life, a necessary part of any political practice designed to produce a society in which essence and appearance are at one.

The status of ethnography in educational research has been transformed dramatically in little more than a decade. Whereas previously it tended to be dismissed as unscientific or subjective, now, embraced simultaneously by policy administrators and research funding organizations, it threatens to become – at least in the sociology of education – the new methodological orthodoxy.

In a recent survey and critique of these developments, Reynolds (1980) has suggested a number of factors which lie behind the current enthusiasm for ethnography. Central to his argument are the preoccupations of idealistic and anarchistically inclined sociologists influenced by the New Left and the counterculture: the theoretical foundations of earlier mainstream approaches are seen to be 'inappropriate to the crisis-torn industrial society of the 1970's.' Disillusionment is felt with structural functionalism and positivism whose reified social models and quantitative procedures have lost sight of human agency and the creative realm of individual consciousness; skepticism is expressed too concerning the policies which seemed to flow from these theoretical and methodological paradigms: moderate, within-system social reformism, planned and orchestrated by 'experts,' policies which were simultaneously ineffective and dehumanizing, characteristic of an administered welfare state (Reynolds, 1980). Against the dominant thrust of mainstream approaches, a variety of 'naturalistic' methods are advocated which allow more scope for voluntarism and self-actualization and facilitate the resuscitation of human agency. Such methods seem more appropriate to the needs and concerns of researchers and to the very nature of the 'objects' studied whose subjectivity previous methods and theoretical frameworks seem to suppress.

Reynolds's account is primarily idealist, focussing especially on the background expectancies, cognitive conceptions, and motivations of social scientists as actors, and is inconsistent with his own apt critique of 'naturalistic' methods. Nevertheless, his description of the changes in methodological fashion does highlight the significance which many educational researchers now attach to the primacy of direct human experience, both as an aspect of social interaction between constituting subjects as they make and remake the social world and as a validating criterion for knowledge about social reality. Both themes are problematic and call for further examination. Both raise ontological and epistemological issues which are by no means resolved through the illusion of rapport and closeness to the real texture of social life, which typically characterizes (and psychologically rewards) ethnography.

The very practice of ethnography tends to reduce social reality to the totality of the real social relationships which can be observed in their givenness through 'naturalistic' methodologies: i.e., 'observing individuals or groups in their natural setting with minimal interference by the observer' (Reynolds, 1980). In field work, the aggregate of these observable face-to-face relationships appears to be sustained by the process of social life as it is produced and regenerated through everyday social practices and routines. Ethnography reinforces ontological and epistemological social atomism: the atoms of social life are individuals; their beliefs, intentions, assumptions, and actions form both the starting point of, and dictate the explanatory procedures for, grasping social reality. The experience of social subjects becomes the prime sociological datum. Methodological individualism in addition leads to the neglect of other dimensions of social reality, and the assumption is sometimes made that only individuals really exist: they socially construct their own reality. As Berger and Luckman (1967) put it:

> The world of everyday life, then, is not only taken for granted as reality by the ordinary members of a society in the subjectively meaningful conduct of their lives; it is a world that originates in their thoughts and actions and is maintained as real by these (pp. 19–20).

Such a perspective overlooks the fact that social beings are born into and are socially constituted by a world already made, that structured patterns of social relations pre-exist the individual and generate specific forms of social consciousness, generate linguistic and hence cognitive possibilities, and socially structure available life chances, technical means, and facilities. In other words, there is a level of social reality, *sui generis*, which is existentially independent of consciousness and which must form part of the object of any science wishing to understand human behavior.

Moreover, despite its self-concept as embodying a methodological procedure which overcomes the blindness of positivism with its empiricist fetishization of the 'objective' fact, ethnography's own method is equally empiricist. In place of 'the facts' as objectified in a computer printout, appear the facts of the raw data of consciousness, of the motivations, purposes, and creative projects of active intending minds in interaction with other minds, and of events and happenings as these are subjectively constructed and mediated through everyday encounters and relationships.

Ethnography follows a classic empiricist inductivist method: observable phenomena are recorded, ordered, and classified; this collating process gives rise to empirical generalizations and hypotheses. Evidence is then sought to further substantiate such empirical generalizations which are then used deductively in explanation to produce plausible interpretations. Atomized observable facts are the starting points from which one can move upwards to theoretical generalization (Adorno, 1976).

As with other empiricist methodologies, the status of reality is only accorded by ethnography to observable phenomena as these are directly apprehended through observation and inferences generated therefrom in the field. In the same way that the social world is a taken-for-granted structure of givenness for the actors, according to Berger and Luckman among others, so for the observer the givenness of observable facts forms the raw data and validating criterion for social understanding.

However, as a number of commentators have pointed out (Bhaskar, 1979; Hindess, 1977; Willer and Willer, 1973) empiricism is by no means to be equated with science. Empiricism is 'the natural attitude' (Schutz, 1962). It characterizes the commonsense mode of being in, and making sense of, the world. Empiricism is the effect of living within ideology, where appearances are taken to be exhaustive of reality. Science, on the other hand, involves a search beyond the way things appear, for the generative mechanisms and processes which causally effect (i.e., set limits on, constrain and enable) activities and consciousness. Science importantly explores the underlying structures and regularities which are not reducible to surface connections that can be observed through empiricist methodologies.

Scientific theory, in both the natural and the social sciences, advances through the generation of theoretical categories and laws which are not themselves reducible to observable phenomena or events. Its goal is the *explanation* of observable realities through establishing the causal and necessary processes which produce them. It does not aim at the mere description of what can be observed. In any case, all descriptions are necessarily theory-laden. Science involves a theoretical construction of the object, an analysis of how it works, its underlying mechanisms and procedures. Science itelf dictates what are the important objects of study and the appropriate procedures for studying them. And the object of science may diverge very considerably from what the realm of observable realities may lead us to define as the scientific object.

Science is guided, not by practical administrative questions, nor by a world already predefined and processed by social actors, but by the essential nature of what is being analyzed. This is especially pertinent for social science which deals, at least in part, with social realities which have already been precategorized; but society's inner relations are not necessarily revealed in and through these precategorizations. For example, in commonsense consciousness, politics is not only analytically separated from economics but *ontologically* also. A scientific analysis of the one or the other would render such separations problematic (Clarke, 1977).

Ethnographic work is necessarily limited in its scope to small-scale locales of social interaction. It involves an examination of the activities and interactions of concrete individuals who are themselves constituted through historically specific structural forms and processes and are acting within historically specific institutional contexts and situations. In order to understand, and more importantly, explain what is occurring we require a theory of the social totality and its inner mechanisms of reproduction and transformation, the *effects* of which are manifest in the surface structure of everyday life. How the social world appears to its participants is an important feature of the processes which reproduce or transform the structural totality, but the latter can by no means be reduced to its forms of appearances as ascertained through ethnography. Naturalistic research methods, by their very nature, can tap only the level of ideology, the phenomenological forms of social existence, and the realm of consciousness materialized in social routines and practices through which people live, in an imaginary form, their relations to their real conditions of existence (Larrain, 1979; Mepham, 1972).

Ethnography can only generate insights superior to those of the actors observed when it is informed by a scientific apprehension of other levels of social reality, hidden or partially obscured by the level of appearances. The ideological or phenomenal forms of everyday life are not mere arbitrary inventions disconnected from underlying reality or simply an objective deception imposed by reality on the acting subject. The realm of appearance is an effect of the essential features of reality, not a mere illusion. Its structure is not indifferent to the way hidden reality itself is structured, its modes of transformation intimately connected to the dynamic at work in the real structure behind and beyond commonsense conceptualizations.

The phenomenal world of everyday life possesses, as ethnographers have shown, an apparent timeless pre-givenness. Its content for the actors is dehistoricized. However, in reality, this phenomenal world is only a particular historic form of social existence, dependent upon and structurally related to the dynamic of the mode of production. As Marx (1974) has shown, it is the internal logic of modes of production in history which is the essence of the social totality, the object of social science.

Knowledge of the structure of social totalities which are really present but phenomenally absent from the surface structure of everyday life cannot be gleaned from the cumulative results of numerous ethnographies. Direct experience of social actors studied in an infinite variety of social settings can, of itself, never transcend the descriptive depiction of phenomenal forms. Many ethnographers, however, would not agree. Douglas (1976), one of the leading systematizers of the methodology of fieldwork, argues:

> We begin with direct experience and all else builds on that, whether we know it and recognize it or deny it . . . The most important implication of this argument for all social research is that we begin with and continually return to direct experience as the most reliable form of knowledge about the social world but it does not mean that all social research has to be direct experience. That depends upon how reliable we want our findings to be. If we want the most reliable truth we can get about the social world then we want as much direct experience as possible, through the direct experience of field research, followed by checking it against the independent direct experience of others and tested out and checked out by us as being true within certain limits in terms of our direct experience . . . (p. 7).

Science, however, advises a certain skepticism regarding our sense impressions and direct experience. Direct experience for those living within the phenomenal world of the Ptolemaic system proved that the sun revolved around the earth. Copernican science on the other hand generated a theory which simultaneously opposed direct experience, i.e., that the earth actually revolves around the sun, and explained how it was that it 'seemed' to do otherwise.

The same is true of a science of social reality. Through an extensive study of human history, Marx, in the mid-nineteenth century, theorized what he thought to be its key, i.e., the internal dynamics of modes of production, their mechanisms of reproduction and transformation. Marx only studied one of these modes of production in detail: capitalism. He provided the basis

for a science of how capitalism worked and in so doing developed a critique
of its forms of appearance as articulated through the theories of bourgeois
political economy in both its classical and (later) vulgar manifestations
(Marx, 1974).

The argument will be developed that for ethnographic work in schools to
move beyond the mere description of phenomenal forms, a scientific theory
is required of schooling systems and the context in which they are embedded.
Such a theory must be predicated upon the analysis of modes of production
and their specific mechanisms of reproduction. Such a theory cannot remain
entrapped by the self-conceptions of capitalist schooling as an autonomous
realm of social life dedicated to the education of a citizenry (Sharp, 1981a).

In order to illustrate the argument let us reconstruct imaginatively an
ethnographic study carried out in a Volkschule in Nazi Germany in 1935. Let
the fieldworker be a hypothetical German ethnographer whose political preferences are decidedly liberal, who is a supporter of the educational reforms
initiated under the Weimar Republic, and who relies on direct experience as
the object and ultimate validator of knowledge of social reality. From
a range of historical and sociological studies,[1] autobiographies, and eye-
witness accounts, it is known that the schooling system under the Third
Reich was characterized by some considerable variety, but let us assume for
a moment that our imaginary ethnography was carried out in a school, the
majority of whose teachers had been active supporters of the NSDAP even
before the fascists gained state power in 1933. What would have been the
main findings? Consider first the teachers' attitudes as expressed in the
educationalist context (Keddie, 1971). The majority of the teachers would
have been opposed to liberal notions of schooling which stress the importance of individual autonomy, self-development, humanism, and egalitar-
ianism. These would have been associated with the iniquities of the Weimar
Republic, the 'democracy of the Jews and the Bolsheviks.' Instead they would
have believed firmly in the idea of 'natural inequalities,' submission to those
born and fit to lead, and the importance of subordinating one's individual
egoistic/materialistic desires through immersing oneself in spiritual goals
collectively pursued for the good of the people, the race, and the nation.
The idea of a 'Volksgemeinschaft' would have figured prominently in
the teacher's vocabulary: a society in which there are no structured divisions, only the collective interest pursued through co-operation and
collective striving. Character training and physical education would have
been given at least as much emphasis as the training of the intellect,
for arid intellectualism leads only to a spurious objectivity (Nyssen,
1979).

Examination of the curriculum would have revealed a strong ideological
content geared to the fascist goal of mass propaganda. The political content
would have been particularly marked in the fields of biology, history, geog-
raphy, German studies, and sport, but no disciplines would have remained

immune. Moreover, ethnographic probing of the hidden curriculum would have demonstrated the implicit biases of the teachers against pupils of working-class origin, girls, and the few still suspected of belonging to the Jewish 'race'.

The study might also have explored inner tensions and conflicts in the school related to the struggles within, and competing spheres of influence of, such groups as parents organizations, the church leadership in the neighbourhood, the Hitler Youth Movement, and the local gauleiters of the NSDAP. It might also have investigated a variety of contexts and forms of resistance to the combination of ideological and repressive controls on the part of both dissident teachers and pupils.

Along with most liberal commentators on Nazi schooling (e.g., Nemitz, 1980), our ethnographer might well conclude that his case study demonstrates how Nazi schooling is characterized primarily by its irrationalism and anti-educational ethos, where the goal of political socialization and indoctrination has superceded education's emancipatory potential.

These hypothetical findings may well be fascinating. The study would probably have been written up in such a way that we can directly experience what it would have been like to be a teacher or a pupil in a school during this period. However, the explanation of the findings revealed through ethnography require a very different kind of study. Fascism was not produced by the schooling system. For a range of questions concerning fascism (Why did fascism come into being in Germany? What was specific about fascism as opposed to earlier or later forms of political domination? How did the schooling system articulate with the fascist state? What was unique and specific about fascist schooling?) we need a *theory* of fascism and that cannot be generated through ethnographies.

Apart from the extensive range of theoretical empiricist studies of various aspects of fascist rule, liberal approaches to the phenomenon of fascism were long dominated by the theory of totalitarianism (Arendt, 1951; Friedrich and Brzezinski, 1956). Arising during the Cold War, this perspective concentrated in a descriptive way on surface aspects of totalitarian parties, as in Stalin's Russia and Nazi Germany, and their relationship to the masses. It operated with a crude elite/mass class analysis, ignored the socioeconomic basis of so-called totalitarian regimes, and failed to recognize the important continuities in class structures characteristic of fascist rule and the discontinuities in Soviet Russia. The elite/mass dichotomy figures prominently in many liberal accounts, especially those informed by recent developments in psychohistory, such as those which focus on the psychological abnormalities of fascist leaders or the psychopathology of the masses produced in the aftermath of the First World War.

The leading contemporary liberal theorist, Nolte (1965, 1970), writing from a position which eulogizes liberal bourgeois democracies in 'liberal capitalism,' explains the growth of fascist movements in Italy and Germany in terms of the weakness of liberal democracy in those countries in the interwar period. Through what he calls a phenomenological analysis of fascist ideology as articulated through its leading exponents, he describes it as an anti-modernist, backward-looking movement seeking to establish a traditional harmonious social order and as anti-socialist in its thrust. For Nolte, the conditions which produced fascism are no longer present and cannot reappear. He fails to explore any essential linkages between fascism and capitalism or to analyze any of the contradictions of bourgeois democracies to which the growth of fascism might, under certain conditions, be related (Kitchen, 1976).

In contrast to the various stances of liberal theory, Marxist accounts[2] of fascism are developed within a theorization of the social totality. They relate the fascist potential to the normal operation of the law of value in capitalist societies which generates periodic crises.[3] Fascism emerges in a classic crisis of capital accumulation, a crisis having simultaneously economic, political, and ideological dimensions. Economically, its preconditions are a serious overproduction crisis with accompanying realization problems, a massive reserve army of labour (unemployment), and conflicts of interest between different fractions of the ruling class concerning possible strategies of crisis resolution (Sohn-Rethel, 1978; Hennig, 1973). In addition, there must be a political crisis caused by the co-existence of strong working-class organizations (trade unions and political parties), a disaffected petit bourgeoisie fearful of the organized power of the working class, and a crisis of political hegemony caused by the disintegration of the mass basis of the parties that have traditionally articulated, politically, the interests of the bourgeoisie (Poulantzas, 1974). Such a situation requires a reorganization of the power bloc in order to re-establish the conditions of class rule (Abraham, 1977). These economic and political preconditions together produce at the ideological level a crisis of legitimation such that liberal democratic solutions are no longer considered viable. It is in such situations that fascist parties, deriving their voting support largely from the peasantry and petit bourgeoisie, can come to power. The balance of class forces is such that under certain conditions a fascist resolution of a major crisis of capital accumulation becomes a necessity if the system of class relations is to be stabilized and maintained (Mason, 1966).

This approach to the preconditions of fascism depends upon a theoretical analysis of the inner structure of capitalism and the logic of the capitalist market place as it manifests itself in specific national conjunctural conditions. An element of this analysis is a theorization of the capitalist state and its mediating role in the accumulation process in the context of the class struggle, a role which has simultaneously economic, political, and ideological dimensions. A Marxist analysis of the fascist state would identify its role in reconstituting the preconditions for capital accumulation and 'resolving' the crisis. The attack by fascism on working-class organizations, the destruction of what Negt and Kluge (1972) have called the working-class public sphere is seen as part of the process of raising the rate of surplus value through lowering the costs of labour power reproduction. Other elements of Nazi economic policy which contribute to crisis resolution for the benefit of stronger fractions of capital are the measures designed to raise the organic composition of capital and to accelerate the process of concentration and centralization, and rearmament (Altvater, Hoffmann & Semmler, 1980).

Fascism involves a decisive reconstitution of the dominant ideology to re-establish hegemony and to ensure the maintenance of the wage labour system and the institutions of private property on which the existing system of class domination depends. Politically, fascism orchestrated a restructuring of the political and repressive apparatuses of the State and, important for the argument of this paper, a restructuring of the apparatuses and institutions of labour power reproduction.

Thus there can be observed under the Nazi rule, a reorganization of the schooling system, intervention in the sphere of family relations, a change in the demarcation between the public and the private spheres, the development of mass organizations for the socialization of youth, housewives, etc., and the establishment of corporative forms of labour control such as the Labour Front (Mason, 1966). Similar developments occurred in fascist Italy (Gramsci, 1978; Togliatti, 1974).

To summarize, the process of reproducing the preconditions for capitalist accumulation and the maintenance of class rule sometimes necessitates fascism. This phenomenon can only be understood given a scientific constitution of the 'object,' the capitalist mode of production, its internal dynamics, its generative mechanisms as they work themselves out in specific historical situations. Reproduction of the capitalist system whether it takes place under bourgeois democratic political forms, fascist forms, or military dictatorship always reproduces simultaneously its own contradictions and forms of resistance. It is never a foregone conclusion but is structured through class and other social struggles and various forms of political mobilization which characterize history's trajectory.

Let us return to our imaginary ethnography. At the level of direct experience some inner mechanisms of the social totality are invisble. What was crucially structuring the constitution of everyday life in a fascist school was the law of value and the dynamics of the class struggle as it manifested itself in a particular set of historical conditions in Germany. Our imaginary ethnographic study shows us only in a descriptive way the *effects* of the specifically fascist mode of crisis resolution in the conditions which then obtained. What is manifest in everyday encounters, what can be ascertained through direct experience obscures a deeper level which can only be revealed through historical and comparative analysis of the changing dynamics of the capitalist mode of production.

The reader will, perhaps, be wondering what this discussion of fascism has to do with the contemporary ethnographer about to embark on a fieldwork study in a Western school. The answer relates to the fact that the capitalist world is again undergoing a major crisis of capital accumulation, not as yet as serious as the one which produced fascism but certainly deeper and of longer duration than any recession since the end of World War II (Mandel, 1975). The way the crisis is mediated politically has important implications for what goes on within schools. The last few years have witnessed the blocking of further social democratic reforms in education in most western democracies, a crisis in educational funding, and a shift to the right in the ideological rhetoric through which educational issues are debated and solutions to problems posed. Public concern through the media is expressed concerning declining educational standards and school discipline, schools are found wanting in that they no longer seem able to mediate successfully a smooth transition between school and the workforce, and pressure is placed on teachers at all levels regarding the issue of accountability (Centre for Contemporary Cultural Studies, 1981).

Individual schools do not remain immune from these tendencies, but again their causal explanation requires us to move beyond the phenomenological reality of social actors to analyze anew the internal dynamics of the capitalist mode of production as it is currently operating in each national setting. The law of value has again generated the phenomenon of overproduction and unemployment, a crisis as yet unresolved through the mobilization of countertendencies by capital and the state. Moreover due to the more advanced level of the internationalization of capital, and concentration and centralization tendencies, the autonomy of the bourgeois state, the political form whereby the domination by capital over labour is ultimately secured, has been undermined. These changes have produced a reorganization of the traditional pattern of political allegiancies of which the growth of right-wing populist political movements committed to the social market economy is perhaps the most significant (Gamble, 1979).

We note through historical and comparative analyses the *changes* in the mode of intervention by the bourgeois state to effect a restructuring of the preconditions for a renewed phase of capital accumulation, changes which necessarily have to take account of the changes in the world system of production and market relationships and the balance of class forces both nationally and internationally in the aftermath of the postwar boom.

Bourgeois schooling systems in such a context are peculiarly vulnerable because of their significance for ideological mediation. At the level of phenomenal forms schooling provides access to the good life, accreditation for the workforce, opportunity for social mobility, and individual self development. On the other hand, schooling has historically had little to do with influencing the actual structure of the work force, the number of jobs available, their range, scope, and level of economic rewards. Given the changes in the international division of labour and technological development, both the result of capitalism's logic, many graduates of the schooling system in the advanced capitalist centres are possessed of bourgeois aspirations but few bourgeois opportunities (Bloch, 1978).

Given such a situation it is hardly surprising that in many capitalist countries there is a tendency for capital and the state to attempt, ideologically, to reconstitute the crisis as nothing but a crisis of schooling which provides both the rationale and the legitimation for a restructuring of schooling systems to render them more in tune with the economic, political, and ideological requirements of capital accumulation, which necessitates, among other things, an acceptance of far higher levels of unemployment than was thought hitherto to be politically feasible (Freeland & Sharp, 1981; Frith, 1979). Such interventions into the schooling system parallel interventions into all the spheres crucial to the process of labour power reproduction, especially the family and trade unions. Schools are not autonomous from the process of capital accumulation and the structure of class relationships. They have to be theorized as instrumentalities for the production of labour power commensurate with capital's needs and as such are a crucial arena for intervention by the capitalist state when the problems of capital accumulation require it. The theoretical analysis of labour power reproduction has to be embedded in a general theory of capitalist reproduction as it is structured by and itself structures the trajectory of the class struggle (Sharp, 1981b).

The restructuring of capitalism which characterizes an accumulation crisis is not a process which passes unchallenged. Active struggles occur between social classes within and over the forms and terms of crisis mediation. Within the schooling system, for example, it is possible to identify many ways in which teachers and others are actively trying, sometimes defensively, sometimes offensively, to effect their own control over the forms and content of schooling (Kallos, 1981).

The theoretical understanding of these tendencies and the mechanisms whereby they impinge upon the structure of the everyday world and the phenomenal forms through which social actors cognize their situation cannot be generated through ethnography alone.

An historical analysis of the development of the capitalist mode of production through its various stages, in different national situations, generates the basis for a scientific theory of the social totalities in which mass schooling systems have evolved. Such a theory enables us to identify the essence of state schooling systems beyond the phenomenal forms of their appearance: they play a vital role, alongside other institutions, in reproducing the system of class domination, the wage labour system, and the ideological forms through which these are sustained and legitimated. They help to reproduce the divisions between mental and manual labour, the sexual and racial division of labour, and other vertical and horizontal divisions necessitated by capitalist labour markets and forms of control over the work force; they help to constitute the bourgeois subject, its selection and qualification for the occupational structure.

The social forms and mechanisms through which this is achieved and the character of the ideological content of formal schooling varies in different stages of the accumulation process and is crucially affected by the class struggle within the social formation. Thus the phenomenal forms of the typical fascist school will be different in crucial respects from the mode of appearance of schools operating under bourgeois democracy, but given that it is a capitalist school, it will share crucial continuities with the latter.

The process of reproduction of capitalist class relations is never an automatic one. Pressures from capital and the state are refracted and mediated through a variety of apparatuses and the practices of differentially constituted social actors with different class ideologies, social allegiances, and alliances. Reproduction is always a double-sided process reproducing simultaneously contradictions and forms of resistance (Gramsci, 1978; Willis, 1977).

Conclusion

> Men make their own history, but they do not make it just as they please; they do not make it under circumstances chosen by themselves, but under circumstances directly encounterd, given and transmitted from the past.
>
> (Marx, 1973)

Ethnography reveals the *effects* of the social totality which itself produces the characteristics of the fieldwork situation and structures possible outcomes. As noted above much of the impetus behind the methodological shift towards ethnography sprang from the commitment to rediscover the individual as an active creator and constitutor of the social world. In structural functionalism, the constituting subject had been swallowed up in the functional 'needs' of the system, in quantitative survey research reduced to an arithmetical element. Some may conclude from the argument presented here that the human individual (as in Althusserianism) is nothing but a 'support' or bearer of structures; no role exists for human agency, ethnography merely charts the dialectic of structures which are beyond human intervention. Such a conclusion would be unwarranted. Ethnography is concerned with the examination of concrete individuals as they are constituted in and through the phenomenal forms of social life.[4] The significance of Marx's analysis of the dynamics of the capitalist mode of production which enabled him to develop a devastating critique of bourgeois political economy, has already been stressed. But Marx tended to examine individuals only as personifications of abstract social categories. Ethnography, on the other hand, concerns itself with the level of practical ideology (Sharp, 1980) and thus provides the basis for a critique of the phenomenal forms of the bourgeois world as it is lived and experienced by concrete individuals in everyday encounters. A critique of the mode of appearance of the everyday world is a necessary component of a practice designed to break through mystifications and fetishisms to reveal the contradictory structures of the social totality which historically generate them. Nevertheless one should stress again that the phenomenal forms are not mere illusions, but real objectifications of a false reality (Larrain, 1979) which itself needs to be transcended not through ideas alone but through practice.

Ethnography thus has a political rationale. A scientific political practice requires knowledge of the fissures, ruptures, and contradictions in capitalism's mode of appearance which can guide political and pedagogical work. Ethnography can offer insight concerning the points at which politicization is possible, feasible, and productive of greater awareness and concerning the processes through which this could be achieved.

Since political practice occurs within the everyday encounter with real concrete individuals who are more than mere personifications of social categories, it can be advanced and assisted by the kind of ethnography informed by a scientific grasping of the essence of capitalist schooling beyond its mere appearance. Such an ethnography is valuable, not because it is the generator of all insights into the social world, nor because direct experience is the ultimate validator of science, but because social forms and structures are reproduced or transformed through human agency. Concrete individuals can move beyond the world of appearances and discover their human creativity through working to produce a world in which essence and appearance are at one.

Notes

1 See Herrlitz et al. (1981) for a recent overview of the history of German schooling. There is an extensive literature on schooling during the Nazi period. Some of the most recent are: Scholtz, (1973); Ottweiler, (1979); Nyssen, (1979); Heinemann (Ed.), (1980).
   See also Nemitz, (1980) for a critique of the liberal paradigm which has dominated research into fascist schooling.

2 The criteria for choosing between theories is an issue which, of itself, is worthy of much fuller discussion than is possible here. The superiority of Marxist science is merely asserted in this article. Internal consistency, coherence, the range of empirical phenomena to which the theory applies, and empirical validation are only four of the most important criteria.
   See Kitchen (1976) for a discussion of rival theories of fascism written from a stance sympathetic to Marxist interpretations; see Laqueur (Ed.) (1979) for a review sympathetic to liberal accounts.

3 See Mandel (1968); Fine and Harris (1976) and Kay (1979) for discussions of the law of value in Marxian economic theory. See Altvater, Hoffman, and Semmler (1980) and Hennig (1973) for discussion of the operation of the law of value in Germany in the 1930's.

4 See Sève (1978) for a discussion of psychology and the science of the individual in relation to historical materialism. Sève argues that whilst Marxism lays the foundation for a scientific theory of the individual, the theory itself still has to be developed. He emphasizes the importance of the distinction between abstract and concrete labour, a distinction found useful for the argument in this paper.

References

ABRAHAM, D. State and classes in the Weimar Republic. *Politics and Society*, 1977, 7, 3, 229–666.

ADORNO, T.W. Sociology and empirical research. In T.W. Adorno et al. (Eds.), *The positivist dispute in German sociology*. London: Heinemann, 1976.

ALTVATER, E., HOFFMAN, J., and SEMMLER, W. *Vom Wirtschaftswunder zur Wirtschaftskrise*. Berlin: Olle und Wolter, 1980.

ARENDT, H. *The Origins of totalitarianism*. New York: 1951.

BERGER, P., LUCKMAN, T. *The social construction of reality*. Harmondsworth, Middlesex: Allen Lane, 1967.

BHASKAR, R. *The possibility of naturalism: A philosophical critique of the contemporary human sciences*. Brighton: Harvester press, 1979.

BLOCH, E. Non synchronism and dialectics. *New German Critique*, 11, 1978.

C.C.C.S. Education Group. *Unpopular education: Schooling and social democracy since the War*. London: Hutchinson, 1981.

CLARKE, S. Marxism, sociology and Poulantzas' theory of the state. *Capital and Class*, Summer, 1977.

DOUGLAS, J. *Investigative social research*. Beverly Hills, Calif.: Sage Publications, 1976.

FINE, B., and HARRIS, L. Controversial issues in Marxist economics. In R. Miliband and J. Saville (Eds.), *Socialist Register 1976*. London: Merlin Press.

FREELAND, J., and SHARP, R. The Williams report on education, training and employment. The decline and fall of Karmelot. *Intervention*, 1981, 14, 54–79.

FRIEDRICH, C.J., and BRZEZINSKI, Z. *Totalitarian dictatorship and autocracy*. New York: 1956.

FRITH, S. Education and industry. *Radical Education Dossier*, 1979, 8.

GAMBLE, A. The free economy and the strong state. In R. Miliband & J. Saville (Eds.), *Socialist Register 1979*. London: Merlin Press.

GRAMSCI, A. *Selections from political writings, 1921–1926*. London: Lawrence & Wishart, 1978.

HEINEMANN, M. (Ed.) *Erziehung und Schulung im Dritten Reich* (Vol. 1 & 2). Stuttgart: Klett-Cotta, 1980.

HENNIG, E. *Thesen zur Deutschen Sozial and Wirtschaftspolitik, 1933–1938*. Frankfurt am Main: Suhrkamp, 1973.

HERRLITZ, H.G., HOPF, W., and TITZE, H. *Deutsche Schulgeschichte von 1800 bis zur Gegenwart*. Regensburg: Athenaum, 1981.

HINDESS, B. *Philosophy and methodology in the social sciences*. Hassocks, U.K.: Harvester Press, 1977.

KALLOS, D. The study of schooling: What is studied? Why? and How? In T.S. Popkewitz & B.R. Tabachnick (Eds.), *The study of schooling: Field based methodologies in educational research and evaluation*. New York: Praeger, 1981.

KAY, G. *The economic theory of the working class*. London: Macmillan, 1979.

KEDDIE, N. Classroom knowledge. In M.F.D. Young (ED.), *Knowledge and control*. London: Collier Macmillan, 1971.

KITCHEN, M. *Fascism*. London: Macmillan, 1976.

LAQUEUR, W. (Ed.) *Fascism: A readers guide*. Harmondsworth, Middlesex: Penguin, 1979.

LARRAIN, J. *The concept of ideology*. London: Hutchinson, 1979.

MANDEL, E. *Late capitalism*. London: New Left Books, 1975.

MANDEL, E. *Marxist economic theory*. London: Merlin Press, 1968.

MARX, K. *Capital* (Vol. 1). London: Lawrence and Wishart, 1974.

MARX, K. *Eighteenth brumaire of Louis Bonaparte. Surveys from exile*. (Vol. 1). Harmondsworth, Middlesex: Pelican, 1973.

MASON, T. Labour in the Third Reich: 1933–9. *Past and Present*, 1966, 112–141.

MEPHAM, J. The theory of ideology in capital. *Radical Philosophy* 2, 1972, 12–13.

NEGT, O., and KLUGE, A. *Offentlichkeit und Erfahrung. Zur Organisationsanalyse von burgerlicher and proletarischer offentlichkeit*. Frankfurt am Main: Suhrkamp, 1972.

NEMITZ, R. Die Erziehung des faschistischen Subjekts. In *Faschismus und Ideologie 1. Argument-Sonderband. A.S. 60*. Berlin: 1980.

NOLTE, E. *Theorien uber Fascismus*. Cologne: 1970.

NOLTE, E. *Three faces of fascism*. London: 1965.

NYSSEN, E. *Schule im Nationalsozialismus*. Heidelberg: Quelle & Meyer, 1979.

OTTWEILER, O. *Die Volksschule im Nationalsozialismus*. Weinheim und Basel: Beltz, 1979.

POULANTZAS, N. *Fascism and dictatorship*. London: New Left Books, 1974.

REYNOLDS, D. The naturalistic method of educational and social research – A Marxist critique. *Interchange*, 1980, 11, 4, 77–89.

SCHOLTZ, H. *N.S – Ausleseschulen*. Göttingen: 1973.

SCHUTZ, A. *Collected papers 1: The problem of social reality*. The Hague: Martinus Nijhoff, 1962.

SÈVE, L. *Man in Marxist theory and the psychology of personality*. Hassocks, U.K.: Harvester Press, 1978.

SHARP, R. Marxism, the concept of ideology and its implications for fieldwork. In T.S. Popkewitz & B.R. Tabachnick (Eds.), *The study of schooling*. New York: Praeger, 1981. (a)

SHARP, R. Beyond the sociology of education: Towards a theory of labour power reproduction. Mimeo. Macquaire University, Sydney: 1981. (b)

SHARP, R. *Knowledge, ideology and the politics of schooling*. London: Routledge & Kegan Paul, 1980.

SOHN-RETHEL, A. *The economy and class structure of German Fascism*. London: C.S.E. Books, 1978.

TOGLIATTI, P. *Lectures on fascism*. New York: International Publishers, 1976.

WILLER, D., and WILLER, J. *Systematic empiricism: Critique of a pseudoscience*. Englewood Cliffs, N.J.: Prentice-Hall, 1973.

WILLIS, P. *Learning to labour: How working class kids get working class jobs*. London: Saxon House, 1977.

Whatever Happened to Symbolic Interactionism?

D. Hargreaves

As yet, we have no comprehensive history of British sociology of education which describes and explains the changing theoretical fashions in the field.[1] But no-one would, I think, dispute that symbolic interactionist studies in the sociology of education are now passing the peak of popularity they have enjoyed in the first half of this decade. Of course, many more studies are currently in press or in process; but nonetheless to be a symbolic interactionist today is to be somewhat behind the times.

Undoubtedly the popularity of symbolic interactionist (SI) approaches in the sociology of education reflected the resurgence of that perspective in mainstream sociology where, in the wake of growing dissatisfaction with structural-functionalism, Herbert Blumer's attempt to restore the sociological implications of Mead's work made their mark. The creation of the Open University's *School and Society* course in 1971 helped to spread that gospel to British sociologists of education, who were in any event looking more closely at schools and classrooms on other grounds, such as the functionalist approach to schools as organisations and the obvious need to investigate in-school processes to complement the heavy concentration of educability studies on the home environment. The question is why, when SI offered such a demanding and extensive programme of work for sociologists, was the perspective to become so rapidly eclipsed before very much of that programme could be realised?[2]

Part of the explanation is external to SI itself. In education, SI encouraged a focus on classrooms, forging important continuities with the earlier work of Waller and Parsons. There was a distinct movement, if not a stampede, to schools and classrooms. But such a neglect of the 'macro' could not possibly last for long. Mainstream sociology, for complex reasons, was moving towards marxist perspectives, which are now beginning to make some impact on British sociology of education. Neomarxist approaches offer a new lease of life to more macro approaches; phenomenology, in many of its European versions, is closely allied to marxism, and so presents a natural direction for future development; and marxist approaches have the distinct attraction of offering radical political commitment for sociologists of education so many of whom are critical of the implicit conservatism of earlier approaches or jaundiced at the alleged failures of liberal reformism.

A second aspect of the explanation for the decline of interest in SI lies in the development of phenomenology and ethnomethodology. In one sense the growth of Schutzian phenomenology injected a renewed vigour into interactionism, especially through the popular conflation of Mead and Schutz in Berger and Luckmann.[3] The future of this marriage between interactionism and phenomenology looked secure and fertile. But it spawned what to most of the anxious sociological relatives was the deformed, monstrous progeny of ethnomethodology, which, after committing matricide against interactionism,[4] and not long after becoming distinctly ambivalent towards Schutz's fatherhood, proclaimed open war against the rest of its sociological kin. It did not, of course, win that war. Some of ethnomethodology's own children turned disconsolately away from what is recognisably sociology (e.g. McHugh), whilst others showed some signs of reconciliation after a period of adolescent rebellion (e.g. Zimmerman and Wieder).

Yet even this is not an adequate account of the problems of SI. For if mainstream sociology and ethnomethodology were offering external attacks, there were also many internal tensions within SI itself. By the middle of the 1960s it was clear that Erving Goffman was the outstanding figure of the movement; indeed so much so that by 1970 Gouldner[5] was able to mount his well known attack on Goffman on the assumption that in criticising Goffman he was also taking to task the whole SI movement. Gouldner's attack is in some respects misdirected, for having conceded that Goffman represents social psychological interests he then proceeds to focus his objections to Goffman at the macrosociological level of analysis. More important, although Gouldner was right in taking Goffman to be the leading proponent of SI, he was mistaken in assuming that he was a *typical* or representative interactionist. One of the greatest achievements of SI is the commitment to ethnography. Goffman aligned himself very closely with this tradition in his early writing – his Ph.D. study of the Shetlands and his work in mental hospitals – but by far the major part of his prolific output has been devoted instead to high quality 'armchair theorising'. In this he makes use of biographies, novels, newspaper cuttings, his own brilliant but unsystematic observation, and other people's ethnographies to illustrate his own indefatigable proliferation of 'mini-concepts'.[6] Indeed, it can be argued that Goffman's fame rests precisely on this capacity to invent his bewildering multitude of concepts – often at the rate of several to the page – which other writers could then use in their work. But Goffman has consistently failed to structure these concepts into any coherent order. He hurries on, inventing concepts ever more frantically, quite unable to stand still and take stock. His work to date is a vast rococo edifice; yet beneath it all there is no solid gothic cathedral but rather the crudest of scaffolding in constant danger of collapse.

Goffman, then, does not adequately represent the other face of SI which consists of detailed ethnographic studies of particular groups and situations, though sometimes good ethnographic studies make extensive use of Goffmanic concepts. Most of these ethnographic studies make interesting if sociologically undramatic reading. Like good television documentaries, they satisfy our voyeuristic inclinations and sometimes arouse our sympathy or even reformist passions, especially in the field of deviance where SI has been notably successful. But for ethnography to appeal widely, researchers have to present 'news' about groups/situations which (as far as the sociological audience was concerned) were relatively unknown or underexplored. As time went on, ethnographers had to explore and expose situations which inevitably became increasingly bizarre, and thus tended to cut themselves off from mainstream sociology with its concerns with mainstream society. If, on the other hand, ethnographers studied mainstream groups, their writing was open to the charge that it was 'obvious'. Simultaneously, SI was foundering at the theoretical level. Ethnography frequently became so entranced in relatively atheoretical reporting of the hidden crevices of society that it failed to produce not only 'formal' theories but also the lower level 'substantive' theories which Glaser and Strauss[7] so rightly perceived as crucial to the future of SI. In its cult of the exotic, ethnography deteriorated into a proliferation of unique case-studies. The early SI rhetoric against the trivial laws produced by positivists proved empty, since that was not replaced by any adequate social scientific substitute. The achievements of SI proved to be non-cumulative and non-generalisable: Goffman and ethnography failed to generate an alternative social science which had any empirical or theoretical coherence. If there is anything today which holds interactionists together, it is their general humanistic assumptions about man and a commitment to certain methods, especially participant-observation. That provides a collective identity, but it fails to provide any clear direction for 'normal science'.

What then is the future of SI? Is it now to be seen as just one more blind alley in the history of social science? Is it to collapse in the wake of ethnomethodology? Does its future lie in carrying its gospel to psychologists rather than sociologists? Or has it still some important part to play in mainstream sociology and in the sociology of education in contemporary Britain? Has it anything to contribute to the recent revival of 'macro' concerns and the development of neo-marxist perspectives? My answer is firmly in the affirmative. Yet whenever sociology changes track, focus or 'paradigm', there is an inherent tendency to discard the achievements of the immediately preceding fashion. Sociologists display a remarkable degree of necrophilia towards the founding fathers, such as Weber, Durkheim and Marx, who are constantly resurrected in various selective guises, but tend to treat the minor heroes of transient fashions in a much more cavalier manner. Specifically, in the current trend in the sociology of education to create a new 'new direction' through various marxist and neo-marxist perspectives, what, if anything, can be retained from SI? Will the new fashion produce a hostile, unfair and foolish rejection or distortion of SI in the interests of making the new, new directions seem more dramatically novel than they are?

If we are to take some aspects of Sharp and Green's *Education and Social Control* (1975) seriously, the answer appears to be yes. I have tried to show in the first part of this paper that SI is replete with faults. In the second part I wish to show, largely through this one book, how there is a real danger of over-emphasising these faults to the point where we deny the real achievements of SI and the role it can play in contemporary sociology of education. What I shall say about Sharp and Green will be generally critical; but it should be borne in mind that I am not attempting a definitive or balanced critique of their book as a whole, to one of whose central themes, the need the link micro and macro levels of analysis, I am not at all unsympathetic.

Sharp and Green never intend to make a thoroughgoing rejection of SI. At first sight they are attempting an integration of SI with a marxist perspective. This is surely a commendable enterprise. They indicate – though rather strangely on the last page of an appendix at the end of the book (p. 234) – that they began their research and collected their data from an interactionist perspective, but changed their stance to a more structuralist/marxist one during the course of their work. This suggests that we must read the two introductory chapters as propounding a theoretical position developed *after* the data collection. (It is a great pity that the structure of the book does not correspond to the history of the project, namely an initial espousal of the interactionist perspective, followed by appropriate data collection, then a rejection of the interactionist position in part, and the final development of a marxist perspective and a re-analysis of some of the data in the light of that change). In essence, the authors came to the conclusion – surely a sound one – that the SI/phenomenological position is, in itself, limited; it is not to be rejected entirely, but is to be placed within a wider, marxist framework.

> Structural factors other than the merely symbolic may be features of interaction. It is crucial to consider the ways in which elements of the interactive situation may well not be acknowledged or understood by the actors involved but that such factors nevertheless structure the opportunities for action in ways that are more complex than has sometimes been thought . . . It is important to understand classroom social structure as the product of both symbolic context *and* material circumstances (p. 6).

The authors fully recognise that any attempt to link SI/phenomenology with a marxist perspective poses serious problems:

> . . . metatheories and theories developed at different levels of analysis should be compatible and logically consistent with each other. Theorists working at their respective levels should be able to articulate the points at which the various levels of analysis link up and interpenetrate (p. 16).

Although some phenomenologists would claim that these problems are beyond solution, many interactionists would agree with Sharp and Green. In any case it seems absurd to deny *a priori* that different levels of analysis cannot be synthesized; rather, we should encourage every attempt to do so and then carefully examine to what extent any such attempt is successful. So let us grant the desirability and possibility of linking together analyses at the interactional and structural levels.

My central argument is that Sharp and Green present an entirely inadequate version of SI/phenomenology and on that ground alone their attempted synthesis fails. Their misrepresentation of SI/phenomenology occurs in two ways: in their general portrayal of the perspective and in their own allegedly SI/phenomenological research.

After claiming that SI/phenomenology are becoming the new orthodoxy in British sociology of education, Sharp and Green note that we must not discard the gains we have made through this perspective, which in particular have drawn attention to members' subjective experience of the world. Sharp and Green have no wish to dispense with notions of intentionality and subjective meaning. But neither do they wish to be limited to that. They seek to go *beyond* subjective meanings and see an important difference between 'things seeming to be the case to the actor and things *being* the case' (p. 21). They argue that phenomenology has no room for the concepts of structure and power, which they (rightly) believe to be important elements that a sociological analysis must take into account.

Sharp and Green's argument is that interactionists are simply unable to cope with power; it is boldly asserted that they 'ignore it and assume that interaction occurs on the basis of democratic negotiation between interested parties who are political equals' (p. 12). Similarly, it is claimed that 'the phenomenologist . . . seems only to be capable of 'grasping' a limited type of social encounter, that between free and equal partners in a truly 'liberal society' (p. 28). This is arrant nonsense. One of the major and most influential of interactionist texts has been Howard Becker's *Outsiders* (1963) in which the question is raised of 'Who makes the rules on the basis of which persons are held to be deviant?' Becker then devoted a considerable amount of space to an answer to this question. I too appear, in Sharp and Green's view, to be guilty of having no notion of power in my analysis of negotiative work in teacher-pupil relations.[8] This seems a very strange charge, since I point out that 'the second distinctive feature of teacher-pupil interaction is the enormous power differential between the two participants' and argue, following Waller, that the dice are heavily loaded in favour of the teachers in their attempts to impose their definition of the situation. Both labelling theory and studies of negotiation would be meaningless if they did not assume that some members of society had the power to impose labels and definitions on others. In short, whilst it can be readily conceded that some interactionists have neglected the notion of power in their analyses, it is simply untrue that all interactionist writing ignores the concept. On the contrary, it can be argued that interactionists have made an important contribution to the study of power by showing how power is frequently *negotiated* in interpersonal encounters.

Equally illegitimate is Sharp and Green's claim that interactionists and phenomenologists have naively asserted that man is 'free'. Goffman's work, for instance, constantly illustrates the nature of situational constraints upon action. Schutz sees man as making choices *and* as being heavily constrained by his inherited 'recipe knowledge' which is treated largely as unquestioned and unquestionable. So SI/phenomenology do not assume that man is 'absolutely free', whatever such a peculiar concept might mean, but rather assert that man is and experiences himself as both free (in some respects) *and* constrained (in some respects). This assumption attempts to restore the notion of human choice in sociological study as against the implicit strict determinism of other perspectives. The contrast is not so much between freedom and determinism, as between (in David Matza's terms) 'soft determinism' and 'hard determinism'.

It soon becomes apparent why Sharp and Green are creating and then knocking down this interactionist straw man; it is but one element in a much broader attack on SI/phenomenology to justify the introduction of a marxist perspective. The next step is the assertion that SI/phenomenology is not really sociology at all, but social psychology (p. 16). I myself take little exception to this, but there is surely little to gain from recategorising 'microsociology' as 'social psychology' which might seem to exclude from the sociological enterprise many interactionists and phenomenologists who wish to identify themselves with that discipline. This exchange of labels is, however, subordinate to the next step, which is central to the thesis of the book, namely the claim that SI/phenomenology is a *descriptive* activity whereas marxism is *explanatory* in nature. Phenomenology gives a description at the social psychological level of man's consciousness and subjective experience; marxism provides a sociological explanation of why it is that man has that experience. SI/phenomenology is not merely made into a different discipline; it is also assigned a quite distinctive and limited role – that of the descriptive under-labourer. It is the function of the phenomenologist to undertake the spade-work of describing man's consciousness, since he is allegedly limited to:

the purely descriptive or illustrative level of enquiry (p. 25).

the meaning of the situation as it appears to the actor (p. 26).

intersubjectivity and the surface structure of meaning (p. 30).

In contrast, the marxist is able to:

look behind the level of immediacy in order to try to develop some sociology of situations, their underlying structure and interconnections and the constraints and contingencies they impose (p. 25).

explain *why* in certain kinds of contexts there are limitations on men's freedom and creativity, and *why* the constraints are so powerful (p. 27). (Italics added).

It is the marxist who has access to this special knowledge, which apparently is unavailable both to our under-labouring phenomenological social psychologist *and* to the persons who are being studied.

This is a remarkable set of claims. Very few social scientists, of any persuasion, would argue that they can write a 'pure description' of any phenomenon. Surely all data collection implies a *selection* from amongst a range of possible data and presentation to a reader betrays an *interpretation* of the data. It is true that social scientists' theories are frequently implicit rather than explicit, but nevertheless all data collection and reporting is a theory-laden activity. That Sharp and Green should allow even the possibility of 'pure description' is the more astonishing when we recall their own preference for a marxist perspective in which they are clearly familiar with the work of Habermas. Further, this (mis) representation of SI/phenomenology ignores the fact that writers of this school have been actively concerned with the development of appropriate *theories*, rather than just descriptions. Such theories are discounted or ignored by Sharp and Green.

For Sharp and Green, then, the problem of articulation between the micro and the macro reduces to the provision of descriptive data by the phenomenologist and the sociological explanation of such data by the marxist. This, I believe, is a profoundly mistaken view. The task is more properly defined as the articulation of *theories* at the micro level (which relate to certain kinds of data) with *theories* at the macro level (which also relate to certain kinds of data which may be quite different from the data that are relevant at the micro level).

The great strength of SI/phenomenology has been the willingness to get close to human phenomena through ethnography. This contribution was to help to put real men back into the abstract theoretical writing of much structural-functionalism. SI's relation to sociology is like that of ethology to psychology: man must be studied in his natural habitat. Some of this writing is relatively atheoretical, but there is a large, if incoherent, body of theory to be found here. In my view we shall not integrate SI/phenomenology with any other perspective unless that perspective can subsume micro theory as well as micro data.

If Sharp and Green portray SI/phenomenology in a highly distorted way, this does not necessarily mean that their attempt to promote a synthesis between phenomenology and marxism be inevitably abortive, for their practice may be less defective than their words. Unfortunately, this appears not to be the case. Chapter Five of the book presents an exposition of the teachers' pespectives or ideologies. Presumably this is intended to be an example of 'pure description'. It can hardly qualify as that, however, since it is clearly a selection which is reported under three analytical headings. Certainly there is no explicit theory here, which renders it inadequate as a piece of symbolic interactionism. The next three chapters are more explicitly phenomenological, for the authors draw on the work of Schutz and develop a model of typification in the classroom.

We then come to the heart of the argument in Chapter Nine. Sharp and Green's aim is to:

> clarify and exemplify our second major problematic: that is to locate or situate the teacher's classroom practice in the wider context of extra-classroom relationships

and

> to understand the degree of teacher's discretion in the classroom by relating it to such extra-classroom influences (p. 176).

It is argued that there are two kinds of 'structural influence' or constraints: intra-classroom (e.g. physical constraints, the teacher-pupil ratio) and extra-classroom (e.g. staff relations, parents).

The authors seek first of all to demonstrate that the teachers' child-centred vocabulary and accounts are 'confused' and 'inadequate' (p. 167). These two concepts are never very clearly explained. To claim that something is 'inadequate' suggests that there are criteria against which we could judge a phenomenon to be 'adequate' or 'inadequate'; but these are never stated.[9] It appears that we, as readers, are to use our commonsense reading of the interview transcripts to recognise the 'confusion' in and 'inadequacy' of what the teachers say. Sharp and Green argue that when they ask teachers to give an account of their actions in the classroom, the teachers' 'child-centred ideology and vocabulary' is unequal to the production of a coherent and clear (i.e. 'adequate') account; in effect, the teachers are 'confused'. For instance, the child-centred ideology proposes that teachers should not intervene and introduce certain curriculum contents for the pupil until he is at an appropriate 'stage' and is 'ready'. Sharp and Green hold that their interview material clearly demonstrates that when teachers are asked to give an account of, for example, how they know that a child is at a certain stage, which would justify teacher intervention, the teachers display an inadequate account which betrays the failure of the teachers to articulate a clear relationship between the child-centred ideology in its abstract formulation on the one hand and their operations or practical decisions in the classroom on the other hand.

Now it may well be that there is a disjunction between the abstract child-centred ideology (as available in books of pedagogy or as uttered by these teachers in non-classroom situations such as the staffroom) and the commonsense knowledge on which these teachers base their mundane and routine classroom decisions about teaching and learning. Indeed, it is phenomenologists (rather than marxists) who would *assume* as a central tenet of their perspective that (a) accounts given in different contexts (e.g. classroom versus staffrooms) or to different audiences (e.g. teachers, head-teachers, parents, researchers) would naturally tend to vary by such situations and audiences;[10] and (b) that it is a basic feature of commonsense knowledge that it is, in Schutz's famous words, incoherent, only partially clear and not at all free from contradiction'. In other words, a phenomenologist would *expect* what Sharp and Green claim to demonstrate. Yet the authors seem to be surprised by the finding and bring it to the reader's attention as if they too should be surprised.

> We are therefore suggesting that there is no direct logical relationships between the child-centred vocabulary and the teacher's actions in all their intricate complexity. The vocabulary does not immediately inform and motivate all their actions. Rather, the teachers' actions are directly informed in an ad hoc manner by routines, habits and motivations, many of which in the immediacy of the classroom work will either be unconscious or only minimally reflexive (p. 175).

It is one thing for a phenomenologist to presuppose or anticipate this; it is quite another to demonstrate it. I shall show that the basis on which Sharp and Green draw this conclusion is highly suspect. If the finding is to stand, we must be sure that the researchers did not *create* this 'confusion' in the teachers by methodological insensitivities. One of the greatest problems of the interview as a method for generating data is that the *questions* asked may be seen by the subject as difficult, strange, ambiguous or meaningless. (It is for such reasons, in part, that interactionists are suspicious of question-naires). If a question is seen as strange or difficult, the interviewee may have great difficulty in formulating a coherent reply to the question. The confusion in the reply might then be a direct function of the form in which the question was asked. It is my contention that this is precisely what occurred in the Sharp and Green data.

They admit that the teachers were 'not used to being closely questioned in this way' (p. 172). As Esland[11] has rightly pointed out:

> Because of their professional isolation the theoretical ideas of their pedagogy are rarely invoked *in the work situation* (italics added).

This places a great obligation on Sharp and Green to examine their own questions with great care. For if the teachers find the questions unusual or difficult – and so probably threatening as well – then one would not, and could not reasonably, expect the answers to flow easily and coherently.

How did Sharp and Green set about asking their questions? Sadly very few of the questions asked by Sharp and Green are reproduced in the text, but the indications are that the questions took a particular form. They appear to be highly *abstract* questions about what teachers do, and usually they are totally *decontextualised* from any actual action the teacher performed. Examples are:

How does one notice what stage a child is at?

How do you know they don't know? (p. 169).

How can you tell their capabilities? (p. 174).

A little reflection (or additional investigation) will show that such abstract, decontextualised questions would be difficult for *any* teacher, whether child-centred or not, to answer. Because when a question is framed in such a way, it indicates that an equivalent abstract, decontextualised answer is required as well. That suggests that teachers ought to be able, as a matter of routine, to turn their everyday commonsense thinkings, their logic-in-use of classroom decision-making, into a series of abstract propositions which would constitute satisfactory answers to Sharp and Green's questions. It is surely hardly surprising that the teachers stumble and falter in their attempts to produce such replies; like typical subjects, they are trying to help the researchers and are reluctant to rephrase the questions. In fact the teachers soon resort to illustrating their points by reference to actual events or individual pupils, where they feel more at home. In other words, they struggle to *recontextualise* the decontexualised question.

The 'confusion' displayed in the answers, then, can reasonably be held to be a methodological artifact. There are good grounds for assuming *a priori* a gap between words and deeds,[12] doctrine and commitment, the educationist and teacher contexts,[13] but we cannot accept that Sharp and Green have clearly demonstrated such a gap in this case. It remains an open question. Moreover, assuming that such a disjunction is a general phenomenon, then there is no reason not to expect it in *all* teachers, not just child-centred ones; and if that is the case, then some of Sharp and Green's comments about child-centred education lose much of their force. But Sharp and Green do not check whether or not non-child-centred teachers display this 'confusion' when asked similar questions. In short, we must regard Sharp and Green's conclusions as unwarranted.[14]

It is clear that Sharp and Green have Keddie's distinction between the educationist and teacher contexts very much in mind, for after quoting her, they argue that the child-centred vocabulary is used by teachers

not so much to provide some detailed operational definition of the situation and the practices, particularly the pedagogical methods expected therein, but as a rhetorical measure of commitment to the organisation and its structure of power relationships (p. 185).

This is an interesting and not implausible notion. There are many reasons for supposing that teachers in the staffroom are, in their talk about education, likely to express a commitment to the dominant school ideology. Keddie, in fact, did not give a single illustrative extract of teacher·talk in the staffroom, so in this aspect her account is no more than suggestive. It appears that Sharp and Green are about to advance that analysis, taking up where Keddie left off, by collecting appropriate ethnographic evidence to support their argument. Clearly this could be done most readily by citing staffroom talk between teachers. Yet Sharp and Green, for unstated reasons, do not do this.

They might argue that the talk given to the researchers in the interviews might constitute such evidence. (Certainly Keddie recognised this possibility). But this would be a poor substitute for 'natural' staffroom talk; Sharp and Green cannot draw conclusions about teacher – teacher talk on the basis of teacher – researcher talk. Again, then, the conclusions are unwarranted. The line of this whole argument may be plausible; but the relevant ethnographic data are either defective or simply uncollected to justify a conclusion that the argument has been demonstrated.

From an interactionist point of view there is yet a further sin of omission in Sharp and Green's analysis. Let us grant that there is a disjunction between the child-centred ideology and teacher practice in the classroom. Let us grant also, for the sake of the argument, that the teachers cannot draw upon the child-centred vocabulary to explain and justify classroom routine decisions. This could then be taken to show what teachers do *not* use to justify their classroom actions, but it ignores what they *do* use to justify those actions. Sharp and Green appear to make little attempt to frame methods or questions which would permit teachers to display their cultural resources and competencies by which they make sense of their own as well as pupil conduct in the classroom. Because they fail to explore this essential research line, Sharp and Green are forced to present the teachers as if they are in some sense deficient; they are presented to us as culturally incompetent 'dopes'. One of the central aims and strengths of SI/phenomenology is thereby discarded.

We must turn finally to the notion of 'structural constraints' on which Sharp and Green rest their claim that a marxist analysis is essential to complement the limitations of SI/phenomenology. Once again, my aim is not to question the importance of structural constraints or the potential of a marxist analysis here; rather my purpose is to show how Sharp and Green distort and under-use SI/phenomenology. The effect is to weaken the foundations of their own analysis, which ironically would have been strengthened by a careful use rather than a careless rejection of interactionist insights.

The heart of Sharp and Green's argument consists of the eminently reasonable view that teachers' actions are subject to a complex variety of social and physical constraints. A structuralist analysis will lay bare the nature and consequences of those constraints. The authors recognise that an awareness of such constraints may be part of the conscious experience of teachers; the issue is raised at several points:

> . . . the teacher who has adopted the ideology of child centredness *may* well find himself *unwittingly* constrained to act . . . (p. viii, italics added).

> . . . the context of social and physical constraints which they *may or may not* perceive . . . (p. 30, italics added).

> . . . constraints on action (which) lead to consequences that the teachers *may not* recognise as primarily the result of material conditions in which they are trying to function' (p. 31, italics added).

Whether the teachers are or are not aware of these structural constraints is crucial to Sharp and Green's argument. If they are not so aware, and if the consequential nature of such constraints can be demonstrated, then Sharp and Green would be correct in claiming that they have exposed one of the limitations of a SI/phenomenological analysis. But if the teachers *are* aware of the structural constraints, then Sharp and Green's attempt to expose the limitations of SI/phenomenology would fail, for their structural analysis would consist of no more than a reiteration of teachers' experience. That is, their sociological, structuralist account would consist of a re-presentation of a commonsense account. Were such an identity between Sharp and Green's and the members' accounts to occur, the strength and importance of an SI/phenomenological analysis would be established.

Sharp and Green clearly recognise the possibility of teacher awareness of constraints, but they do not appear to understand the empirical imperatives that are consequential upon such a recognition. It follows that Sharp and Green must make a careful *check* on the extent of teacher awareness, for only if teachers are not fully aware of the nature and consequences of the constraints, and demonstrably so, will their own structuralist account be enhanced and their attack on the limitations of SI/phenomenology be sustained. Astonishingly, however, Sharp and Green give no indications that they have undertaken the required empirical checks; they simply do not bother to ask the teachers about their awareness of constraints.

A critic must ask: why not? Only Sharp and Green know the answer to this; in default of their explanation, several possibilities suggest themselves. My own guess – and it can be no more than that – is that the failure to undertake the checks arose because Sharp and Green made the analysis some time after completing the field work; that is, they recognised the need for the test when all the field data had been completed. If this is the case, we are witnessing a common problem of field research, namely that during the writing-up the researcher recognises the significance of questions he did *not* ask during the original field-work. For such a failure, Sharp and Green cannot reasonably be faulted, though it does appear from the data reported in the book that in their field-work Sharp and Green greatly emphasised the teachers as explainers of their pupils and too rarely explored the teachers' explanations of *themselves*, which is so central to any phenomenological analysis. The fault lies rather in Sharp and Green's failure to undertake the tests after developing their analysis, or, if that could not be done, in failing to tell the readers of the book of the importance of the check and ·in not admitting that they had not done the check.

Instead, Sharp and Green struggle with the data they had collected without the insights generated by later analysis. Yet the data are, strictly speaking, inadequate to that analysis. In the interview data there are clear indications that the teachers are indeed at least partially aware of the constraints upon them and Sharp and Green do not hide the fact – e.g. '. . . the headmaster experiences constraints impinging upon him . . .' (p. 184). A careful reading of Chapter Nine shows that Sharp and Green allow the teachers to be aware of constraints on occasions, presumably when their interview data gave indications of such an awareness. But when the teachers do not betray indications of such an awareness, Sharp and Green impose their *own* analysis of constraints. But this is completely unjustifiable. The fact that the teachers do not mention their awareness of certain constraints and their consequences cannot be taken as evidence that they do not have such an awareness, unless the authors have carefully probed the teachers and their understandings of constraint, which was not the case. Sharp and Green merely add to and sophisticate the awareness which the teachers volunteered in interview, and it may well be the case that the teachers had such a degree of awareness all the time. Indeed, it is possible that the teachers had an awareness which is more sophisticated than that offered by Sharp and Green; on the evidence we cannot tell.[15]

In short, in the light of these serious methodological defects, Sharp and Green's analysis becomes suspect. It is possible that what they claim is a sociologist's structural account is nothing more than a commonsense member account. Their analysis does not show the limitations of a SI/phenomenological analysis as such; rather it shows how they have failed to use SI/phenomenology in all its potential. Had they done so, they would have recognised the power of SI/phenomenology to explore and expose the teachers' understandings of constraints and their nature and consequences. This would be the essential first step in their analysis. They would then have been justified in using their more structuralist analysis either in claiming that, from the perspective of a sociologist, the members' accounts are incomplete, and/or in seeking to show that the members' accounts are themselves in need of explanation.

Few interactionists/phenomenologists, with the exception of a small number of ethnomethodologists, have argued that their own form of social scientific analysis is the only valid form of analysis. Hopefully we shall see in coming years a serious attempt to articulate the gains of SI/phenomenology with more 'macro' approaches in sociology. But this will not be achieved, I think, if we misrepresent the nature of SI/phenomenology or use it in a highly defective manner as, I have contended, Sharp and Green have done. Future attempts to link micro and macro analysis must, if they are to be successful, be grounded in ethnographic work of the highest quality.[16] Otherwise, we are just exchanging fashions in which rhetorical victories take precedence over substantive achievements. In conclusion, I wish to turn from a defence of SI/phenomenology to a more positive statement about its future role in the sociology of education. In a sense I am making a plea for tenacity[17] among adherents of the perspective. From what I said in the opening sections of this chapter it is clear that among the most important tasks are the generation of better theory, at both the substantive and formal levels, and greater attention to the production of empirical and conceptual generalisations in place of the proliferation of unique, isolated case-studies with their *ad hoc* employment of minor concepts. Those tasks are, in part, internal to SI/phenomenology itself. But we are poised between two worlds, those of education and sociology. Educationists demand that more of our work be policy-related, yet many interactionists and phenomenologists have eschewed policy issues in favour of a 'science for science's sake' motto. Fellow sociologists ask for connections with their work – currently with the development of neo-marxist ideas – yet interactionists and phenomenologists often display a myopic complacency in their cosy corner of the sociological enterprise. It need not be so. SI/phenomenology has a complex of strengths and capacities, of which I shall briefly mention five.

1 Its Appreciative Capacity

This is the most widely proclaimed strength of SI/phenomenology, which rests in its basic model of man and in its preferred methodology. This readiness to explore and expose social action from the point of view of the actor, with empathetic fidelity, stands at the root of SI/phenomenology's finest achievements, even if at times, as Gouldner has asserted, this humanistic liberalism has fallen prey to a romantic identification with underdogs. In education this perspective can, as a wide range of studies illustrates, display the nature, meaning and existential rationality of pupil conduct to teachers and to others. It can also, though this has been done too rarely (a political bias), display the nature, meaning and existential rationality of teacher conduct to pupils.

2 Its Designatory Capacity

Phenomenologists have focused much of their work on the painstaking analysis of the complex commonsense knowledge of members of society. In exposing the nature, content, structure and dynamics of this knowledge, much of which is tacit, phenomenologists have *named* features of what is normally taken for granted, both by members and by social scientists who draw upon it as a resource in their work. Through this process of designating or naming these features, phenomenologists have provided us with a language for speaking about that which is not normally spoken about; the ineffable is rendered articulate. Recent interactionist work in the field of education shows the extent to which teacher skills rest upon this tacit knowledge. Teachers have no explicit conceptual apparatus in which to express and communicate these skills – and they reject the traditional language of the educational sciences as inadequate to that end. By its designatory function, SI/phenomenology can provide such a language, so enriching the working vocabulary of teachers and teacher-trainers. At present we are merely beginning to see the possibilities for analysing communicating and teaching these newly designated skills.[18]

3 The Reflective Capacity

Once a language for the analysis of the unspoken or unnoticed is created, it can be offered not only to fellow social scientists (usually the primary audience) but also to the members themselves. SI/phenomenology can act as a mirror which reflects man back to himself. Man is provided with an opportunity to judge and appraise the reflection he sees: he may, if he dislikes what he sees, seek to change himself and the world in which he acts. In education far too rarely have the teachers' and pupils' reactions to an ethnographic research report been followed up as an integral part of the research.[19]

4 The Immunological Capacity

Social scientists are often outspoken in describing social ills and in providing prescriptions about how the world might be a better place if only the practical implications of their analyses were implemented. Yet many of these policies fail and nowhere is this more evident than in education, where innovations frequently fail quite disastrously. I would argue that one common reason for this is that, in grafting our new ideas onto schools, we do it with so little knowledge about the nature of the everyday world of teachers, pupils and schools that our attempted grafts (and various forms of major or minor surgery) merely arouse the 'anti-bodies' of the host which undermine our attempts to play doctor to an educational patient. SI/phenomenology, through ethnographic studies of schools and classrooms and through the phenomenological analysis of the experience of headteachers, teachers and pupils, can help to provide us with the necessary immunological understandings; for only when we understand the precise nature of the host body can we design our innovatory grafts with any confidence that they will prove to be acceptable.

5 *The Corrective Capacity*

Many sociological (and psychological) models of man, and the theories and policy prescriptions which are based upon them, prove to be defective in some regards when applied at the micro level of social interaction. Good-quality ethnography is always a potential source of correction to macro theories, which frequently oversimplify, underestimate or ignore the complexity of the detailed operation of relevant factors in actual social settings. Willis's recent *Learning to Labour* is a good example of how fine ethnography can generate problems for macro theories of social reproduction. However, it is still almost unknown for interactionists/phenomenologists to use their perspective as a basis for a critical reading of a macro theory, and then actively to seek out the micro implications with a view to undertaking the necessary ethnographic work to provide an empirical testing ground. There is much scope for ethnographers in the works of writers such as Bourdieu, Gramsci or Bowles and Gintis.

Four of these capacities (the appreciative, designatory, reflective and immunological) have clear implications for policy, and three of them (the appreciative, immunological and corrective) offer important points of articulation with macro level work. Most of these capacities are still badly underdeveloped and they need urgent attention. The fashion may change in the sociology of education; but we must recognise it as a change of fashion rather than as a rejection of SI/phenomenology *in toto* because it has been found wanting in principle. A fashion change soon engenders a disheartened defensiveness among the unfashionable, when it should stimulate a renewed but self-critical vigour. The task is to continue with its programme of work, whilst nevertheless being responsive to the challenges of those in other perspectives. If it can thus realise its own potential SI/phenomenology has an assured future in the vast sociological enterprise, whatever changes in fashion it may encounter in its path.

Notes:

1 This is not to deny the relevant work of B. Bernstein in *Class, Codes and Control*, Volume 3 (London, Routledge and Kegan Paul, 1975) and G. Bernbaum, *Knowledge and Ideology in the Sociology of Education*, (London, Macmillan, 1977), as well as papers in L. Barton and R. Meighan (eds) *Sociological Interpretations of Schooling and Classrooms*. (Driffield, Yorks, Nafferton, 1971).

2 I do not have space to show how it may be that it is psychologists rather than sociologists who will play the major role in the realisation of that programme.

3 P.L. Berger and T. Luckmann, *The Social Construction of Reality*, (London, Penguin Books, 1966).

4 See D.H. Zimmerman and D.L. Wieder, 'Ethnomethodology and the problem of order', in J.D. Douglas (ed.) *Understanding Everyday Life* (London, Routledge and Kegan Paul, 1971).

5 A. Gouldner, *The Coming Crisis of Western Sociology*, (London, Heinemann, 1970).

6 J. Lofland, 'Interactionist imagery and analytic interruptus', in T. Shibutani (ed.) *Human Nature and Collective Behaviour*, (Englewood Cliff's, Prentice-Hall, 1970).

7 B.G. Glaser and A.L. Strauss, *The Discovery of Grounded Theory*, (London, Weidenfeld and Nicolson, 1967).

8 D.H. Hargreaves, *Interpersonal Relations and Education*, (London, Routledge and Kegan Paul, 1972).

9 A stimulating critique of Sharp and Green's imputations of 'inconsistency' to the teachers they studied is offered by M. Hammersley, *Teacher Perspectives*, Unit 9 of Schooling and Society (Open University Press, 1977).

10 See for example M.B. Scott and S.M. Lyman, 'Accounts', *American Sociological Review*, Vol. 33, 1968.

11 G. Esland, 'Teaching and learning as the organisation of knowledge', in M. Young (ed.) *Knowledge and Control*, (London, Collier-Macmillan, 1971).

12 See I. Deutscher, 'Words and deeds', *Social Problems*, Vol. 13, 1965.

13 See N. Keddie, 'Classroom knowledge', in M. Young (ed.), *Knowledge and Control*, (London, Collier-Macmillan, 1971).

14 The book is replete with unwarranted assertions of which one of the most remarkable is 'Those pupils whom their teachers regarded as more successful tended to be given far greater attention than the others' (p. 115), a 'finding' for which no evidence is given.

15 The sophisticated understanding of structural constraints among young teachers is very apparent in the literature, for example, D. Hanson and M. Herrington, *From College to Classroom: The Probationary Year*, (London, Routledge and Kegan Paul, 1976). For researchers the danger is that older teachers may regard these constraints as too obvious to be worth mentioning under normal circumstances.

16 A recent example is P. Willis, *Learning to Labour*, (Farnborough, Hants., Saxon House, 1977). Whilst this is an important book, it contains, from the point of view of this paper, some important deficiencies. For instance, Willis fails to develop and articulate the linkage between macro and micro *theories*.

17 I am, of course, making reference to Feyerabend's principle of tenacity, by which scientists adhere to a perspective even when it encounters considerable difficulties. Contemporary sociologists of education would advance their field much more readily through a healthy conflict between this principle of tenacity and its partner, the principle of proliferation, than through the current tendency to indulge in

polemical denunciations of competing perspectives. 'Tenacity: this means that one is encouraged not to follow one's inclinations, but to develop them further, to raise them, with the help of criticism (which involves a comparison with the existing alternatives) to a higher level of articulation and thereby to raise their defence to a higher level of consciousness'. P.K. Feyerabend, 'Consolations for the specialist' in I. Lakatos and A. Musgrave (eds.), *Criticism and the Growth of Knowledge*, (London, Cambridge University Press, 1970).

18 See D.H. Hargreaves, S.K. Hester and F.J. Mellor, *Deviance in Classrooms*, (London, Routledge and Kegan Paul, 1975), pp. 257-8 for some elementary examples.

19 The important, but often rather inaccessible, work of CARE at the University of East Anglia is the best exception known to me.

The Micro-Macro Problem in the Sociology of Education

A. Hargreaves

Organized education is a highly political affair. It shapes and channels life opportunities, it opens up and blocks off careers for those who work within it, it draws heavily on scarce resources from the state budget, and it is subject to a range of competitive pressures from all sectors of society. One does not have to be a sociologist to appreciate this point. Since the late 1970s, cuts in educational expenditure and their effect on the everyday practices of teaching and learning have become a matter of widespread public concern (HMI, 1982). And a whole range of new initiatives to bring about a fundamental restructuring of the educational system, through the provision of assisted places in independent schools, the development of programmes of vocational education and training for less able 14–19 year olds, and the mooting of educational voucher schemes, have all served to heighten public consciousness about the extent to which state provided education is saturated with political significance. For the public at large, education is, in this sense, being subjected to increasing politicization (Hunter, 1983; Dale, 1979; Bush and Kogan, 1982). But for those of us who are fortunate enough to continue earning our living as sociologists of education, these policy changes and their implications for school practice only emphasize in a particularly dramatic way what should perhaps always be at the heart of our professional concern in any case: the explanation of everyday school practices in the context of their wider outcomes and determinants. Among professional sociologists of education the understanding of such connections has come to be known as *the micro-macro problem.*

The micro-macro problem is central to much sociological theorizing of a general kind where it has been taken up in a particularly creative way by such writers as Giddens (1976 and 1979) and Habermas (1976). Nor is it confined to sociology and its derivative sub-disciplines. In the physical sciences, for instance, practitioners have worried for a long time about the troublesome connection between those 'macro' objects given to our sense experience – planets, pendulums and the like – and the sub-atomic micro-particles with which much current theoretical physics is concerned (note here that it is the *micro* objects which cannot be apprehended through immediate sense experience). Our concern here, however, is with the sociology of education, and that is where I shall focus my attention. Here, the micro-macro problem has been the subject of a great deal of theoretical debate, though not much empirical research, since the mid 1970s onwards. Until that point, the sociology of education had been broadly divided into two broad camps – into somewhat insulated small-scale empirical studies of teacher-pupil interaction, pupil sub-cultures and so on on the one hand, and ambitious, speculative, grand theoretical explanations of the relationship between schooling and society on the other. The sociology of education, in other words, was segregated into what might be called studies of the schools and studies of 'the system'. Hardly any attempts, it seems, were made to connect the two.

Furthermore, from the relative security of their respective camps, the students of the schools and the scholars of the system made sniping criticisms of each others' work. On the one hand, classroom researchers were strongly criticized for their idealism and 'bourgeois individualism', for the emphasis that writers like Keddie (1973) placed on the possibility that educational change might be brought about through raising individual rather than class consciousness. Michael Young and Geoff Whitty, for instance, (1977) in their introduction to a collection of Marxist readings in the sociology of education, complained that 'Many classroom studies, seem to present education as being carried on in a social vacuum' (p. 7).

But if 'micro' researchers often seemed, like ostriches, to be so preoccupied with the fine-grained detail of school and classroom life, that they rarely took their heads out of the sand to see what was happening in the world outside, theorists of 'the system' appeared all too often to have little contact with the 'real world' at all. As David Hargreaves (1978) put it in his paper with the pleading title 'Whatever happened to symbolic interactionism?'

> Marxist positions appear to offer a new 'paradigm shift' in which sociologists of education in their disturbing flight from the empirical can indulge in polemical pieces which take the format of 'a critique of position X from a Marxist perspective' through which theoretical kudos is achieved without getting one's hands dirty with research.

Not everyone was happy with this state of affairs though, and a number of writers, including myself, began to advocate a synthesis of 'micro' and 'macro' approaches, a binding together of those parts of the discipline which had hitherto been separate. Their arguments took many different forms, not least, as I shall go on to show, because there was a good deal of uncertainty and confusion about what exactly it was that was being connected. But one general view ran through all their recommendations – that each approach had something to offer the other, and that together, they might help us understand a little better how society shapes and is in turn shaped by the schooling system.

Spirited and impassioned as they were though, the various appeals were also extremely unclear about what kinds of bridges needed to be built (Hargreaves, A. 1980). They gave little indication of what was to be joined together and *how* any synthesis was to be achieved. At some points, the synthesizers appeared, myself included, to be proposing links between different levels of reality, between patterns of educational structure and the texture of daily life. At other points, the bridge was a theoretical and conceptual one, between different ways of looking at reality, between 'interpretative' and 'normative' approaches. And David Hargreaves' disdainful remarks about the unwillingness of macro theorists to venture from their ivory towers and 'get their hands dirty' with empirical research suggests yet another kind of connection – between theory and evidence. In pleas for synthesis, these different possibilities with their own particular difficulties have typically been run together. What we have come to know as the micro-macro problem actually subsumes them all (and more besides). It is not, in that sense, one problem, but several. Not surprisingly, then, when all the various difficulties have been compounded together, that problem has often seemed to be insuperable; just too formidable a challenge to one's time, energy and imagination as an educational researcher. While I myself sought to unravel some of these difficulties by developing and giving some empirical illustrations of the concept of *coping strategy*, and while indeed Olive Banks (1982) in her review of thirty years of the sociology of education concluded that such bridging concepts point to important ways forward for the discipline, it is now clear to me that I have been just as remiss as my colleagues in specifying with due precision what the making of 'micro-macro' connections entails – at some points implying that this involves linking 'structural questions to interactionist concerns' and at others suggesting it as a matter of analyzing how 'classroom matters may relate to the nature of the socioeconomic and political structure' (Hargreaves, A. 1978).

In view of the vagueness of guidelines for synthesis, then, it is not altogether surprising that in recent years, barring a few important exceptions, the sociology of education has become even more strongly characterized by a proliferation of approaches, its proponents becoming ever more firmly entrenched in their own camps, confined to their own 'problematics', blissfully or wilfully ignorant or dismissive of the literature and research findings being produced by their opponents (Hammersley, 1984a). While, in the late 1970s there were at least brief skirmishes between members of the different camps, stereotyped, distorted and hostile as they were, they did at least amount to some kind of communication. What is sadder is that with the cessation of theoretical hostilities, so too has there been an ending to communication. In this sense, perhaps too many of us have settled for the theoretically easier life. By and large, interactionists have gone back to their classrooms and staffrooms, while macro theorists have moved into 'the state' and educational policy. When the current and intensifying educational crisis and its effects on schooling begs decent sociological explanation, this unproductive division of theoretical labour is, in my view, regrettable.

In the rest of the chapter, therefore, I want to try and outline and clarify just three of the different dimensions which make up the micro-macro problem, to outline the problems contained in each, to assess how well these problems have been dealt with in existing studies devoted to making micro-macro connections, and to suggest how these problems might be overcome.

1 Theory and Evidence

The first interpretation of the micro-macro link is that which sees it in terms of the relationship between theory and evidence. It is on this very dimension that much influential Marxist scholarship has 'written off' the possibility of any micro-macro project at all, or interpreted it as involving the subsumption of (usually ethnographic) data within a broadly unquestioned Marxist theory. Since this position is both an influential and controversial one, and since it raises most of the issues concerning the difficulties of relating theory to evidence, I shall concentrate on it here.

One of the most extensive sociological objections to the general worth and possibility of micro-macro work has been advanced by Louis Althusser. Basically, Althusser (1977) indicts those adhering to what he calls an *empiricist* position for advancing *experience* as the ultimate reference point for all knowledge claims about the world. The problem with this, Althusser contends, is that such experience is inescapably suffused with ideological meaning and for that reason cannot provide an adequate discourse of proof (pp. 183–4). Being blind to the ideologically loaded character of their 'evidence', empiricists, Althusser contends, falsely equate the object of their knowledge with the 'real world' object to which it relates. They confuse appearances with reality, that is (for example, Althusser and Balibar, 1970, p. 133). Instead, Althusser proposes, what the social scientist ought to do is purge the 'facts' or 'evidence' with which the theorist is presented of their ideological content, to reveal their inner truth. This, he suggests, can only be achieved by the use of theoretical procedures *alone*, and, much as in mathematics, it is the inner logic of these procedures, not the ideologically-laden world of 'experience', that provides the only acceptable criterion of proof.

Althusser outlines these views in the context of general sociological theory, but interpretations deriving from them have made their mark within the sociology of education too. Rachel Sharp (1980) for instance, has taken issue with the 'retreat into empiricism, the collection of a mass of data and its analysis in terms of low level hypotheses which ultimately do little more than reproduce a more articulated version of common-sense'. And Kevin Harris (1982) in his Marxist analysis of *Teachers and Classes* offers an even more elaborate defence.

> All investigations and analyses are made from the perspective of some particular theory or theories: they are theory-dependent or theory laden, and this is so regardless of whether or not the underlying theory is declared, admitted to, or spelt out. There can be no such thing as a neutral examination, or an examination which is objective either in the sense that it is a-theoretic or else sufficiently eclectic so as to encompass all theoretical perspectives . . .
>
> Theory-ladenness of investigation gives rise to a large number of methodological issues and problems, and it is hardly our purpose to discuss these here. On the other hand, it is our purpose to undertake an investigation, and this we shall do by . . . casting our investigation into the context of a research programme (or problematic) wherein certain basic or 'hard core' hypotheses and propositions are accepted as being secure and inviolable for the purpose of operating or working with the research programme.

Having laid the philosophical groundwork, Harris then sets out how he proposes to conduct his own research.

> The investigation which follows here is carried out within the framework of Marxism or historical materialism, and thus certain 'hard core' propositions of that theory or research programme, propositions regarding the nature of the State, the nature of classes, and the role of class struggle, for example, will form the basis for our investigation: that is, they themselves will not be argued for here (they are being accepted as viable starting points because a wealth of previous argument, along with practical outcomes, has established their value for investigations of social relations).

Now Harris makes a number of appeals here as to why we should accept his claims about the relationship between theory and evidence. Setting aside his exceedingly shaky appeals to 'traditional authority', to the previous, unnamed work of anonymous writers of supposed erudition, I shall concentrate on the other two: the appeal to the irreconcilability of 'problematics' and the appeal to pragmatism.

(a) The Irreconcilability of Problematics

Harris claims that theoretical 'problematics' are irreconcilable, providing different possible starting points for analysis, the soundness of which is to be judged by the logical consistency of the argument that follows. In response to this, it is important to state at the outset that few sociologists would dispute the contention that the adequacy of a theory is dependent upon its logical consistency and internal coherence. Alfred Schutz and Max Weber, for instance, placed great stress on the fact that explanations ought to follow the postulate of adequacy at the level of meaning *and* that of logical consistency.

However, these selfsame sociologists would almost certainly add the rider that logical consistency is only a *necessary*, not a *sufficient* criterion of proof. As E.P. Thompson (1978) states, there are 'other (and equally difficult) procedures of research, experiment and of the intellectual appropriation of the real world, without which the secondary (but important) critical procedures would have neither meaning nor existence' (p. 203). Indeed, without these procedures how would we *know* that capitalist states are *really* as Marxist writers describe them, or if there is any such thing as a 'capitalist state' at all? These should not be resources for analysis but central topics for critical and searching inquiry, not least because if they are not, if state and class struggle remain immune from questioning and justification, it is likely that all but the already converted – the left intelligentsia – will switch off. Empirical research, of one kind or another, then, (though obviously the more rigorous the better), is ultimately indispensable to sustained theoretical advance.

Admittedly it has to be said that a good deal of empirical research is far from rigorous, and if it were brought to Althusser's court of theoretical enquiry, it would quite rightly be found guilty (even if the court were one where 'ignorance of the law' of theory-ladenness did not count as a defence). The highly fashionable and heavily funded tradition of abstracted empiricism, much favoured by certain kinds of psychologist, where masses of data are avidly collected and computed, then generalizations (barely worthy of the designation 'theory') abstracted from them, would certainly be extremely vulnerable to most of the charges that Althusser makes against empiricism – since the very selection of possible variables is based on unexplicated theories of possible causation (for example Bennett, 1976; Rutter, *et al.*, 1979; Galton, Simon and Croll, 1980). So, as I have argued elsewhere (Hargreaves, 1981) could many ethnographic studies of school life be criticized for adopting a posture of 'splendid isolation', a false claim that their analyses of microsettings like classrooms and staffrooms are uncontaminated by assumptions about the workings of the wider society when, in fact, they are in many cases based on a loose commitment to pluralist values (for example, Woods, 1979). Furthermore, many of those studies which attempt to link detailed accounts of school processes to 'macro' theories about the operations of social structure would also fare badly against the Althusserian critique. In the details of analysis, they rarely communicate a sense of data having been scrupulously checked, of disconfirming cases having been searched for, and so on (e.g. Sharp and Green, 1975;

Willis, 1977; Anyon, 1981). But the real irony in all this, is that those studies which appear to have been *most* susceptible to the selecting and squeezing of data in order to fit a preconceived theory, i.e. those which seem to be most open to the charges of 'empiricism' laid out by Althusser, are not, as Sharp (1980) alleges, 'bourgeois' and 'liberal' at all, but Marxist (Hargreaves, A. 1982).

To be candid, then, educational research, whether Marxist or non-Marxist is often much less rigorous than it ought to be. But this offers no warrant for discarding *all* empirical research as worthless. The best empirical work does *not*, as Althusser contends, use and interpret evidence uncritically, but treats it as constantly problematic. Empirical work of high quality consists of a continuing *dialogue* between theory and evidence where each is continually interrogated against the other *as well as* being tested for its internal consistency and coherence. It is only through such a dialogue that understandings of the social world can ever come to approximate to valid knowledge. Indeed, the greatest impediment to the achievement of such knowledge is the total immersion of the researcher within the worlds of either empirical evidence (empiricism) or 'pure' theory (theoreticism – as in Althusser's work).

Of course, Althusser is correct in saying that evidence is selected, that it is not neutral and self-evident, but produced for particular audiences and purposes. And many ethnographic researchers, it must be said, have too often overlooked the point, failing to note for instance, that what teachers say to researchers during a brief interview may differ from what they say to one another or even from what they puzzle about themselves (Sharp and Green, 1975). Althusser is also right to alert us to the ever-present danger that the theorist's identification and interpretation of data will reflect his or her particular theoretical and value orientations and that the resulting explanations will therefore be prone to ideological contamination. The crucial point, however, is that few empirical researchers would dispute these charges. Moreover, at their best, empirical researchers actually take account of these difficulties in their analyses – they can note the audiences for which documents were produced and deduce the political significance of this fact, they can check out the contaminating influence of their theoretical preferences by actively seeking out disconfirming cases in the data that would challenge their initial prejudices and hunches through cross-referencing (triangulating) different kinds of data on the same topic, or comparing different methods (observation and interview, for instance) in order to check the consistency of what a particular teacher or pupil says between settings, or triangulating the interpretations that different observers make of the same data, and so on (Denzin, 1970; Hammersley, 1979). The processes of analytic induction (Robinson, 1952) or grounded theorizing (Glaser and Strauss, 1967) contain similar procedures for checking the validity of interpretations. And as David Hargreaves (1981) and Pollard (1982) point out, such procedures might be included in forms of ethnographic enquiry directed towards testing theory too, and not just generating it.

Ethnographic practice is, of course, not always, or not even usually, as the handbooks tell us. In a sophisticated defence of the very possibility of Marxist ethnography, for instance, West (1984) criticizes the practice of British educational ethnography in general and of Marxist ethnographies of writers like Willis (1977) in particular on this count. He takes issue with Willis especially for 'spot welding' a Marxist analysis with descriptive ethnographic material. Similarly, one might say that in the case of Woods' (1979) *Divided School*, the author's Weberian claim that the teachers and pupils he studied were trapped within and trying to break free from institutional pressures brought about by increasing bureaucratization and growing disenchantment in society as a whole are also 'bolted on' to the descriptive accounts of subject choice, the typologies of pupil adaptation and teacher survival and so on.

Fortunately there are emerging signs that these weaknesses might now be on the wane as the principal figures involved in the first exploratory phase of British educational ethnography move into a second wave of research, where, aware of their errors and anxious to remedy them, they can produce studies which are more rigorous, tightly focused and theoretically informed than their first efforts (Hammersley, 1980; Woods, 1985; Pollard, 1984). The switch of emphasis is, to be fair, but a glint in the ethnographer's eye at the moment, but it remains to be seen if Marxist ethnographers are willing, at least, to recognize the importance of this challenge too. In this respect, West's (1984) injunctions for greater methodological rigour within Marxist ethnography are both provocative and encouraging. But one would hope here that the interest in testing and therefore in being sceptical about prior theoretical claims will extend not only to the details of analysis, to the characteristics of particular pupil cultures and so on, but will extend to those central concepts and categories, those fundamental domain assumptions, those commitments to a particular view of the social totality, to which West and many of his Marxist colleagues (for example, Wright, 1979) curiously seem to want to attach continued privileged status, to keep immune from and above methodological test, to leave unthreatened by the possibility of incorrectness. If the interrogation of theory with evidence and vice versa is to have any meaning, then, the most basic assumptions of the paradigm (Marxist, Weberian, or otherwise) must be left open to doubt (Hammersley, 1984a), otherwise the supposed validity of our analyses will rest only on the force of our belief, in which case we are likely to continue preaching only to the converted.

That such procedures of checking and testing *are* possible rests on the fact that while the interpretations of phenomena can and often do reflect the theoretical predilections of the researcher, the range of possible explanations is not entirely limitless, not completely the product of theoretical/

ideological bias; for the object itself as a real object places definite limits on the interpretations that can be made of it (Thompson, 1978, p. 210). Thus, had Althusser sat with Willis' lads at Hammertown Secondary School, he might have been able to view their conduct as 'larking about', institutional defiance or class resistance, but I sincerely doubt whether he would have been able to sustain his claims about how working-class pupils conform to the demands of their teachers in preparation for their role in the workplace.

Maintaining a dialogue between theory and evidence therefore demands both theoretical creativity *and* rigorous methodological checking in a context which credits the 'real world' with some potential to impose itself upon the way we think about it. It should be stressed that a great many empirical researchers, whether historians of education or ethnographers of schooling, for instance, would see themselves as contributing to just this sort of enterprise. The major flaw in the Althusserian critique and its derivative in educational study is that this important tradition of theoretically imaginative and methodologically cautious work which is cast in an *empirical mode*, is confused with a quite narrow *empiricism* (which rests on the view that knowledge claims are valid only if tested against the 'irrefutable' data of our sense experience) (Thompson, 1978, pp. 63-4 and p. 198). Whether this deceit is an innocent or a guilty one is impossible to say, but it is a deceit nonetheless, and one which has constituted a sizeable barrier to the advancement of sociological understanding in all fields of enquiry including education. It is perhaps salutary to note that Marx himself was, at one point in his writings at least, much less confused by this distinction. He drew a clear dividing line between shallow *empiricism* and well-conducted *empirical research*. In the *German Ideology*, he argued that . . .

> Empirical observation must in each separate instance bring out empirically, and without any mystification and speculation, the connection of the social and political structure with production. The social structure and the state are continually evolving out of the life process of definite individuals, however, of these individuals, not as they may appear in their own or other people's imagination, but as they *actually* are, i.e. as they act, produce materially, and hence as they work under definite material limits, presuppositions and conditions independent of their will . . . This manner of approach is not devoid of premises. It starts out from the premises and does not abandon them for a moment. Its premises are men, not in any fantastic isolation and fixity, but in their actual, empirically perceptible process of development under definite conditions. As soon as this active life process is described history ceases to be a collection of dead facts, as it is with the empiricists, or an imagined activity of imagined subjects, as with the idealists. Where speculation ends, where real life starts, there consequently begins real positive science, the expounding of the practical activity, of the practical process of the development of men . . .
> (Marx and Engels, 1976, pp. 35-7)

What is interesting about the comments of Marx and Engels here is that their defence of the role of empirical observation is made not just against a quite narrow empiricism, but also against 'speculation' and 'mystification' which, at the time Marx was writing, were characteristic defects of German Idealism. The irony of this second part of their argument, though, is that as well as being an effective attack on German Idealism, it now amounts to a trenchant critique of the speculative character of much contemporary neo-Marxist writing, and its refusal to acknowledge the admissability of empirical evidence.

Paradoxically, the theoreticist position with its refusal to take account of empirical evidence actually allows the most iniquitous kind of empiricism of all to creep in, in the shape of unacknowledged, unexamined, and unchecked assumptions of what, as a result of the capitalist system, 'really' happens in schools and elsewhere. Althusser and his followers, that is, have indulged in some of the worst empiricist excesses of all – erecting whole theoretical edifices on the basis of unacknowledged and unchecked assumptions – leading to what some have rightly called an 'indefensible dogmatism' (Cutler *et al.*, 1977, p. 211). Indeed, in one of the more extreme instances of this, a scathing critique of 'uncontexted' ethnography, by Rachel Sharp (1982), not a single example of the kind of work she is taking issue with is cited. Instead, she presents us merely with her own *imaginary* ethnographic account of a Fascist school in Nazi Germany, and the political context of that school which the account would allegedly ignore. If uncontexted ethnography really is as defective as Sharp claims, could she not have found a single example of 'bad' practice to support her case? Why should she feel the need to fall back on an (albeit dramatic) fictional case rather than a real one to provide her burden of proof? And if such neglect and fictionalized critiques run through her assessments of alternative research traditions whose texts and arguments are tangible and easily accessible, what faith can we reasonably have in her similarly unsupported claims about the nature and functions of schooling?

Judging by the work of both Sharp and Althusser, then, it seems that unbridled theoretical speculation and assertion offers a most suitable environment for crude empiricism to flourish[1].

(b) Pragmatic Necessity

If the objections in principle to incoherent theoreticism and vulgar empiricism seem well founded, if the ideal case for a carefully nurtured *rapprochement* between theory and evidence seems well made, that task may still be impeded by strong and perhaps insurmountable practical difficulties. In this sense, one might say, with Harris (1982), that while a rigorous dialogue between theory and evidence, a dialogue which involves adjudicating between competing theories as well as modifying existing ones, is desirable in an ideal world where researchers have unlimited resources of time, money and energy, in practice, a choice has to be made between one seemingly arbitrary set of concepts and categories and another on *pragmatic* grounds.

There is something in this. For one thing, at the 'micro' end of the research scale in studies of face-to-face interaction and so on, it is not possible, as ethnomethodologists discovered to their cost, to deal with all data literally and exhaustively, to notice and interpret every word, every gesture, every glance that passes between participants. Nor are these difficulties resolved by adopting increasingly sophisticated techniques of recording, such as videotape, for while such techniques may increase the amount of data we have available, this in turn only magnifies the problem of selecting which data we should attend to, and of how those data, those forms of talk and gesture, should then be interpreted. Attempts at providing entirely presuppositionless accounts of such phenomena have not been promising, and while a certain degree of reflexivity in our accounts, while deep aware-ness of why we interpret the data this way and not that, is to be applauded, there does come a point when the reflexivity has to stop, when some working assumptions, however provisional, have to be made in order to organize the data into some coherent, intelligible form. This is what David Hargreaves and his colleagues (1975) discovered, for instance, when they tried to pro-vide an assumption-free account of classroom rules. In the end, they found it necessary, on practical grounds, to construct what they called a 'working platform', a theoretical model of the rule system, against which their observations could then be compared. At the 'micro' end, then, there *are* times, even in the most methodologically rigorous research, when the reflex-ivity has to stop; when working assumptions must be *made*, however provisionally.

Similarly, it is also expedient, indeed necessary, to make arbitrary cut-off points at the 'macro' end of the scale too. Many writers have spoken of the importance of situating small-scale ethnographic accounts of particular aspects of school life in a larger context that takes account of the structural pressures that move the school and its participants one way and not another (Sharp, 1980; Apple, 1979 and 1982; Harris, 1982; Pollard, 1984). And elsewhere I have rekindled Mills' (1959) conception of the sociological imagi-nation as a way of encouraging sociologists of education to 'grasp the rich-ness of personal and interpersonal experience', while also noting the ways in which social structures impinge upon and partially shape the organization of peoples' everyday lives' (Hargreaves, A., 1981, p. 162). However, persua-sive as they might sound, these appeals leave unanswered the vital question of just how far this process of situating should go. Should the internal processes of schooling be placed in the context of the local community, the demands and pressures of the local education authority, changes in the local economy and so on? And should these local patterns in turn be related to changes at the national level – to the nature of class struggle, the requirments of the economic mode of production, the nature and demands of the capitalist state and the extent of its dependence on and independence from the capitalist economy? But why stop there? For states, economies and politics are not insulated systems, but part of a vast and complexly inter-connected global pattern – in which case, it might be argued, studies of pupil peer groups, staffroom cultures, teaching methods, subject subcultures and so on, should perhaps be related not just to the local and national context, but to the whole social totality (Sharp, 1980), to the entire world system, no less (Wallerstein 1974).

For researchers whose immediate concern (and the thing for which they have been funded) might be something as specific as 'gifted children', the establishment of tertiary colleges, pupil profiles or whatever, this is clearly a daunting prospect. For one thing, data on some parts of the 'world system', on some non-capitalist modes of production, for instance, may be severely restricted. Nor, given the shortness of our lives and the finite nature of human effort, would it be feasible, even if such data were available, to show the extent to which and ways in which schools in all known societies pro-duced patterns of reproduction and/or resistance to the social, political and economic orders in which they were located. And again, from a practical perspective, there are clear limits to just how many concepts can be rigor-ously interrogated for their validity in any particular study, just as there are to the exhaustiveness of that interrogation. Moreover, as cartographers of the social world, we must also be mindful of the mapmaker's dilemma – that the more complex and comprehensive our maps become, the more closely they resemble the actual territories they represent, the less useful they serve as guides through it.

For a host of sound practical reasons then, some things must be left out. Neither the world system, nor the smallest interactional encounter can be described in their entire complexity, nor is it obvious that they should be. Life, as they say, is simply too short.

Faced with such awesome tasks of macro-micro integration, of inter-rogating theory with evidence and vice versa, a solution recommendead by Hammersley (1980) begins to sound extremely attractive. What Hammersley suggests is that 'any piece of research should be explicity directed predominantly towards' one of four different areas: *micro-formal* (for exam-ple, the rules of conversation); *micro-substantive* (for example, differ-entiation and polarization of pupils); *macro-formal* (for example, the division of labour); and *macro-substantive* (for example, the history of education in France). Turner (1983) seems to interpret this as implying a policy of 'live and let live' – 'you do your research and I'll do mine!' – a policy which would allow us all to sleep more soundly in our beds (or under them!). Turner argues:

It is surely quite legitimate to pursue a particular project from a particular standpoint, such as interactionism, whilst accepting that this work will have deficiencies which can be compensated for by other researchers perhaps from a different theoretical standpoint . . . Indeed it seems naive to assume that any research project could achieve anything other than a partial explanation of the workings of society. Thus what is important about a piece of research is not so much its scope, but its validity (pp. 4–5).

This, it seems to me, is a naive solution. It promotes the misleading idea that work located in different traditions will somehow 'add up' to produce a more rounded picture of schooling or whatever. And it implies, as a characteristic piece of 'splendid isolation' that matters of scope are unrelated to matters of validity when, as I have noted, and as Turner's own study of 'conformist' pupils illustrates, interactionist studies of schooools and classrooms, by ignoring the context in which their 'cases' are situated, often exaggerate the moment by moment fluidity and variability, the pluralistic diversity of pupil conduct. Moreover, having recognized the impossibility of achieving total integration of theories, Turner's solution, his policy of 'separate develop-ment' is of dubious virtue for it is likely to lead not to greater understanding between the adherents of different perspectives, but to a reinforcement of theoretical prejudice and intolerance.

Actually, what Hammersley proposes is more subtle than Turner sug-gests. Hammersley's argument is for work focused *predominantly* at one level, but sensitive to work in other traditions pitched at other levels, too (see also, Hammersley, 1984b). In this sense it would not be unreasonable to expect interactionist researchers who are studying deviance and disruption to take account of Marxist work on pupil resistance, for instance (and vice versa), and to make some attempt to argue through the continuities and discontinuities that arise from such a comparison. Similarly, it is fair to ask that the validity and utility of some of the most contestable concepts that sociologists of education use, like 'state', should be justified against competing ones. Clearly, it is not possible to explain everything, but we should not use this as an excuse to bury our heads in small-scale empirical studies, or to become exclusively preoccupied with speculation about the nature of 'the social totality'. Though we cannot say everything, the solution is not to say almost nothing. There may be disagreements about just how far we should be sensitive to one another's work, about the number of competing perspectives and concepts we should take on board when justi-fying our own and so on, but the case for heightening that sensitivity, for leaving at least some of our concepts open to question and to empirical test is clearly very strong. Theory and evidence, that is, do have something to say to one another. They should be allowed to do so.

Some time ago, in his essay on 'The bearing of sociological theory on empirical research', Robert Merton (1968) 'pointed to the need for a closer connection between theory and empirical research'. 'The prevailing division of the two', he argued,

> . . . is manifested in marked *discontinuities* of empirical research, on the one hand, and systematic theorizing unsustained by empirical test on the other. There are conspicuously few instances of consecutive research which have cumulatively investigated a succession of hypotheses derived from a given theory (pp. 153–4).

'It is a commonplace', Merton concluded, 'that continuity can be achieved only if empirical studies are theory-oriented and if theory is empirically confirmable'. How sad it is, then, *pace* Althusser, Sharp and Harris, that this commonplace still needs to be reasserted.

2 Micro Theory – Macro Theory

In educational research, as in other forms of social enquiry, then, it is important to connect theory with evidence and to modify each accordingly if they do not fit. It would be a mistake to infer from this, however, that evidence is necessarily 'micro' and provides a testing ground for theory which is necessarily 'macro'. Statistical generalizations which point to the tendential characteristics of whole collectivities, to the social origins of university students, or to the destinations of secondary modern as against grammar school pupils (Halsey, Heath and Ridge, 1980), for instance, are not at all 'micro' in character. Similarly, not all theory is what Mills (1959) called Grand Theory: interrelated propositions on a vast scale about whole societies, their forms of economic organization and so on. Many theories are, in fact, directed to 'micro' concerns – to aspects of interpersonal relations, peer group dynamics and the like.

In clearing up this possible muddle, I am, of course, now raising a further distinction between micro and macro, one which lies within theory itself. The contrast between micro and macro in this sense is between explanations of social behaviour and interaction in particular settings like classrooms or staffrooms on the one hand, and explanations of supra-individual forces like social classes and the state which are more than aggregates of the individuals which make them up, and which transcend particular settings on the other. Some might see this as the difference between interaction and structure, but that would be a misleading distinction, for it is not only things like classes and economies that have structures, but forms of interaction too, as in structures of conversational turn taking or of classroom discourse.

How, then, do micro and macro theory interconnect? Can they be so connected? And if so, by what mechanisms? These are surely important questions for anyone who is attempting to deal with the problem of micromacro integration. But before they can be treated properly, there is a more fundamental issue still that must be tackled – the serious allegation that macro theory may be of no worth at all, that it is just an assemblage of unverifiable speculation which ought not to be treated seriously. According to this view, the objects of macro theory are not real but simply fictionalized products of the fertile imaginations of those sociologists who, as Merton (1968, p. 139) puts it 'seek the grandeur of global summaries'. Thus, Paul Rock argues that:

> In a rigorous scheme, it is impossible to derive a totality from the partial and ambiguous fragments which are alone available to observational science . . . Interactionism discards most macro-sociological thought as an unsure and over-ambitious metaphysics. It claims that the realm described by macro sociology is not open to intelligent examination.

Macro sociology, then, allegedly refers to a realm which lies outside, of, or beyond, direct observation, and is, therefore, either unknowable or non-existent. This view has been echoed by a number of ethnomethodologists who have likewise discarded the idea that macro theories refer to anything of substance in the real world, and instead have used these theories only as an occasion for investigating the peculiar practices in which social scientists engage when they go about the business of theorizing (Philippson, 1972). But one of the clearest and most forceful atacks on the very possibility of macro sociology has been mounted by Rom Harré (1982).

Macro concepts, Harré argues, are nothing more than rhetorical devices which social scientists employ to score points off one another in seminar debates. At the very best, Harré concedes, concepts like class refer only to what he calls taxonomic collectivities – to groups who might happen to have some attribute in common, but have no collective agency or causal powers. In that sense, the working class, for instance, is no more interesting, real and effective than the group of British passport holders. For it to be any more than this, for it to be a real entity, Harré argues, the existence of the working class would need to be demonstrated through evidence concerning real relations among its members. The working class, that is, would presumably have to be seen picketing the gates of factories in their thousands, or storming through the streets waving red banners. The fact is, Harré claims, that no such relations exist. 'In consequence the status of alleged large scale macro groupings must be equivocal. At the very best, they might be conceived as theoretical entities whose existence . . . must be hypothetical' (pp. 148-9). According to this view, the only things that do exist in the social sense are phenomena which are bounded in space and time and which have causal powers – classroom groups, not class groups; interpersonal relations not relations of production. This, therefore, is where research should be focused.

This is a powerful argument. Unlike the debate about the relationship between theory and evidence, it does not suggest that macro theory *happens to be* speculative, that it is neglectful of evidence; but that it is *necessarily* and *unavoidably* speculative, since the objects to which it refers do not, as such, exist. Macro theorizing is, in that sense, not just a flawed venture but a futile one. No good can come of it. These objections are persuasive, not least because they cohere with a good deal of commonsense prejudice – if we cannot *see* the logic of the capital accumulation process, or the new middle class, or the *conscience collective*, or the reproduction of cultural capital, why should we believe that these things exist other than as pretentious bits of sociological mystification? Running against the grain of such prejudice, there are, I want to propose, at least two good reasons why these objections should be reconsidered.

First, members of social groups often belong not only to the same social category (like passport holders) but also share the same experiences. Nor does that sharing have to be self-conscious, or expressed in one time and place either on the miners' picket lines or in the Gdansk shipyards, for that group to be real. This, in a sense, is the classic difference that Marx drew between class-in-itself and class-for-itself. Many people will be familiar with Aldous Huxley's (1959) account of *Brave New World* where, through hypnopaedia and other techniques, the four different caste groupings – the alphas, the betas, the gammas and the epsilons – were made aware of their group identity and of the advantages of their own group compared to the others. Presumably not even Harré would question the existence, the reality of these four different groups. But supposing that hypnopaedia and all the other techniques of socialization in Huxley's *Brave New World*, had been directed towards softening senses of group identity, to instilling powerful if false ideologies of individual opportunity and mobility, meritocracy and so on. Would their resulting lack of sense of group belonging have made the common experiences of these groups any less real? Would it have made the differences between the conditions and lifestyle of the alphas, betas, gammas and epsilons, any less marked or causally significant? I doubt it. And so it is with such things as social class. It may be that the clear community basis of working class groups has been eroded by the decline of heavy manufacturing industries and the movement of council housing to the estates of the city periphery, and that if anything, this weakening of class identity has been reinforced by the mass media, the schooling system, and the very organization of production itself with its growing tendency to individualize the labour process. But this does not detract one bit from the fact that experiences of working are often similar from assembly line to assembly line, factory to factory, or office to office, where people are caught up in similar relations to their product and to those who exercise authority over them; and that the efforts of these relations carry over into family life, leisure, voting behaviour and so on.

Classes, in this sense, are very real things, even if their members are not fully aware of the fact. How exactly such groups should be defined is, of course, properly a matter of vigorous debate. And some definitions – especially those which help us to make sense of peoples' experience – are clearly more useful than others. Here, I am thinking in particular of the rather sterile exercise some theorists engage in of trying to assign occupational groups like teachers to one class or another according to whether they are engaged in productive or unproductive labour, a distinction which seems to have virtually no implications for teachers working or life experience at all (Ozga and Lawn, 1981; Ginsburg *et al.*, 1980; Poulantzas, 1973; Carchedi, 1975). But while particular definitions at the macro level may be subject to dispute, it does seem unduly restrictive to suggest that only those social collectivities which are bounded in time and space are worthy of our serious sociological attention.

This leads to a second point. It is not the case that only those things which can be observed are the ones which have any real existence. Theoretical physicists deal all the time with sub-atomic particles whose existence they posit by mathematical inference rather than direct observation. Likewise, in astronomy, the existence and location of the planets Neptune and Pluto were established mathematically as a way of explaining observable disturbances in the motions of Uranus. The existence of Neptune and Pluto, that is, was inferred through empirical observation of their effects. Bearing in mind the analogy with such things as social class and similar constructs it makes no difference that Neptune and Pluto were at the time of their discovery still observable in principle and that indeed they did become visible later through the use of powerful telescopes in one case, and sophisticated photography in the other. The point is that at the time of their discovery, these sources of tangible empirical confirmation were not available, nor, for all their discoverers knew, might they ever be. Sometimes, then, if only as a starting point for further investigation and testing, it is useful to see a range of disparate phenomena as the effects of some common, yet unseen, cause. Thus, one might propose, for instance, that the growth of pupil disruption in school, and the declining rate of student applications to university (even at a time when places are more scarce), coupled with a massive rise in youth unemployment are all effects of a growing crisis of pupil and student motivation (why bother subscribing to a system which offers you no rewards), which is in turn linked to an intensifying crisis in the economic system. This hypothesis would require further test, of course – other effects would need to be predicted then tested for (the growth of girls' interest in marriage rather than job or career might be one). But the principle of inferring systems and structures at the macro level through their effects, remains a sound one. Theories of what is unobservable can, therefore, stand up, if, that is, they are made to work in relation to available evidence of what *is* observable.

It seems reasonable to suggest, then, that we need theories of what occurs in particular settings bounded in time and space, *and* of the supra-individual entities which provide a context for what goes on in those particular settings. But this still begs the question of how exactly these theories at the micro and macro level are to be combined. Some solutions to this problem are impressive in their elegance and sophistication, most notably in the highly acclaimed work of Giddens (1976 and 1979). Giddens speaks with teasing persuasiveness about what he calls the *duality of structure*, about how 'structure is both the medium and the outcome of the social practices it recursively organizes' (Giddens, 1981; p. 171). Structures, he points out, are not only constraining but enabling too. And given that they are reproduced through interaction, every act is therefore a moment of possible change, an act of production as well as reproduction, containing within itself both the likelihood of continuity and the seeds of change. What Giddens achieves with great skill here, is a subtle resolution of the conventional dualism between action and structure. He demonstrates their mutual dependence, their logical entailment. However, while Giddens' writings are peppered with a most attractive collection of phrases and arguments which affirm the interdependence of action and structure, micro and macro, they are also largely devoid of empirical examples. There are no suggestions as to what implications his observations on social theory might have for any particular programme of empirical research.

I suspect the reason for this is not just Giddens' personal preference for 'Grand' theory of the classical kind, but that the gap between the elements he seeks to draw together is too great – a gap between the world of small scale face-to-face interaction, on the one hand, and vast social structures of immense proportions on the other. Such a gap is unbridgeable without the provision of some additional support. That kind of support, I want to propose, might well be found in the form of what Merton (1968) calls *theories of the middle range*. These theories, Merton argues

> lie between the minor but necessary working hypotheses that evolve in abundance during day to day research and the all-inclusive systematic efforts to develop a unified theory that will explain all the observed uniformities of social behaviour, social organization and social change . . . Middle range theory is . . . intermediate to general theories of social systems which are too remote from particular classes of social behaviour, organization and change to account for what is observed and to those detailed orderly descriptions of particulars that are not generalized at all. Middle range theory involves abstractions, of course, but they are close enough to observed data to be incorporated in propositions that permit empirical testing (p. 39).

In this sense, between the rules, negotiations and bargainings of classroom interaction, and the dynamics of the capitalist economy, or the relative autonomy of the state, lie a whole range of intermediary processes and structures which have been largely neglected in sociological accounts of education; such things as school ethos, or institutional bias (Rutter *et al*, 1979; Pollard, 1982), teacher cultures (Hargreaves D., 1982), teacher coping strategies, (Hargreaves, A., 1978), and so on. Were more attention paid to structures and processes at this middle or 'meso' level of analysis, then researchers like Anyon (1981) and Sharp and Green (1975) would not find themselves forced, in their wish to make micro-macro links, to leap from highly localized observations of teacher-pupil interaction in a small number of classrooms, to speculative assertions about how far these processes are determined by class struggle and other forces within capitalism. The existence of such leaps between classroom and society, as it were, in sociological accounts of schooling brings me on to my third and final interpretation of the micro-macro distinction – the difference between school and society.

3 School and Society

Of the many interpretations of the micro-macro relationship, one of the most dominant has entailed a usually implicit but nonetheless powerful distinction between schools and society. In particular, in case study work which attempts to make macro linkages, there is a tendency to bolt on observations of what goes on in schools, to speculative understandings and assertions about the very nature of society. This, in turn, tends to reinforce the divisions I have already discussed: between theory and evidence, between what comes across as unsubstantiated assertions about the requirements of capitalism, for instance, and detailed observations of school life. Moreover, when vast generalizations are made about the whole of society, about the needs of the capitalist economy, the effects of class struggle and so on, and these are then set alongside data on three teachers in one infants' school (Sharp and Green), or twelve working class lads (Willis), or five US elementary schools (Anyon), we, as sociologists of education, start to look as if we have badly overreached ourselves, as if we have seriously overstated our case. Worse still, when the case study analysis is presented as describing educational appearances, and the grand scale theorizing about 'society' is said to document some underlying fundamental 'reality', claims about that reality, given the shaky empirical foundations on which they rest, start to look at best like acts of sociological arrogance, and at worst like downright bias. None of this, as Nisbet and Broadfoot (1980) point out, impresses those teachers or administrators who might otherwise be in a position to make use of the findings of educational research.

Fortunately, these difficulties are to some extent, avoidable. There is no necessary reason, for instance, why 'society' must be dealt with or explained as an undifferentiated unit. It is true that those who have tried to bring off some kind of micro-macro integration in their work, have in fact tended to focus their empirical energies on the classroom, and to bracket off everything else that happens outside those walls as belonging to 'society', but this weakness need not continue. For instance, many of the so-called macro constraints which teachers face that are usually attributed to the operation of vast social structures could actually be analyzed by studying interactions *outside* the classroom – in the headteacher's office, County Hall, the Department of Education and Science, and so on. Admittedly, it is not so easy gaining access to the office of a senior administrator as it is to the classroom of a low status teacher. But the barriers are not insuperable and even if direct observation is not possible much can still be gleaned from interviews or from the careful scrutiny of historical documents such as LEA memoranda (Hargreaves, A. 1983).

One very fruitful way of clarifying the micro-macro relationship, then, would involve undertaking a number of studies of different educational settings and spelling out the links between them. My own work on middle schools is an attempt to do this, to show how the constraints that middle school teachers and heads faced in the mid 1970s, could in many cases be traced to accumulated decisions that policy makers made about the establishment of middle schools during the late 1960s (Hargreaves, A., 1985). It is a mistake, then, to regard educational policy as belonging exclusively to the world of macro theory (as in Ahier and Flude 1983; Dale, 1981) not just because classroom teachers have policies too (Pollard, 1984), but also because even outside the school, policy still has to be negotiated and implemented through interaction, be this face to face, on the telephone or via correspondence.

The growth of linked micro studies could be one of the most significant future developments in the sociology of education, not only for micro-macro integration as an interesting if esoteric theoretical project, but also for the much needed attempt to understand the schooling process in the context of policy changes, economic pressures and so on, and not in isolation from them. One might, in this sense, reasonably hope to see future research projects which are based not just on a single school or classroom, nor even on a number of schools or classrooms, but on processes in two or more linked settings, drawn from such places as classrooms, staff meetings, LEA offices, teacher union branches and so on. Given such research programmes we might just begin to gain a serious, well grounded understanding of the complicated mechanisms by which economic, political and social constraints on teaching and learning are filterd down to school level. Of course, these linked micro-studies would still not remove the need and relevance for concepts like state, class and economy which transcend space and time, but they *would* prevent us relegating much of our analyses to that level by default simply because we *chose* not to study them empirically. And in broadening the areas of empirical enquiry beyond the classroom, we would also be widening the base of evidence according to which our theories could be tested and modified. If linked empirical studies can sharpen our procedures and heighten our awareness on all these fronts, then they are to be recommended strongly, not only for those with lofty theoretical ambitions but also for those who have a strong sense of political urgency too.

Note

1 This perhaps explains why, on those occasions when Althusser drops his vague and bewildering formulations of the complicated relationships between the economic, political and ideological 'levels' of the capitalist social formation, and tries instead to outline the processes that occur in one particular sphere – in the educational system, say – his argument, shot through with unchecked assumptions, then degenerates into an exceedingly deterministic account of schools as efficient servants of capitalism. Beneath the vagueness of Althusser's general social theory, then, lies a deep-seated empiricism which comes to light in his analyses of more specific issues. Contrary to initial appearances, there are not, in that case two Althussers, as it were – an Althusser of vulgar reproduction theory (the Althusser of 'Ideology and ideological state apparatus'), and an Althusser of indeterminate relative autonomy theory (the Althusser of *For Marx*) – but one, whose theoretical scheme is at once a speculative theoreticism (leading to relative autonomy theory) and a most pernicious kind of empiricism (leading to direct reproduction theory), each of which supports the other in a mutually self-confirming scheme of dogmatic explanation.

References

AHIER, J. and FLUDE, M. (Eds.) (1983). *Contemporary Education Policy*, London, Croom Helm.

ALTHUSSER, L. (1971). 'Ideology and ideological state apparatus', in Cosin, B. (Ed.) *Education, Structure and Society*, Harmondsworth, Penguin.

ALTHUSSER, L. (1977). *For Marx*, London, New Left Books.

ALTHUSSER, L. and BALIBAR, E. (1970). *Reading Capital*, London, New Left Books.

ANYON, J. (1981). 'Social class and school knowledge', *Curriculum Inquiry*, 11, 1, pp. 3–41.

APPLE, M. (1979). *Ideology and Curriculum*, London, Routledge and Kegan Paul.

APPLE, M. (1982). *Education and Power*, London, Routledge and Kegan Paul.

BANKS, O. (1982). 'The sociology of education 1952–1982', *British Journal of Educational Studies*, 30, 1, pp. 18–31.

BENNETT, N. (1976). *Teaching Styles and Pupil Progress*, London, Open Books.

BUSH, T. and KOGAN, M. (1982). *Directors of Education*, London, Allen and Unwin.

CARCHEDI, G. (1975). 'On the economic identification of the new middle class', *Economy and Society*, 4, 1.

CUTLER, A. *et al.* (1977). *Marx's Capital and Capitalism Today Volume I*, London, Routledge and Kegan Paul.

DALE, R. (1979). 'The politicisation of school deviance: reactions to William Tyndale', in Barton, L. and Meighan, R. (Eds) *Schools, Pupils and Deviance*, Driffield, Nafferton Books.

DALE, R. (1981). 'The state and education: Some theoretical approaches', Unit 3, E353, *Society, Education and the State*, Milton Keynes, Open University Press.

DENZIN, N. (1970). *The Research Act*, Chicago, Aldine.

GALTON, M., SIMON, B. and CROLL, P. (1980). *Inside the Primary Classroom*, London, Routledge and Kegan Paul.

GIDDENS, A. (1976). *New Rules of Sociological Method*, London, Hutchinson.

GIDDENS, A. (1979). *Central Problems in Social Theory*, London, Macmillan.

GIDDENS, A. (1981). 'Agency, institution and time-space analysis', in Knorr-Cetina, K. and Cicourel, A.V. (Eds) *Advances in Social Theory and Methodology: Toward an Integration of Micro and Macro Sociologies*, London, Routledge and Kegan Paul.

GINSBURG, M.B., MEYENN, R.J. and MILLER, H.D. (1980). 'Teachers' conceptions of professionalism and trades unionism; an ideological analysis', in Woods, P. (Ed.) *Teacher Strategies*, London, Croom Helm.

GLASER, B. and STRAUSS, A. (1967). *The Discovery of Grounded Theory*, Chicago, Aldine.

HABERMAS, J. (1976). *Legitimation Crisis*, London, Heinemann.

HALSEY, A.H., HEATH, A.F. and RIDGE, J.M. (1980). *Origins and Destinations: Family Class and Education in Modern Britain*, Oxford, Clarendon Press.

HAMMERSLEY, M. (1979). 'Analysing ethnographic data', Part 1, Block 6, DE304, *Research Methods*, Milton Keynes, Open University Press.

HAMMERSLEY, M. (1980). 'On interactionist empiricism', in Woods, P. (Ed.) *Pupil Strategies*, London, Croom Helm.

HAMMERSLEY, M. (1984a). 'The paradigmatic mentality: a diagnosis', in Barton, L. and Walker, S (Eds) *Social Crisis and Educational Research*, London, Croom Helm.

HAMMERSLEY, M. (1984b). 'Some reflections upon the micro-macro problem in the sociology of education', *Sociological Review*, 32, 2, pp. 316–324.

HARGREAVES, A. (1978). 'The significance of classroom coping strategies', in Barton, L. and Meighan, R. (Eds) *Sociological Interpretations of Schooling and Classrooms: A Reappraisal*, Driffield, Nafferton Books.

HARGREAVES, A. (1980). 'Synthesis and the study of strategies: A project for the sociological imagination', in Woods, P. (Ed.) *Pupil Strategies*, London, Croom Helm.

HARGREAVES, A. (1982). 'Resistance and relative autonomy theories: Problems of distortion and incoherence in recent Marxist sociology of education', *British Journal of Sociology of Education*, 3, 2, pp. 107–26.

HARGREAVES, A. (1983). 'The politics of administrative convenience', in Ahier J. and Flude, M. (Eds) *Contemporary Education Policy*, London, Croom Helm.

HARGREAVES, A. (1985). 'English Middle Schools: An historical and ethnographic study', unpublished Ph.D thesis, University of Leeds.

HARGREAVES, D. (1978). 'Whatever happened to symbolic interactionism?', in Barton, L. and Meighan, R. (Eds) *Sociological Interpretations of Schooling and Classrooms: A Reappraisal*, Driffield, Nafferton Books.

HARGREAVES, D. (1981). 'Schooling for delinquency', in Barton, L. and Walker, S. (Eds) *Schools, Teachers and Teaching*, Lewes, Falmer Press.

HARGREAVES, D. (1982). *The Challenge for the Comprehensive School*, London, Routledge and Kegan Paul.

HARGREAVES, D., HESTER, S. and MELLOR, F. (1975). *Deviance in Classrooms*, London, Routledge and Kegan Paul.

HARRÉ, R. (1982). 'Philosophical aspects of the micro-macro problem', in Knorr-Cetina, K. and Cicourel, A.V. (Eds) *Advances in Social Theory and Methodology: Towards an Integration of the Micro-Macro Problem*, London, Routledge and Kegan Paul.

HARRIS, K. (1982). *Teachers and Classes: A Marxist Analysis*, London, Routledge and Kegan Paul.

HER MAJESTY'S INSPECTORATE (1982). *Report by Her Majesty's Inspectorate on the Effects of Local Authority Expenditure Policies on the Education Service in England, 1981*, London, HMSO.

HUNTER, C. (1983). 'Education and local government in the light of central government policy', in Ahier, J. and Flude, M. (Eds) *Contemporary Education Policy*, London, Croom Helm.

HUXLEY, A. (1959). *Brave New World*, London, Chatto.

KEDDIE, N. (1973). *Tinker, Tailor . . .* , Harmondsworth, Penguin.

MARX, K. and ENGELS, F. (1976). *Collected Works*, 5, London, Lawrence and Wishart.

MERTON, R. (1968). *Social Theory and Social Structure*, New York, Free Press.

MILLS, C.W. (1959). *The Sociological Imagination*, New York, Oxford University Press.

NISBET, J. and BROADFOOT, P. (1980). *The Impact of Research on Policy and Practice in Education*, Aberdeen, Aberdeen University Press.

OZGA, J. and LAWN, M. (1981). *Teachers, Professionalism and Class: A Study of Organized Teachers*, Lewes, Falmer Press.

PHILLIPSON, M. (1972). 'Theory, methodology and conceptualisation', in Filmer, P., Phillipson, M., Silverman, D. and Walsh, D., *New Directions in Sociological Theory*, London, Collier-Macmillan.

POLLARD, A. (1982). 'A model of classroom coping strategies', *British Journal of Sociology of Education*, 3, 1, pp. 19–37.

POLLARD, A. (1984). 'Ethnography and social policy for classroom practice', in Barton, L. and Walker, S. (Eds) *Social Crisis and Educational Research*, London, Croom Helm.

POULANTZAS, N. (1973). *Political Power and Social Classes*, London, New Left Books.

ROBINSON, W.S. (1952). 'The logicl structure of analytic induction', in McCall, G. and Simmons, J. (Eds) (1969) *Issues in Participant Observation*, Reading, Mass., Addison Wesley.

ROCK, P. (1979). *The Making of Symbolic Interactionism*, London, Macmillan.

RUTTER, M., MAUGHAN, B., MORTIMORE, P., OUSTON, J. and SMITH, A. (1979). *Fifteen Thousand Hours: Secondary Schools and Their Effects on Children*, London, Open Books.

SHARP, R. (1980). *Knowledge, Ideology and the Politics of Schooling*, London, Routledge and Kegan Paul.

SHARP, R. (1982). 'Self-contained ethnography or a science of phenomenal forms and inner relations', *Boston University Journal of Education*, 164, 1.

SHARP, R. and GREEN, A. (1975). *Education and Social Control*, London, Routledge and Kegan Paul.

THOMPSON, E.P. (1978). *The Poverty of Theory*, London, Merton Press.

TURNER, G. (1983). *The Social World of the Comprehensive School*, London, Croom Helm.

WALLERSTEIN, I. (1974). *The Modern World System: Capitalist Agriculture and the Origins of the European World-Economy in the Sixteenth Century*, London, Academic Press.

WEST, G. (1984). 'Phenomenon and form in the interactionist and neo-Marxist qualitative educational research', in Barton, L. and Walker, S. (Eds) *Social Crisis and Educational Research*, London, Croom Helm.

WILLIS, P. (1977). *Learning to Labour*, Farnborough, Saxon House.

WOODS, P. (1979). *The Divided School*, London, Routledge and Kegan Paul.

WOODS, P. (1985). 'Ethnography and theory construction in educational research', in Burgess, R.G. (Ed.) *Field Methods in the Study of Education*, Lewes, Falmer Press.

WRIGHT, E. (1979). *Class, Crisis and the State*, London, New Left Books.

YOUNG, M. and WHITTY, G. (Eds.) (1977). *Society, State and Schooling*, Lewes, Falmer Press.

Some Reflections Upon the Macro-Micro Problem in the Sociology of Education

M. Hammersley

Abstract: The macro-micro problem has been a prominent feature of British sociology of education since the early 1970s. In this discipline macro and micro have each come to be associated with particular theoretical perspectives, notably Marxism and interactionism respectively. This has had several unfortunate consequences. First, arguments about the value of macro and micro work have often been little more than dismissals of one perspective by advocates of another. Second, the macro-micro debate has conflated several quite distinct methodological issues. This article focuses on one of these issues: the question of whether social events can best be explained as the product of large or small scale structures. It is claimed that this issue cannot be resolved by philosophical analysis alone, the answer is a matter for empirical discovery. Moreover, the problem cannot be settled at the moment because we have insufficient well-established theories. Only when more such theories are available will we be able to resolve the question of whether valid macro *and* micro theories are possible. What stands in the way of achieving this, however, is precisely what led to the fruitless character of the macro-micro dispute in the first place: the organization of the sociology of education around theoretical perspectives rather than around substantive research problems.

Over the last ten years there has been considerable debate among sociologists of education, and indeed amongst sociologists generally, as to the proper relationship between macro- and micro-analysis. Nor of course is this debate restricted to sociology. One finds it in other social sciences, including economics, and even in the natural sciences.

Within sociology the debate has raged on and off for years, though the particular versions of macro and micro analysis at issue have changed over time (O'Neill, 1973; Homans, 1967; Knorr-Cetina and Cicourel 1981). The salience of the macro-micro issue within the sociology of education is more recent, stemming from the split that took place in the 1970s between various forms of interpretive sociology on the one hand, and Marxist approaches on the other. One consequence of this history is that within the field of education micro-sociology has come to be identified with interactionism and macro-sociology with Marxism; and the debate has been about the validity of these different theoretical perspectives in toto, rather than about the macro-micro issue in particular. Indeed, often there has not been much real debate at all, the macro-micro distinction has simply been used to dismiss work in other traditions. There is a strong element of this in Woods's (1977:10) description of macro theories as 'not "scientific" ' and his appeal to Jack Douglas's (1970:11) recommendation that 'We must stop treating macro-analyses as if they were scientific arguments, that is, arguments based on carefully done systematic observations of concrete phenomena'. Interactionists in the sociology of education might equally take comfort from Paul Rock's (1979:238) declaration that macro-sociological thought is 'an unsure and over-ambitious metaphysics' dealing with a realm which is 'not accessible to intelligent examination'.

From the other side of the barricades, Rachel Sharp, in the course of a critique of Stephen Ball's *Beachside Comprehensive*, has claimed that 'the study of individual schools can never be more than illustrative of a more fundamental order of structuring mechanisms which requires macro-analysis' (Sharp, 1981:282). And she claims that the concerns displayed in Beachside Comprehensive are those of 'policy-makers and experts rather than theoretically derived from a framework which is geared to grasping the 'whole' with its richness of texture and underlying structural logic' (Sharp, 1981:281).

Perhaps because arguments about macro versus micro analysis have generally amounted to justification of one sociological approach and rejection of others, one of the striking features of the literature is the variety of meanings given to the terms 'macro' and 'micro'. Typically, a number of different issues have been run together in the debate. Some of these are as follows:

In sociological research, should one assume determinism or free will?

Is the goal of sociology to produce generalized explanations which abstract from the details of social phenomena, or is it to document the process of social life in all its detail and complexity (its 'richness', if you like)?

Can theories be tested against empirical data or can one only judge them by their internal coherence since all data are theory-laden?

Do sociologists produce scientific theories which document what is 'really' going on while participants' views are simply myth or ideology? Or must sociologists' accounts in some sense build upon the interpretations of participants?

Can social events be best explained as the product of the structure of national (or international) society, or can valid explanations be provided which appeal to the features of relatively small-scale organizations and groups or even the characteristics of individual people?

It is important to recognize that these issues are logically distinct. While resolving one of them in a particular way may have implications for how the others are to be dealt with, we are not faced with opposition between two coherent positions taking contrary views on each of the issues. The conflation of these issues has, in my view, been one of the major reasons why little advance has been made towards resolving the macro-micro problem. They are all important issues, but for the purposes of this article I shall restrict discussion to the last of them since this corresponds most closely to usage of the terms 'micro' and 'macro' in other disciplines. Nevertheless, what I have to say about this issue is in many respects applicable to the others.

On this definition, it is clear that macro-micro is a dimension rather than a dichotomy. We can rank theories according to the scale of the units to which they apply, from individual human beings (or even genes) at one end of the spectrum to the world system (Wallerstein, 1974) at the other.[1] Equally obvious, it seems to me, is that this issue is not one which can be resolved by philosophical analysis alone. Whether there are valid macro and/or micro theories is a matter for empirical investigation.

One might think, given the amount of work which has been done in the sociology of education over the last twenty years, that we would already have a clear answer to this question. That we do not is perhaps partly a product of the rather descriptive character of the political arithmetic tradition which dominated the early years of British sociology of education. More important, though, I suspect, is the anti-positivist backlash which fragmented the sub-discipline in the 1970s, and indeed produced the macro-micro dispute itself. Neither the macro nor the micro tradition within the sociology of education has been very successful in developing and testing theories about educational institutions and processes. Indeed this enterprise itself has often been dismissed as positivist. Many sociologists of education have concerned themselves with developing general macro theories, but few have subjected these to serious test. Indeed, such theories have rarely been developed to the point where the claims they make are clear enough to be tested (Hargreaves, 1981). Interactionists, phenomenologists and ethnomethodologists, on the other hand, have been primarily concerned with *describing*, albeit in a theoretically informed manner, the perspectives of teachers and pupils and the process of classroom interaction. While they have produced some interesting theoretical ideas, once again these have not been systematically developed or tested. (For an attempt to spell out what the development and testing of theory involves, see Hammersley, Scarth and Webb 1985).

There are few exceptions to this dismal performance in the area of theorizing. One is the sequence of work carried out by David Hargreaves (1967), Colin Lacey (1966, 1970) and Stephen Ball (1981) on the effects of streaming, banding and mixed ability grouping. The theory which they develop and test, expressed in abstract terms, claims that if pupils are publicly ranked in terms of some set of values, their attitudes to these values will become polarized, with those placed at the bottom of the rank order rejecting the values. Hargreaves, Lacey and Ball test this theory by showing that the attitudes of pupils and their behaviour towards the school, and towards one another, do vary in the way the theory suggests; and not only in the case of a predominantly working class secondary modern school, but also in a grammar school where the pupils enter with a strong commitment to school values (Lacey, 1970). Moreover, Ball (1981) shows that if the differentiation of pupils is reduced through a change from banding to mixed ability grouping, polarization of pupil attitudes also declines. What we have here, it seems to me, is a theory very similar in form to those which are to be found in the natural sciences (Homans, 1967). Moreover, while it still requires further development and testing, it is reasonably well-established. (For a discussion of this body of work as a research programme and paradigm, see Hammersley, 1985.)

Interestingly, because the analysis embodied in this sequence of studies is located midway along the macro-micro dimension, it has been attacked by both micro-theorists and macro-theorists. From the micro side Hammersley and Turner (1980) have criticized it on the grounds that, even on the authors' own reported data, top stream and band pupils do not simply conform to the values and rules of the school. They also point out (following Werthman, 1977 and Furlong, 1976) that contextual variations in the behaviour of pupils are at least as noticeable as differences between the behaviour of pupils in top and bottom groups. Meanwhile, Rachel Sharp's critique of Beachside Comprehensive accurately reflects the attitudes of some macro-theorists to this set of studies. She argues that because he largely neglects the structure of the wider society Ball is incapable of providing an adequate explanation for events at Beachside Comprehensive:

> What indeed was going on at Beachside Comprehensive was the reproduction of labour power in a docile form to meet the economic, political and ideological requirements of a capitalist system based on exploitation . . . In Ball's study we learn much about the middle class and its superior access to educational provision. We learn, however, nothing about the bourgeois class and its strategic location in a system whose logic structures the conditions in which *all* the teachers and school pupils at Beachside Comprehensive are constrained to live out their lives. This is the reality of the social processing that takes place at Beachside Comprehensive, the reality of selection for the wage labour system which characterizes capitalist production and its profit-seeking dynamic.
>
> (Sharp 1981:283)

Each of these two critiques is premised upon a general sociological perspective which is taken to be mutually incompatible with that embedded in the work of Hargreaves, Lacey and Ball. Underlying the arguments of Hammersley and Turner is the idea that any sociological account must grasp social process in all its rich complexity so that, for example, contextual variability should not be ignored, nor should pupils' perspectives be 'reduced' to pro-school and anti-school categories. These criticisms are, however, beside the point. The differentiation-polarization theory does not require top group pupils to be fully conformist, only significantly more conformist than bottom group pupils. Furthermore, any theory must abstract from reality, none can capture it in its fullness. The division into pro- and anti-school perspectives cannot be legitimately criticized on those grounds. Similarly, the fact that pupils' behaviour is contextually variable is irrelevant. While it is an interesting fact, it would be the subject of a different, and probably non-competitive, theory.

The commitment to an alternative perspective is even more obvious in the case of Sharp. But once again what she proposes is not a competing theory. While she appears to be challenging the validity of Ball's claims, she is actually arguing that the research problem he is addressing is not the most important one. That is clearly a matter for debate, in which political as well as scientific criteria would be relevant. But whatever the conclusion drawn, contrary to Sharp's argument, this would have no implications for the *validity* of differentiation-polarization theory, only for its importance.

The nature of the criticisms made of the work of Hargreaves, Lacey and Ball highlights what I think is the most serious problem facing the sociology of education at the present time: the fact that it is organized around competing theoretical perspectives rather than around research problems (Hammersley, 1984a). The macro-micro dispute is a symptom of this, as is the paucity of theory (in the sense I have used the term here). As George Homans (1967:87) notes:

if most of the social sciences did possess widely general propositions about social aggregates, they would be less worried about the question of reduction. [i.e. whether macro can be reduced to micro and vice versa – M.H.] After all, thermodynamics can handle most of its problems of explanation and prediction without ever calling for the help of statistical mechanics. The fact that the former can be reduced to the latter is of greater intellectual than practical interest . . . Scientists argue about reductionism only when it is not clear what is to be reduced and how it is to be done.

And, of course, there are areas of natural science where the development of theories dealing with types of phenomena of different scale has not reached the point where theories at different levels can be integrated. This has not held up the work of natural scientists, though. As Hans Margenau has remarked:

though most of us hope, it is true, for an all embrace future theory which will unify the various postulates of physics, we do not wait for it before proceeding with the important business of science.

(Margenau 1949: quoted in Merton 1967)

This has important implications for those concerned to show by philosophical argument that either macro or micro theory is untenable. It also suggests that attempts at 'synthesis' (Hargreaves, 1978; Pollard, 1982) are premature. What the search for synthesis leads to are futile efforts to 'map' the whole range of causal chains thought to be relevant to the explanation of a particular phenomenon. But even the *description* of these lines of influence, without any attempt to check their reality, is an inexhaustible task. Ironically, perhaps even more than macro or micro chauvinism, the drive for synthesis is likely to discourage the systematic development and testing of theory.[2] No theory is likely to encompass all the factors that influence the behaviour of teachers and pupils. Theorizing necessarily involves selective attention to a group of interrelated factors which seem to represent a plausible explanation for some aspect of the events which make up the research problem. It seems to me that at the present stage of sociological development such theories are likely to operate at a single level of the macro-micro dimension. Of course, I would not want to deny that at some point in the future we might be able to combine macro and micro theories into a theory that spans several levels, and I can accept that this might add to the explanatory power of the component theories. Equally, when we set out to explain a particular event or phenomenon, we may well want to draw on both macro and micro theories.[3] But the point is, as Homans makes clear, that the validity of any theory or explanation synthesizing macro and micro levels is dependent on the validity of the theories at each level. The problem in the sociology of education, and in sociology generally, at present, is that well-established theories of any kind are few and far between.

Conclusion

Rather than wasting time in fruitless polemic between theoretical perspectives over the macro-micro issue, sociologists of education should in my view put their efforts into trying to develop and *test* theories at both macro and micro levels. Whether valid theories are available at all points of the macro-micro dimension, and if they are whether these theories can be reduced to one another, in either direction, are issues which can only be resolved through empirical investigation. The way in which the sociology of education is currently organized, around theoretical perspectives rather than substantive research problems, obscures that fact however; it turns a methodological problem into a political dispute. It also discourages the systematic development and testing of theories on which the solution of the macro-micro problem depends.

Notes

1 What I mean by the units to which theories apply is the categories of phenomena specified by the theories. Macro theories can, of course, be applied to explain micro-scale phenomena which fall within their categories. Thus, a theory of class structure can be used to explain the relations between teachers and pupils where these actors are treated as representatives of particular social classes. Conversely, micro theories can be used to explain macro phenomena, as when the policies of a government are ascribed to the personality of a prime minister or head of state.
2 For a more extended discussion of synthesis as a solution to the macro-micro problem see Hammersley (1984b).
3 See, for example, Lacey (1982). In my view it is important to make a clear distinction between theorizing and explaining; see Hammersley (1984b and 1984c).

References

BALL, S. (1981). *Beachside Comprehensive*, Cambridge University Press.
DOUGLAS, J.D. (1970). *Understanding Everyday Life*, Aldine.
FURLONG, V.J. (1976). 'Interactions sets in the classroom', in Hammersley, M. and Woods, P., *The Process of Schooling*, Routledge & Kegan Paul.
HAMMERSLEY, M. (1984a). 'The paradigmatic mentality: a diagnosis', in Barton, L. and Walker, S. (eds) (1984), *Social Crisis and Educational Research*, Croom Helm.
HAMMERSLEY, M. (1984b). Interpretive Sociology and the Macro-Micro Problem, Unit 22, Course E205, *Conflict and Change in Education*, Open University Press.
HAMMERSLEY, M. (1984c). 'Making a vice of our virtues: some notes on theory in history and ethnography', in S. Ball & I. Goodon (eds), *Defining the Curriculum*, Falmer.
HAMMERSLEY, M. (1985) 'From ethnography to theory', *Sociology*, 19, 2, 244–59.
HAMMERSLEY, M., SCARTH, J. and WEBB, S. (1985). 'Developing and testing theory', in R.G. Burgess (ed.), *Issues in Educational Research*, Falmer.
HAMMERSLEY, M. and TURNER, G. (1980). 'Conformist pupils', in Woods, P. (ed.), *Pupil Strategies*, Croom Helm.
HARGREAVES, A. (1978). 'The significance of classroom coping strategies', in Barton, L. and Meighan, R. (eds), *Sociological Interpretations of Schooling and Classrooms*, Nafferton.
HARGREAVES, D.H. (1967). *Social Relations in a Secondary School* Routledge & Kegan Paul.
HARGREAVES, D.H. (1981). 'Schooling for delinquency', in L. Barton and S. Walker (eds), *Schools, Teachers and Teaching*, Falmer.
HOMANS, G. (1967). *The Nature of Social Science*, Harcourt, Brace & World.
KNORR-CETINA, K. and CICOUREL, A.V. (1981). *Advances in Social Theory and Methodology*, Routledge & Kegan Paul.
LACEY, C. (1966). 'Some sociological concomitants of academic streaming in a grammar school', *British Journal of Sociology*, XVII, 3.
LACEY, C. (1970). *Hightown Grammar*, Manchester University Press.

LACEY, C. (1982). 'Freedom and constraints in British education', in Frankenberg, R. (ed.), *Custom and Conflict in British Society*, Manchester University Press.

MARGENAU, H. (1949). 'The basis of theories in physics', unpublished MS.

MERTON, R.K. (1967). 'On sociological theories of the middle range', in Merton, R.K., *On Theoretical Sociology*, Free Press.

O'NEILL, J. (1973). *Modes of Individualism and Collectivism*, Heinemann.

POLLARD, A. (1982). 'A model of classroom coping strategies', *British Journal of Sociology of Education*, 3, 1.

ROCK, P. (1979). *The Making of Symbolic Interactionism*, Macmillan.

SHARP, R. (1981). 'Review of Stephen Ball's *Beachside Comprehensive*', in *British Journal of Sociology of Education*, 2, 3.

WALLERSTEIN, I. (1974). *The Modern World System*, Academic Press.

WERTHMAN, C. (1977). 'Delinquents in school', in Cosin, B. *et al.*, *School and Society*, Routledge & Kegan Paul.

WOODS, P. (1977). 'The ethnography of the school', Units 7–8, Course E202, *Schooling and Society*, Open University Press.

PART FOUR
Case Study and Action Research

The Conduct of Educational Case Studies: Ethics, Theory and Procedures

R. Walker

Introduction

A glance at the literature reveals that it is usual for the case study researcher to encounter severe problems over such issues as conduct in the field, confidentiality, publication, and control over the use of data (McCall and Simmons, 1969; Becker, 1964). A key element of such studies is that they usually involve the immersion of the researcher in the field for relatively long periods of time. Long-term study is justified in terms of the need to determine areas of significance and to check the reliability and consistency of data. Long-term studies also have the incidental effect that personal relationships are established with those being studied, and to some extent these relationships protect the case study worker during the period of research and after its publication.

In the field of education there are now a number of such long-term field studies, for example Smith and Geoffrey (1968), Becker (1961, 1968), Lacey (1970), Hargreaves (1967), Wolcott (1967), and we take these along with related studies in criminology, industrial sociology and community studies, to constitute something of a research tradition. This is a tradition that finds some roots in the Chicago Sociology of the 1920s, that finds inspiration in the methods and techniques of social anthropology and, in the case of Education, has established a niche for itself in the Child Development field and in the sociology of education.

Recently this research tradition, with its stress on naturalistic observation, and on the study of individual instances in some depth, has received considerable attention in other areas of educational research, and particularly in the evaluation of educational development programmes (Parlett and Hamilton, 1972; Hamilton *et al.* 1977). It is an approach highly suited to the problems being pursued by SAFARI, which, as we have framed them, demand the close study of individual events, institutions and people. Yet the long time-scale of appropriate research methods imposes restrictions that we find difficult to handle. If we set out to provide the information people need to know in order to make particular policy decisions we often find ourselves committed to timetables that preclude use of 'anthropological' methods in the collection of data.

It is this double-bind resulting from simultaneous commitments to study in depth *and* to rapid reporting, that creates the starting point for this paper. It is also this double commitment that leads us to attempt to formulate a position for the case study worker that is midway between the worlds of academic research and educational practice.[1]

The Central Dilemma[2]

Our conception of the case study starts from a double-bind. We find ourselves advocating two things that often seem to be in conflict with one another.

> 1. First is a commitment to studies of the individual instance. We feel that the study of curriculum innovation in its post-development phase has been weighed down by generalities and theories and that there is a need to confront and portray what is actually happening in schools, classrooms and LEA offices at a level of some detail. At the surface level the problem is less one of theory and more one of access to knowledge.

> 2. Second is a commitment to forms of research that start from, and remain close to, educational practice. This involves us in a form of action research that attempts to inform decision-taking and policy-making by, for example, the fast turn-round of data to those being studied. This has action implications if we accept that knowledge is often the spring for action and that access to knowledge is frequently used as a mechanism of control.

These aspirations conflict in that the first tends to push us towards methods of research that seem to require long term immersion both in the field and subsequently in the data. On the other hand the second tends to push us towards short-term, almost journalistic styles of reporting in which the researcher has little time to check his interpretations against either the data or continuing events.

What we propose is a way out of the dilemma which involves a shift away from reliance on the personal integrity and authority of the researcher. That is to say a shift away from the notion of the researcher as the prime inter-preter. We propose instead the establishment of sets of rules and procedures which to some extent free the researcher from responsibility for what is reported, and which allow rapid access to, and publication of, information. At the same time such procedures are designed to protect those being studied from the consequences of the research.

Are the Problems Really Technical?

We have already noted that case study research is a field commonly thought to be fraught with problems of method and technique:

> Should the observer become involved in the situation being studied?
>
> Is it possible to offer informants confidentiality?
>
> Is it right to do so?
>
> How should requests for access to data during the course of the study be handled?
>
> What procedures should be adopted in obtaining release for final publication?

Usually these problems are considered to be technical problems. That is to say, given accepted notions about the nature of research and the role of the researcher, then the problem is essentially one of evolving procedures which mobilise the normal ethics of research in fieldwork situations.

In this paper we take a different view. We believe that the difficulties of doing case study research do not stem primarily from technical issues, that is, issues about means, but from deeper value concerns. In order to create a way out of the case study research dilemma with which we opened this paper we feel it is necessary to raise questions about what research and researchers in the field of education should be doing. We intend to challenge the frame.

Case Study – A Definition

Case study is the examination of an instance in action. The study of particu-lar incidents and events, and the selective collection of information on biography, personality, intentions and values, allows the case study worker to capture and portray those elements of a situation that give it meaning. In educational evaluation or research the case study worker may attempt to study and portray the impact in a school of a particular innovation, the

erience of a curriculum development project team, the development of an
a through a number of social organisations, the influence of a social and
professional network, or a day in the life of a teacher, administrator or pupil.
These very different studies have in common some commitment to the study
and portrayal of the idiosyncratic and the particular as legitimate in
themselves.

Case Study – Background to the Definition

In the past, case study methods have generally been utilised and developed
where there has been a clear need to confront the idiosyncrasy of individual
instances, (for example, in attempting historical reconstruction, or in
biography, journalism and documentary film making). Or where there has
been no clear vision of an appropriate theoretical base from which to operate
(for example, in applied social science research). Of academic disciplines (as
opposed to practitioner-disciplines like clinical medicine, town planning and
social work), only anthropology and ethology appear to have developed procedures for using case study research cumulatively. As a result case study
research has a generally low status as a research method. The Open University Course E341 on Educational Research dismissed case study in a
section of three brief paragraphs whose opening sentence was: 'The
simplest approach to educational research is the case study' (Entwistle, 1973,
p. 19).[3]

Case Study – Pros and Cons

The justification usually given for case study research is that it gives insight
into specific instances, events or situations. The case study reveals, 'what
institutions *mean* to individuals (and) helps us get beyond form and structure
to the realities of human life, or to use Malinowski's term, "it puts flesh and
blood on the skeleton" ' (see Lewis, 1959, p. 3). Part of the appeal of case
study is that it offers some escape from the language of theory, but the case
study may contribute *to* theory, for it promises to reveal how theoretical
abstractions relate to common sense perceptions of everyday life.

   The objection most often raised to case study is the 'generalisation problem'.
This is seen in terms of the limited reliability and validity of the case study and is
often framed in terms of two questions:

> How can you justify studying only one instance?

> Even if it is justifiable theoretically, what use can be made of the study by
> those who have to take action?

The first question touches on the problem of studying representative situations and events. The case study worker seems to reject ideas of sampling and control, both key aspects of experimental design.

In one sense the criticism is inappropriate. The vast readership of books like Bel Kaufman's *Up the Down Staircase* (1964) testify to the fact that large numbers of people find truth even in the fictionalised instance. The problem for the case study worker is not whether it is *worth* studying individual events, but whether he can do so in a way that captures the attention of his audience. Yet in research terms a fundamental problem of design is raised by single-sample studies (though to phrase the problem in this way is itself misleading; to define case study research as 'research on samples where N equals 1' is to allude to a set of research values that are not necessarily appropriate). When only one instance is studied it does not really matter *which* instance is studied. The sampling problem is not really a problem at all; one instance is likely to be as typical and as atypical as another. The problem of generalising ceases to become a problem for the author. It is the reader who has to ask, what is there in this study that I can apply to my own situation, and what clearly does not apply?

The question 'What use is the case study?' raises more clearly the issue of the relationship of research to the making and taking of decisions. In some ways this is a more serious issue and it is a continuous concern in this paper. At this juncture we simply make the point that many educational practitioners are in fact 'natural' case study workers. Teachers, advisers, heads, administrators, curriculum developers – they all tend to make judgements on the basis of knowledge of the particular instance, rather than by reference to research findings. Some researchers may disapprove of practitioner-lore as a basis for action, but if that is how the system works we would do well to know more about it.[4] Perhaps we might even try to improve such 'research' rather than merely condemn it.

To Restate the Argument

Users of case study methods have encountered a number of difficulties in conducting their research. As we have seen, a list of these difficulties would include:

  problems of the researcher becoming involved in the issues, events or situations under study;

  problems over confidentiality of data;

  problems stemming from competition from different interest groups for access to, and control over, the data;

problems concerning publication, such as the need to preserve anonymity of subjects;

problems arising from the audience being unable to distinguish data from the researcher's interpretation of the data.

Problems of this kind are usually considered as 'methodological' problems, that is to say they are seen as isolated technical problems that can be overcome within existing frames of research. Whenever they dominate particular studies there is a suspicion that the research has been poorly executed; that unspoken professional norms have been violated. The risks that case study workers run are frequently reflected in the hesitancy with which sponsors approach proposals for such research. Any proposals we make that attempt to resolve the dilemma posed between depth study and rapid reporting will have to cope with these issues and this may mean recasting accepted notions about the nature of research and the role of the researcher.

Evaluation and Research

The tradition of case study research that has emerged in the social sciences has evolved under conditions rather different from those which constrain the work of the evaluator. The social scientist normally reports to his peers rather than to his subjects, and usually he is relatively free from pressures either to complete his fieldwork fast or to report quickly. Field studies typically involve periods of several months in the field and final reports are often delayed by several years.

The evaluator, however, usually works in situations which are more politically intense. The people he studies may well be part of the audience he reports to; he may have the opportunity to spend only a few days in the field and have to produce his report in weeks or months rather than years.

The evaluator often finds himself in situations where he has to account for his research in terms outside the normal constraints and values of the researcher; his need to reconcile research and practical affairs is consequently more urgent and compulsive than it would be in pure research. Not only in relation to case study, but more generally, evaluators have tended to find accepted notions of educational research wanting when they have been applied to evaluation problems.

This difference between research and evaluation is essentially one of degree, for the researcher too in choosing to respond to the interests and needs of one group rather than another, enters a web of political relationships, perhaps less pressing but just as real as those enclosing the evaluator. Whether we are working as researchers or evaluators we are primarily concerned with the creation, production and communication of knowledge. We enter the political arena because that knowledge is often the basis on which power is legitimated. As researchers and evaluators we are frequently hired by those with power to study those who are powerless; and in the particular case of education, knowledge is not only the basis of power but the medium through which power is exerted.

In a related paper, Barry MacDonald (1974, pp. 11–12) has looked more closely at the inherently political nature of evaluation and sketched out three models by which evaluators can secure their enterprise. He outlines his three types of evaluation as follows:

Bureaucratic evaluation
Bureaucratic evaluation is an unconditional service to those government agencies which have major control over the allocation of education resources. The evaluator accepts the values of those who hold office, and offers information which will help them to accomplish their policy objectives. He acts as a management consultant, and his criterion of success is client satisfaction. His technique of study must be credible to the policy makers and not lay them open to public criticism. He has no independence, no control over the use that is made of his information, and no court of appeal. The report is owned by the bureaucracy and lodged in its files. The key concepts of bureaucratic evaluation are 'service', 'utility', and 'efficiency'. Its key justificatory concept is 'the reality of power'.

Autocratic evaluation
Autocratic evaluation is a conditional service to those government agencies which have major control over the allocational resources. It offers external validation of policy in exchange for compliance with its recommendations. Its values are derived from the evaluator's perception of the constitutional and moral obligations of the bureaucracy. He focusses upon issues of educational merit, and acts as expert adviser. His technique of study must yield scientific proof, because his power base is the academic research community. His contractual arrangements guarantee non-interference by the client, and he retains ownership of the study. His report is lodged in the files of the bureaucracy, but is also published in academic journals. If his recommendations are rejected, policy is not validated. His court of appeal is the research community, and higher levels in the bureaucracy. The key concepts of the autocratic evaluator are 'principle' and 'objectivity'. Its key justificatory concept is 'the responsibility of office'.

Democratic evaluation
Democratic evaluation is an information service to the community about the characteristics of an educational programme. Sponsorship of the evaluation does not in itself confer a special claim upon this service. The democratic evaluator recognises value pluralism and seeks to represent a range of interests in his issue formulation. The basic value is an informed citizenry, and the evaluator acts as broker in exchange of information between groups who want knowledge of each other. His techniques of data gathering and presentation must be accessible to non-specialist audiences. His main activity is the

collection of definitions of, and reactions to, the programme. He offers confidentiality to informants and gives them control over the use of the information they provide. The report is non-recommendatory, and the evaluator has no concept of information misuse. The evaluator engages in periodic negotiation of his relationships with sponsors and programme participants. The criterion of success is the range of audience served. The report aspires to 'best-sellers' status. The key concepts of democratic evaluation are 'confidentiality', 'negotiation' and 'accessibility'. The key justificatory concept is 'the right to know'.

Recasting Notions of Research

We see the democratic mode as particularly appropriate in case study research, or in evaluation activities using case study techniques. This places the case study worker in the position of having to *negotiate* his interpretations with those involved in the study rather than being free to impose them on the data. The shift involved is a shift in power, a move away from *researchers'* concerns, descriptions and problems towards *practitioners'* concerns, descriptions and problems. This is essentially what we mean when we talk about recasting our notions of the nature of research and the role of the researcher. Put this way we may seem to be back in the mainstream of contemporary sociology, but we are not simply arguing for the validity of 'members' categories', we are arguing for the rights of informants over the control of what is published. In relation to our central dilemma we see the democratic mode of evaluation as a possible source of resolution but in terms of MacDonald's typology this shift towards acknowledging practitioners' perceptions could also be accommodated within the bureaucratic mode. The difference is a fundamental difference in the answers each mode gives to the questions 'Who is the research for?' and 'Who owns the data?'.

The possibility of a move towards the bureaucratic mode as a means of moving from researchers' to practitioners' problems is clear in Mrs Thatcher's statement about DES sponsored research:

> There was clearly only one direction that the Department's research policy could sensibly take. It had to move from a basis of patronage – the rather passive support of ideas which were essentially other people's, related to problems which were often of other people's choosing, to a basis of commission. This meant the active initiation of work by the Department on problems of its own choosing, within a procedure and timetable which were relevant to its needs. Above all, it meant focussing much more on issues which offered a real possibility of yielding usable conclusions.
>
> (Quoted in Nisbet, 1974)

Perhaps the difference between the views of Mrs Thatcher and the 'democratic' mode evaluator is a fine one, but one which almost certainly will work out to be significant in practice. On a DES commission the democratic mode researcher would include the DES in the field he was studying, and the DES would be involved in the negotiations that could constitute a significant element of the research. Ideally the researcher would act as a communication point between the commissioners of the research and those being studied.

The general issue is not which of MacDonald's modes of research is 'best' but which is most appropriate to certain problems and conditions. Our feeling is that the democratic mode is best suited to exploratory studies or to the study of situations of some political sensitivity, for it is a mode of research in which all those engaged have the means continuously to direct and to influence the research from the proposal stage through to publication. Democratic evaluation studies can only work when there is involvement by all the significant people and groups implicated in the problem area.

The major limitation of the democratic mode is likely to be its inherent inertia. Any proposal that requires the support of multiple audiences before decisions are taken is likely to lead to complication if not to confrontation. As Oettinger points out, 'The observation that decisions were made by relatively few people is true of most of the major military-industrial developments of recent decades, including not only the Manhattan Project but the development of the national air defence system . . . the design of the Polaris submarine, and the race to the moon'. He quotes Alvin Weinberg, Director of the Oak Ridge Laboratory, on the same point: 'Many fewer people were involved in our decision to go ahead with the Manhattan Project than were involved in our decision to adopt pay-as-you go income tax. In consequence it was easier to start on the atomic bomb than to modify the income tax laws' (1969, p. 59).

The democratic mode of evaluation is conservative in that it presupposes values in the existing situations that need protection. Its negative aspect is inertia, which is inherently conservative precisely because it offers support, perhaps even unthinking support to the *status quo*. It seems clear therefore that democratic evaluation ought logically to attract support when a threatened system appears capable of being shored up by a restatement of consensus values. But it should also attract conservative support where the activity under review is commonly perceived as likely to get *dramatically* worse. Here the necessary changes would be arguably better controlled by establishing as wide a basis as possible for fully-discussed cautious progress. It is potentially a way of screening out the possibility of really radical review. Whether this logic ever gets turned into practice is another matter.

Case Studies in Education

Case study research has previously been used in education but mostly in an autocratic mode. That is to say it has been carried out primarily as a piece of 'pure' research directed to an audience of research professionals. The interpretations made have been essentially the interpretations of the researcher. The responsibility for the final account has been his alone.

In evaluation this approach has been complicated by the fact that the evaluator has often had a dual role, that of case study worker *and* that of change-agent, and the assumption has been that these two roles are not incompatible. We hold strongly to the view that the two roles are incompatible and that the evaluator should strive for neutrality. A problem that highlights this issue, and which frequently emerges at the design stage of a study, is how to set up procedures that ensure the credibility of the evaluation. In other words how to insulate the roles of evaluator and change-agent from each other even when the same people are operating in both roles.

To return to the dilemma with which we opened this paper, what is distinctive about the use of case study in evaluation as opposed to research is that the case study worker hopes to work in such a way that he is not overtaken by events. He has to design the research so that he can report before the normal passage of events irretrievably changes the situation under study. In contrast to an evaluation report most educational case studies read to the practitioner like history. Howard Becker writes in the introduction to *Making the Grade* (1968):

> We started our fieldwork in 1955 and completed it in 1961. The university has changed greatly in the interim, and it should be clear that the figures we present and other organisational features we describe represent the university at that time. Some of the things we describe are characteristic of most American universities. Others are to be found only in certain kinds of universities, particularly the large state schools. Still others may be unique to Kansas. The generalisability of our analysis is problematic (p. 16).

Educational case studies, within a democratic mode, will have a commitment to feeding back information quickly to participants in the situation under study. For the evaluator it is less important to generalise than it is to report accurately. If case studies are to be used in evaluation this will involve some reappraisal not only of the time scales involved, but also of the social context within which the 'meanings' will be generated. The 'generalisability' problem can be to some extent ameliorated if the initial audience is confined to *those involved in the study*. The final report then becomes a report on the process of research and publication becomes part of that process.

Characteristics of the Case Study

Application of the democratic mode to case study research reveals a number of questions which all relate to accepted notions of the nature of research and the role of the researcher:

to whose needs and interest does the research respond?

who owns the data (the researcher, the subject, the sponsor . . .)?

who has access to the data? (who is excluded or denied?)

what is the status of the researcher's interpretation of events vis à vis the inter-pretations made by others? (who decides who tells the truth?)

what obligations does the researcher owe to: his subjects, his sponsors, his fellow professionals, others?

who is the research for?

The implications of such questions is to reaffirm that research is inherently a social process leading to a social product. Case studies are public docu-ments about individuals and events with consequences for the lives of those portrayed as well as for the reader. In order to maintain the integrity of both the record and those under study the fine line between what is public and what is private needs to be carefully negotiated.

Equally, case studies are identifiable, at least to those involved and usually to wider audiences. By this we do not mean that people and institutions can always be recognised, but that the kinds of issues, problems, paradoxes, conflicts, situations and events portrayed ring true. In this way case studies may create images of reality that become part of the reality itself. Thus Elizabeth Richardson's study of Nailsea School (Richardson, 1973), and Roger Graef's film 'Space Between Words' (Graef, n.d.), have become part of the vocabulary of thinking of many teachers, headteachers and administrators.

The best case studies transcend the boundaries between art and science, retaining both coherence and complexity. Inevitably, the case study worker finds himself part historian, part psychologist, part sociologist and part anthropologist. Often he is also part scientist and part artist, sometimes to his own surprise. (Freud wrote: 'It still strikes me . . . as strange that the case studies I write should read like short stories' (1953, p. 160).)

The difficulty that case study workers within the democratic mode are likely to encounter in retaining their identity as specialists in particular disciplines raises major problems for the status of the case study itself as a form of knowledge. In related papers, Hans Brugelmann and John Elliott (1974) have pointed out that a triangulation approach such as we suggest in this paper tends to lead to a relative view of truth in terms of the reports and perceptions of differently located observers. There is little attempt in this paper to locate those reports relative either to objective truth or to theoreti-cal propositions at the level of subject disciplines. The case study worker may produce a study which is internally consistent and acceptable to all those involved, but which in fact relates only marginally to the 'truth'. This is not to claim that all reality is necessarily relative, but simply to suggest a methodological stance in relation to fieldwork situations. The stress on

'definitions of the situation' and the application of increasingly rigorous
procedures in order to validate subjective data, constitutes a method and
related sets of techniques which I feel are applicable in the particular case of
educational case studies. It is not intended to prescribe a world view or to
exclude the validity of alternative approaches. I am not claiming that all
truth is relative, and all reality necessarily multiple, but that in some situations it is a useful strategy to treat them as if they were.

Research and Policy

Recognition of the issues raised has consequences for the conduct of
research. Yet questions of this kind have only recently been considered by
educational researchers, perhaps because the social sciences have themselves
rarely been taken seriously by decision-makers, but also because those areas
of study that *have* influenced decision-making (economics, demography,
psychometrics) have held a strong allegiance to a positive, rational, scientific
model which has effectively precluded research from asking reflexive questions. For the most part the questions we have outlined here have not been
asked because the answers have not been required.

Within policy making bodies, despite an apparent increasing sophistication of research, there has been a growing sense of unease at the lack of fit
between research and practice; a feeling that research defines its own problems irrespective of the problems faced by practitioners and that its audience
is primarily an audience of fellow researchers rather than its sponsors, subjects or fellow citizens. Mrs Thatcher's statement echoes this feeling clearly.

Perhaps the main appeal of measurement data is that it is relatively easy to
condense, and so amenable to rapid handling. On the other hand case study
data does offer some things to the practitioner that conventional educational
research does not. Louis Smith has summarised some of these aspects of the
case study in relation to the educational administrator as follows:

> . . . case studies . . . have a quality of *undeniability*. That is someone is actu-
> ally doing something; it is not hypothetical. As such cases accumulate, in
> varying settings and with varying support, personnel and rationale, it becomes
> difficult to excuse one's own inaction. It forces one to back off from his 'ratio-
> nalisations' and to confront the basic choices and dilemmas in values under-
> lying his decisions in his district.

> Second, the case studies are totalities, that is they have a 'holistic' or 'systema-
> tic' quality. By their very nature, they constrain or attend to all the elements.

> Third, a cluster of elements seem summarisable as a particularistic quality.
> There is a concreteness, vividness . . . and detail. The nooks and crannies of a
> phenomenon, an event, an experience, are explored.

> Fourth . . . the case study can be individualised. Each person can clarify the

similarities and the differences in his own setting, his own organisation, his own personality. With even minimal discussion he can ask the questions which 'bug him', work through the immediate perceptions of possible difficulty 'at home', test his experience against the elements of the case.

Fifth, the case studies accent process, change over time. This has a particular utility for 'men of action', persons who want to do something – administer, supervise, teach. Data are revealed on where and how one begins, implements and terminates. The critical decisions at each point in time are highlighted, along with such elements as alternatives, prediction systems, subjective probabilities, value systems, utilities, costs and benefits.

(Smith, 1974, p. 7)

What is interesting here is that case study is seen as close to the real world of the administrator, in a way that research produced by orthodox experimental design or survey research is not.

Louis Smith writes about the relationship between the *completed* case study and its audience. The problems we are looking at concern the *production* of case studies – and here there are often tremendous difficulties. For example, since educational case studies are usually financed by people who have, directly or indirectly, power over those studied and portrayed, the case study worker may be operating, or perceived as operating, under a series of constraints from sponsors. This effect may be amplified by the fact that case study methods rely heavily on human instruments (researchers and subjects) about which only limited knowledge can be obtained and whose private expectations, desires and interests may bias the study in unanticipated and unacknowledged ways. Lack of rules for case study leaves research opportunities open to abuse. Not only will people and institutions studied give their own accounts as to why they are being studied, they might well have their own reasons for *wanting* to be studied and these may not always be made explicit to the researcher. This again may influence and constrain the research in unacknowledged ways especially when, as we are suggesting, their own perceptions and responses may be built-in to research procedures.

Recently some Local Education Authorities have established their own research units, or attempted to move their advisers into research roles. Research has been established in colleges of education, polytechnics and even schools. If research roles become diffused through the system then as research gets closer to practice it may face the need for new forms of theory and new methods which allow audiences to generalise directly *to* other situations and not simply generalise *from* situations into areas of abstraction. If this happens on a large scale it is likely that the specialist research role will once again turn to problems which will sophisticate methodology rather than pursue raw data. This in turn will involve small scale, situationally specific research pursued through limited funding and access.

Beginning to Resolve the Dilemma – Condensed Fieldwork

Characteristic of traditional case study research in the social sciences is the long time spans involved – both in the field and in analysis and presentation. If case study methods are to be used within a democratic mode it is inevitable that one of the key features of the method will have to be revised – the use of *long term* participant observation or fieldwork.

In developing ways of using case study methods within a democratic mode of research we have to think in terms of *condensed fieldwork*; we have to find ways of collecting and presenting our data with some speed.[5] Inevitably this takes us even closer to the endemic problems of case study research, especially the problems of reliability and validity, confidentiality, consultation, publication and control over data. It is one thing to publish a study five years after the period of fieldwork, but quite another to spend a week in a school and to produce the case study a week later.

The notion of condensed fieldwork in part cuts us off from the traditions of case study research in the social sciences and draws us closer to other traditions in journalism, documentary film making and the writing of biography. What we retain most strongly from social science is the attempt to be objective, impartial and well-informed.

In part condensed fieldwork is an inevitable consequence of the demands of a democratic mode of research. If the researcher is to engage in continuous negotiation with his sponsors and subjects he is unable to make a long term study his main preoccupation. He cannot insulate himself from his sponsors or his subjects. People will not only want to know what he is doing, they will want results. Another facet of the democratic mode, however, is that the method of research should, through the process of the research, become available to those being studied, so that when the project terminates they will have, not just a copy of the report, but access to skills which allow them to continue to research unaided. 'Anthropological-style' research which is usually held up as the distinguishing mark of case study research is rarely feasible in democratic mode evaluation or research, there is simply not time for such methods as they are normally practised and they are rarely accessible to practitioners.

Reliability and Validity

Perhaps the heart of the problem is that case studies are inevitably always partial accounts involving selection at every stage, from choosing cases for study, to sampling events and instances, and to editing and presenting material. Since educational case studies are almost always conducted under severe constraints of time and resources, reliability and validity pose considerable problems.

Superficially case study is often set against quantitative research as belonging to a different 'paradigm', but in some ways this distinction is misleading, the case study worker is often more 'quantitative' in orientation than is realised. Howard Becker writes:

> The observer, possessing many provisional problems, concepts and indicators . . . wishes to know which of these are worth pursuing as major foci of his study. He does this, in part, by discovering if the events that prompted their development are typical and widespread, and by seeing how these events are distributed among categories of people and organizational sub-units. *He reaches conclusions that are essentially quantitative*, using them to describe the organization he is studying (1958, p. 656).

Although Becker works primarily within a descriptive frame, his concern is often with what is recurring, typical or widespread. Even when he looks at single instances the focus is often on the single instance as running counter to the main trend. For example, in the study *Boys in White* a major theme concerns the development and functioning of the 'perspectives' of medical students. The data used to construct perspectives was generated by studying the frequency with which items appeared in field notes but 'the final step in the analysis . . . was a consideration of those cases found in the field notes which run counter to the preposition that students shared a particular perspective' (Becker, 1961, p. 43).

The analysis of these 'negative cases' was used to explore the boundaries within which the perspective in fact operated.

The approach we are exploring moves further away from quantitative methods than that developed by Becker and his colleagues. As a result it is not easy to apply to accepted notions of reliability and validity to the kinds of data we collect and the forms of presentation we adopt. We find, instead, that we need to start by questioning the meanings of these concepts and then to see if we can rework them into our methods and procedures.

Reliability

We see reliability as concerned with the degree of fit between construct and data. Given high reliability it should be routine for other researchers to reach the same representations from the same events, and further to gather their own data and be able to handle that in a manner that is free from ambiguity or confusion. This seems to us essentially the same definition as that used in testing. For instance, Guilford defines reliability as 'the accuracy with which a score represents the status of an individual in whatever aspect the test measures him' (1954, p. 398). The critical point is that reliability is concerned with the relation between events and representations.

In the case study, however, the emphasis is towards '*collecting* definitions of situations' (multiple representations) and the presentation of material in forms where it is open to multiple interpretations. If it proves feasible to do this, to some extent we are by-passing the usual problems of reliability by passing responsibility for them on to the audience. In other words, the relationship between our representations of events and the events themselves is not critical because no claim is made for our representations as against those made by anyone else. What we have done is to put the audience in a situation where *their* representations are as significant as ours; the fit between events and their representations of it presenting a more subtle set of problems than is usual in testing or survey research.

It is common in research to use the term reliability to refer to a further difficulty and one which often dominates discussion of case study research: the problem of replicability. Would another researcher entering the same situation produce similar results? We suggest that in our emphasis on procedures rather than personal intuition we are moving to a kind of case study research that has high reliability in this sense. Educational situations are rarely replicable and this proposition would be difficult to test, but in theory it would seem that where procedures are clear and explicit then reliability in this sense would be higher than it would given a free hand to the researcher in the design and conduct of the case study.

Validity

Consideration of validity takes us to the interface between the findings of the study and the reality from which they were extracted, with what Guilford describes as 'the concern with *what* a test measures and with what it will predict' (p. 400). Validity is essentially about truth conditions.

The news the educational researcher brings is generally of one of two kinds. He may enter the system in order to seek truth through explanation, or alternatively he may enter it to seek truth through the portrayal of reality. Case study belongs to the second tradition. The news it brings is news which gives the reader a feeling of vicarious experience (Stake, forthcoming). Case study research relies heavily on face validity – the judgement that the results *seem* to fit the reality. This is a form of validity strongly distrusted by psychometricians:

> Looking valid by itself is no guarantee of any form of genuine validity, even to experienced psychologists, one can have little confidence in such information. This is why some psychologists facetiously refer to the acceptance of some tests as a matter of 'faith validity'. Apart from any confidence in superficial appearance, or lack thereof, it is sometimes said that for the sake of good public relations it often pays to make a test relevant to the layman who takes it, or who has any administrative decisions to make concerning it.
>
> (Guilford, 1954, p. 400)

In the case study, face validity is of much greater significance, for the case study worker is critically concerned to capture just those 'commonsense' meanings which constitute mere interference to the test designer. The case study worker constantly attempts to capture and portray the world as it appears to the people in it. In a sense for the case study worker what *seems* true is more important than what *is* true. For the case study worker as opposed to the psychometrician the internal judgements made by those he studies, or who are close to the situation, are often more significant than the judgements of outsiders.

This brings us to a further problem of validity which arises when the audience is not a research audience but an audience of practitioners. Descriptive accounts of individual instances may be accepted as true by practitioners but they are not likely to create appropriate and convincing bases for policy or decision making. The problem seems to be that such descriptive accounts are highly persuasive to a primary audience, but not to secondary audiences. Case studies do not readily lend themselves to 'data collapse', and where it may be easy to extract key statistics from a set of tables in order to pursue a course of action it seems less credible to extract an incident from a descriptive account. This might seem at first sight a convincing argument against case study research. However, our point is that when descriptive or personal data is missing from a research report, then those taking decisions will 'fill-in' from their own experience. Our conception of the case study is basically concerned with how to systematise this informal data. The question the decision-taker has to ask him, or herself, is how well do they really want to be informed?

What we are suggesting is that in educational research we need to go beyond the effective portrayal of individual instances and to find ways to be on guard against using case study to smuggle our own, or single values into the system.

Some will see this emphasis on practitioner lore as a dismaying denial of a basic value distinction between high order and lower order conceptual frameworks of understanding. (Rather as some educational reforms are seen a conceding high standards in order to gain popularity with the pupils.) Perhaps a warning analogy can be drawn here with what has happened to the theory of film, with the implications that has for education. Since the war, film theory has received considerable interest, encouraged by the formation of the British Film Institute's Education Department. But despite its concern with popular film and the mass media (as opposed to what were disparagingly referred to as 'Art House Movies'), the kind of theory it developed was mainly derived from academic literary criticism and from sociology. As such it was often largely inaccessible to the audience who watched the films. What set out as an attempt to produce an accessible theory of the mass media often became a purely esoteric intellectual pursuit.

We feel it is important that educational research should attempt to avoid a similar fate. It is rare for educational researchers not to claim teachers as a primary audience, but in practice few researchers can claim the audience of teachers captured by John Holt or Bel Kaufmann. Most educational research simply does not directly connect with the world it purports to study.

New Models of Procedure

In the case study worker's search for models of procedure, conduct and technique he/she often turns to the ethnographer working in an exotic culture. Recently the terms 'anthropology', 'ethnography' and 'participant observational' have begun to appear in education research studies (e.g. Parlett and Hamilton, 1972; Cronbach, 1974), but we believe that although the ethnographic analogy is in some ways helpful, in other ways it is misleading.

Perhaps the attraction of the ethnographic model stems from the recognition that the research itself is *social*; it proceeds through a set of social processes that influence and shape it from its inception through the fieldwork phase and into its final presentation, reception and usage. Social and cultural anthropologists seem particularly sensitive to the social processes involved in the fieldwork phase of research and echo many of the feelings felt by educational researchers who work within the educational process.

At the heart of this is a problem of identifying for the researcher how he relates his own sense of self to the person he feels himself becoming in the field situation. One anthropologist, Alan Beals, writes:

Except under extraordinary circumstances, there will always be a kind of clear plastic film separating the fieldworker from the rest of the community. The fieldworker does not fully understand the motives of others, he may in fact come to display a kind of paranoia arising in the fact that he knows that he is a centre of attention, but is not sure why. The fieldworker who behaves like a mechanical man, who treats others as subjects, or who coldly calculates the degree of friendship to be extended in each case, is going to appear less than human. People will be puzzled and dismayed by his behaviour. Certain kinds of information are available to the dispassionate observer. He is not likely to make enemies or become involved in disputes. On the other hand, he may have a considerable impact simply because his behaviour is impossible to understand or predict. Perhaps the ideal fieldworker would be a person who learned to behave in a natural and predictable manner, involved but not strongly involved. For our part, we came to feel at home in Gopalpur. Even today we can remember each friend and each enemy as we remember our friends and enemies at home. We were a part of the community and we shall not forget it.
(Quoted in Spindler, 1970, p. 40)

The fieldworker engaged in long-term participant observation in an exotic culture, has this curious and periodic identity crisis about being part in, and part outside the culture; of being, as Hortense Powdermaker (1967) puts it, both 'stranger and friend', or what the linguist Labov (1973) describes (adopting the vernacular of the Harlem youth groups he studied) as 'being a lame'. The short-term case study worker rarely meets these problems, yet there is something in the way an anthropologist like Alan Beals writes that seems familiar. He seems to be describing what it is like to 'make a strange journey in a familiar land' (Blythe, 1969).

Ethnographers often talk about 'culture shock' resulting from sudden immersion in an alien culture. The effect is to put the fieldworker in the position of constantly asking: what kind of person am I in this situation? For the fieldworker can never fully take himself for granted. Lacking the knowledge to become a real member of the culture the ethnographic fieldworker is frequently seen by those he is studying as incompetent, in the way that a child is seen as incompetent. Perceiving this view of himself only compounds the psychological disorder accompanying 'culture shock':

> At first we had a hard time just getting along from day to day among people in whose terms we were weird and barely comprehensible outsiders with the social and technical skills of a Semai four-year old. This initial social situation produced in us a psychological condition anthropologists call 'culture shock'. We felt depressed, incompetent, unattractive, and very lonely. I can easily understand the response of the great anthropologist, Malinowski when he writes in his field diary that one trivial frustrating incident, 'drives me to a state of white rage and hatred of bronze-coloured skin, combined with depression', a desire to 'sit down and cry' and a further longing to 'get out of this'. For all that I decide to resist and work today – 'business as usual', despite everything.
>
> (Dentan, in Spindler, 1970, p. 88)

For the educational case study worker the world being studied is mostly mundane, part of our commonsense experience. Yet you do not have to travel far to encounter the paradoxes, ambiguities and curiosities which constitute the exotic.

Charting Multiple Realities

In the educational case study we are dealing with more familiar worlds, yet when we being to collect data we soon realise that the perceptions of our informants often differ. Somehow we have to produce 'research' which fits in to a grammar created by multiple rules; we have to find ways of working where what we do fits to some extent the language, norms and expectations of diverse groups. We cannot do this by immersing ourselves in the field for a period of time and then extracting ourselves with no obligations to return, and besides, we are part of the culture we portray.

The study of multiple realities belongs to a considerable academic tradition stemming particularly from the work of William James (1890) in psychology, from Alfred Schultz in social psychology and from W.I. Thomas in sociology. Nevertheless, the scientifically trained fieldworker often finds it hard to suspend his belief in his own reality, and to find a way of capturing the complexities of multiple interpretation. This may create for him a sense of inner confusion. An anthropologist working in Chicago writes:

> When you are an infant in age, it is one thing to be helpless, but when you are 29 years old, it is quite something else. This feeling of helplessness was very difficult for me to handle. In the early part of my research it often made me feel so nervous and anxious that the events occurring around me seemed to merge in a blur of meaningless action. I despaired of ever making any sense out of anything. Vice Lords sensed my feelings and I could see it made some people uncomfortable. This increased the difficulty of gaining the rapport necessary to carry out successful research.
>
> (Keisar, in Spindler, 1970, pp. 234–5)

The educational researcher may share some of these feelings on entering a school, classroom or an LEA office, but is unlikely to be perceived as quite so helpless, and indeed may often be seen as an authority or expert. Yet the extent of his or her own sense of confusion constitutes some sort of test for the researcher, for it would seem that the degree of 'culture shock' experienced in the initial stages of fieldwork is in part a function of the degree to which the taken-for-granted assumptions of the world under study have become problematic. It is unlikely that an educational researcher will experience the kind of cultural shock met by anthropologists working in exotic cultures – to do so within one's own culture would perhaps be classified as insanity.

Conduct in the Field

As you read accounts by anthropologists about the experience of fieldwork (e.g. Spindler, 1970; Malinowski, 1967; Powdermaker, 1967; Mead, 1975), it is clear that the research is highly personal – that the knowledge gained is often personal knowledge gained by the researcher. Little comes out of the final monograph for the reader that is not carefully worked and understood by the writer. This marks the process off from the kind of case study role we have been suggesting – for we have talked about the possibility of case study sustaining multiple interpretations, of portraying reality rather than explaining it. To this end we have suggested relying on carefully considered procedures rather than on personal intuition.

This is not to say that some of the initial problems met by the field anthropologist are not very similar to those met by the educational case study worker. Consider for instance this point raised by an experienced ethnographic fieldworker:

> I became aware of another factor which happens everywhere I think, and which should be carefully watched by every fieldworker. In another society, the anthropologist, (stranger or outsider) is taken in and made welcome by one group or faction, who henceforward tend to monopolise him. He, therefore, becomes an object of suspicion or (at best) indifference to rival groups or factions. One has always to find a way to break away from one's original welcomers or sponsors.
>
> (Hart, in Spindler, 1970, p. 46)

This is a familiar problem in the case study of schools. How to gain acceptance by the Head, the staff and the pupils without being captured by any one interest, or group. To gain access to the school you need to first approach the Local Education Authority; to gain access to the staff, you need to approach the Head; to gain access to the pupils you need to approach the staff. Each fieldwork contact is thus sponsored by someone in authority over those you wish to study, and relationships between 'sponsors' and researchers cannot be broken if the research is to continue. Somehow the fieldworker has to construct some kind of compromise, relying on the passage of time for him to become known as a *person* rather than in his official status. This, in fact, is one of the main reasons that fieldwork takes so long to conduct – it is not so much that the data itself demands long immersion in the field, but that the mutual trust required in research relationships takes time to create.

This is part of what is involved when Alan Beals writes of 'feeling at home in Gopalpur', 'being part of the community', and of 'remembering each friend and enemy as we remember our friends and enemies at home'. The point is not the field anthropologist is in *danger* of becoming part of the situation under study, but that he fails unless he does. This, perhaps more than any other single issue, stands between the view of research held by those with a commitment to 'objectivity' derived from experimental design and personal non-intervention and those who believe in 'objectivity' acquired from *within* the situation under study. John Dollard, who probably more than any other social scientist has attempted to reconcile the difference and conflict between the research methods of the anthropological fieldwork, the methods of psychoanalytic case study and the methods of experimental psychology, finally recognised a significant discontinuity in method when he wrote 'but not every *n*th person can be a friend' (Dollard, 1949).

Those who have been involved in fieldwork recognise truth in this and are aware of the critical and often precarious friendships they have made in the course of their work. But to the untrained observer such statements only serve to mystify even further the methods and procedures of the anthropological fieldworker. Margaret Mead recalls how, having trained in psychology, she attended anthropology classes given by Franz Boas:

Professor Boas always spoke of the Kwakiutl as 'my dear friends', but this wasn't followed by anything that helped me to know what it was like to live among them . . . there was, in fact, no *how* in our education. What we learned was *what* to look for. Years later Camilla Wedgewood, on her first trip to Manam Island, reflected on this point when she wrote back: 'How anyone knows who is anybody's mother's brother, only God and Malinowski knows'.

(Mead, 1975, pp. 148–51)

Later Margaret Mead attempted to teach her own students more explicitly about the methods and procedures involved in fieldwork and evolved a view close to the one we want to promote in the context of educational research:

For fieldwork is a very difficult thing to do: to do it well, one has to sweep one's mind clear of every pre-supposition. In the field one can take nothing for granted. For as soon as one does, one cannot see what is before one's eyes as fresh and distinctive, and when one treats what is new merely as a variant of something already known, this may lead one far astray . . . the point of going into the field at all is to extend further what is already known, and so there is little value merely in identifying new versions of the familiar when we might, instead, find something wholly new. But to clear one's mind of pre-suppositions is a very hard thing to do and, without years of practice, all but impossible when one is working in one's own culture or in another that is very close to it.

(Mead, 1975, pp. 154–5)

Margaret Mead's stress on fieldwork to extend what is already known despite the difficulties she foresees, is critical for the use of case study research in education as we envisage it. Many people in and around education today detect a growing feeling of cultural fragmentation. People at different points of the educational system feel increasingly isolated from people at other points. Classroom teachers becoming divorced from the concerns of teachers whose roles are managerial or pastoral. Schools becoming isolated from the concerns of local authorities; colleges of education from the concerns of schools. The ultimate effect is one of division and suspicion at a number of levels in the system, anarchy at the periphery as seen from the centre; malign conspiracy at the centre as seen from the periphery.

There seems also a distinct move in the administration of research funds towards the adoption of criteria of social usefulness and towards accountability of researchers to their sponsors. For researchers this means justifying their research as a means and not as an end, and so demands either that they commit themselves to non-technical values, or that they take up roles in bureaucratic institutions where value positions relating to their research are taken by others. Other trends could perhaps be added, but these seem to indicate a growing separation between the worlds of controllers and controlled throughout the educational system. Under the conditions brought about by these kinds of change, case study research offers glimpses of the culture of the other groups. It offers to short-circuit the insulation each interest group has accumulated for its protection. More than any other reason, this explains the delicacy with which the case study worker has to proceed.

A Democratic Ethic

In fieldwork most of the researcher's time and energy is frequently taken up in initiating and sustaining the relationships that make the research possible. Once the relationships are established the business of data collection can often be accomplished quite quickly. One of the main suggestions we make in this paper is for 'condensed fieldwork' to replace long immersion in the field as the legitimate methodological basis for case study in educational research. Rather than waiting for personal relationships between researcher and subjects to create trust we believe it may be possible to substitute sets of rules and procedures which synthesise an ethic that makes feasible a research strategy that is genuinely 'democratic'.

There are, of course, a number of dangers in using a word like 'democratic' in the context of educational research. The word itself has so many associations, subtle shades of meaning, and raises many paradoxes. For example, in the way we have used it here there is some conflict between, on the one hand, the attempt to formulate a set of research practices which give those being studied more control over the study itself, and on the other hand a move on the part of the researcher towards more freedom from the constraints of the academic community. More fundamentally there is a tension between the claim that individuals and interest groups have a right to know about what is happening in areas of the system that are structurally invisible to them, and the claim that such knowledge is personal, that people own the facts of their lives and have the right to deny others access to them.

Normally in case study research the case study worker is heavily dependent on personal trust. Instead of relying entirely on personal trust we feel that in the contexts we work in it may be possible to maintain trust through holding strongly to a carefully formulated ethic. The trust we seek depends on generating a style of educational research in which methods and procedures are explicit and visible. We are interested in attempting to play down the *personal* expertise of the researcher in order to enhance his professionalism. Just as people will put trust in a doctor, or policeman (while knowing some doctors are unprofessional and some policemen corrupt) so we believe it should be possible for the educational case study worker to establish a similar professional identity. In other words for people to trust us because of what we do rather than because 'we are people just like them'. The cost may be the loss of personal freedom now allowed to the researcher, but the gain could be that case study research will gain in credibility and begin to be used more effectively by educational practitioners.

The researcher attempting to produce a case study of a school or curriculum project faces a problem, for in presenting *his* interpretations of persons and events, how does he account for the interpretations made by others? What kinds of responsibility do they have for the finished product? Marie Kurchak (1974) describes the educational researcher's problem as well as the film maker's when she writes:

> What the film maker has presented is her private vision, packaged in celluloid. The family's isolation is reinforced as the film maker impotently withdraws the camera and hopes the message will reach someone 'in a position to do something about it'.

Since the case study is a *selective* mirror of events, accounts and definition of what happens, then whenever selections are made they must be related, as far as possible, to named issues and negotiated with participants as to relevance and accuracy. By according confidentiality to informants for the term of the study and thereafter negotiating for release of material when it is needed for publication many initial field problems can be overcome, but the deeper issues remain.

Film as Example and Analogy

In documentary film making as in educational research the confusion of roles between observer and change agent recurs. The film maker feels impotent because he expects to bring about change, but in the way we have described a democratic mode of research that would be no part of his responsibility. The non-involved stance of the observer being validated by the increased involvement of his subjects in, and their responsibility for, both the process of research and its finished product.

Some of these ideas have already been practised by documentary film makers. Through its 'Challenge for Change' programme the National Film Board of Canada has been experimenting with ways of overcoming the alienating effects of the social documentary film on those portrayed. One of their most influential projects involved making a film on the island of Fogo, off Newfoundland, and the procedures adopted there have become known by film makers as 'The Fogo Process':

> Film maker Low shot 20 hours of footage oriented around several personalities and events. He screened the film, unedited, to the participants, and asked them to approve screenings to other members of the community. They had the option of cutting out film they might later regret.
>
> Low then made a series of short films (which he called 'vertical' films) each about a single personality or event. The films were screened for groups all over

the island. In their work as a catalyst to discussion of mutual problems, the films allowed people, who may have been reluctant to speak in public, to allow their films to speak for them. People with opposing views had something external to mediate the hostility that might have occurred in face-to-face confrontation.

One of the members of the film team remarked that in a 'horizontal' documentary intercutting of opinions immediately creates a hierarchy of who is right and who is wrong, thereby putting down some members of the community. The goal of trying to get people to talk to each other is then impeded.

With the permission of the islanders, the films were shown to the decision makers, and their comments were recorded for the islanders.

The technique of using film as a catalyst, mirror and third party mediator has been used since the Fogo experiment from the Mississippi Delta to Alaska. In some cases, half inch video (vtr) has been used in place of, or in conjunction with, film.

(Kurchak, 1974)

Educational research, like film making, has traditionally worked with the notion of producing a final, 'finished' product. It too has seen its work left unrecognised, become suddenly popular, misinterpreted or misused, leaving the researcher with uncertain responsibilities.

Vertical Studies

The film makers' idea of the 'vertical documentary' coupled with Barry MacDonald's notion of 'democratic evaluation' raise intriguing possibilities for the case study worker. Perhaps rather than engage in lengthy fieldwork and finally producing an account (as both Howard Becker and Louis Smith did), it might be possible to work by producing initial case studies on the basis of limited fieldwork and then using responses to these to redirect later work.

For example, after a week in a school the case study worker could produce limited 'vertical' studies – an account of a single event, a recording of a lesson, an interview with the Head. After working through these with the people involved they could circulate to a limited audience, and on the basis of that audience's response perhaps circulate more widely.

Visual Records

In producing 'vertical' studies there are considerable advantages in using visual presentations, even in educational research. We have worked

previously mainly with classroom recordings though more recently we have
been experimenting with other visual records. For example we have recorded
on tape-slide a whole working day in the life of an LEA adviser as he visits
schools. We have also considered using an exhibition of photographs of a
school and its immediate environment as a stimulus for interviewing pupils.
The visual record has advantages for the researcher who has to work fast,
what Collier (1967, p. 12) calls its 'can opener' effect. It gives the researcher a
clear identity and an immediate visible product, and used skilfully this can
provide him with a rapid introduction to the field. Since the early 1960s,
video-tape recording has become more easily available, accessible and sim-
pler to use. This increased availability of the technology represents a considerable challenge both to research and teaching. Video-tape makes it possible
to capture and to replay some aspects of classroom action, so creating an
enormous potential for research in the form of new kinds of data.

Negotiating Interpretations

In terms of research design the point is not simply that vertical studies are
circulated for approval, but for validation; the responses to the study perhaps being added to the study itself when they reveal significant new interpretations. Like works of art, case studies are never finished, only left.

This is the kind of process we have in mind when we suggest that democratic mode research may demand school case studies that can be completed
within a week. Under such circumstances the researcher cannot become an
expert in the detailed workings of the institutions under study, and is unable
to become the person who knows the full story of the schools. Unable to
produce the authoritative study from personal own resources the case study
worker needs to proceed in such a way that his or her accounts are viewed as
tentative and provisional. In admitting the fragility of their own interpretations case study workers might strengthen their accounts by mobilising
the responses of participants as part of the final study.

For example in SAFARI one of the projects we are studying is Nuffield
Secondary Science. Quite early on we realised that people in science
education were referring to a range of different and often complex issues
when they used the phrase 'The Nuffield Approach'. When we asked what
the phrase meant we failed to obtain a clear, unambiguous formulation
which might constitute a definition. What we did in this instance was simply
to collect a range of comments, definitions, anecdotes and accounts which
surrounded the phrase and seemed as a collection to retain some of the
complexities of meaning the phrase has in use. By circulating this collection
to people with an interest in the area we continuously obtained new frag-
ments to add to the collection, it thus became self-validating and as our

research continued a source for checking later ideas and by hypotheses. The point is that we produced this collection at the *start* of the research and then used it as one way into the field, rather than simply opening a file which we wrote up at the end.

Confidentiality

For the case study worker confidentiality represents a continuous rather than an intermittent concern. It is not simply a question of negotiating access to the field at the start of the research and publication at the end. Given the sort of research we have outlined, and the constraints of the democratic model, confidentiality necessarily assumes the status of a continuous and predominant concern. At every stage of the research and with almost every encounter the case study worker must continually monitor what is said in order not to breach the confidentiality given to other participants.

The nature of case study is such that participants can often only judge the full consequences of release of data in retrospect, when the full study is available. We have adopted the procedure of offering blanket confidentiality in order to gain faster access to relevant data and to protect informants from the need continuously to monitor what they say. Release of data is then progressively negotiated between case study worker and informants according to the context of publication and the audience being informed.

We emphasise that confidentiality is not simply a mechanical procedure but a continuous methodological concern closely related to the values contained and communicated by the research. To return to the analogy with documentary film making:

> The problem with social documentaries is that they can be exploitative. The film maker may be sensitive as he goes about the act of embalming their misery, but when the lights are gone the family is still hungry. This is not the only problem: after *The Things I Cannot Change* was aired on CBC TV, the family was exposed to the teasing and mocking of their neighbours.
>
> (Kurchak, 1974)

The researcher attempting to produce a case study of a school of curriculum project faces similar problems. In presenting *his* (or her) interpretation of persons and events, what account is made of the interpretations made by others? The researcher is caught in the tension between meeting the obligations owed to the audience and the obligations owed to the subjects. The democratic model does not dissolve this tension but formalises the need for negotiation.

Interviews[6]

One of the implications of using condensed fieldwork methods is a much heavier reliance on the unstructured interview than is usual in participant observation. Few of the handbooks available on interviewing, however, describe adequately the kind of interview often adopted in case study of the kind we have described. The reason is perhaps that those we interview not only have greater knowledge than we do about the areas under study, but that they assume that we have some knowledge too. The educational researcher is part of the educational scene in a way that, say, the organisational sociologist is not. Areas of knowledge and expertise overlap. This also gives the unstructured interview a certain cutting edge. Many of the procedures we are recommending here are necessary because the interview is a penetrating device which requires greater protection for those studied than is necessary for observation of their routine social behaviour.

In the hands of a skilled interviewer most people are inexperienced and will reveal things they do not intend. Only by allowing retrospective control of editing and release of data to informants can the case study worker protect his subjects from the penetrative power of the research as well as checking his own misinterpretations or misunderstandings. Ethically this involves taking the view that people own the facts of their lives and should be able to control the use that is made of them in research.

The sharing of control over data with participants does mean that the researcher often has to face the fact that some of the finest data is lost, diluted or permanently consigned to the files. On the other hand access to knowledge about what are sensitive issues to his (or her) informants may guide the research in significant and unexpected ways.

The critical skills for interviewing are perhaps psychological mobility and emotional intelligence. 'Psychological mobility' is a phrase used by the American anthropologist Hortense Powdermaker (1967) to describe the fieldworker's ability 'to step in and out of the role of people with different value systems'. She ascribes her failures in conducting a study of the Hollywood film industry to her inability to make psychological transitions smoothly. In retrospect she wrote:

> I think of what the book might have been if some of my involvement had not been hidden, if I had possessed the psychological mobility and the sociological opportunity to enter and understand all the contending groups, if my value system had not so aggressively dominated the whole study, if I had known more humility and compassion.

In an interview the interviewee will often react to or against what is perceived to be the interviewer's frame of reference and definition of the situation. He will attempt either to 'tell the interviewer what he wants to know' or to take issue with what he perceives as the interviewer's point of view. Either way the interviewer's values enter the interview, and unless he/she is 'psychologically mobile' the interviewer may not realise the extent to which he or she is dominating or controlling what is said. Hortense Powdermaker warns, 'Conscious involvements are not a handicap for the social scientist. Unconscious ones are always dangerous' (Powdermaker, 1967).

The phrase 'emotional intelligence' extends the psychological mobility of the interviewer in order to empathise with the interviewee. It is not enough simply to be self-aware and to know how your own values are entering the situation. You need to enter the world of the other. As the novelist Sybille Bedford writes of the interview, 'it takes two to tell the truth':

> It takes two to tell the truth.
> One for one side, one for the other?
> That's not what I mean. I mean one to tell, one to
> hear. A speaker and receiver. To tell the truth
> about any complex situation requires a certain
> attitude in the receiver.
> What is required in the receiver?
> I would say first of all a level of emotional intelligence . . .
> Imagination,
> Discipline.
> Sympathy, Attention
> And patience.
>
> (Bedford, 1968, p. 18)

For most interviewees the research interview clearly presents a novel and somewhat paradoxical situation. It is quite common to find people who treat the interview as mildly inconveniencing, who initially offer to talk for 'twenty minutes' but then go and talk for two hours. Given an interviewer who is both emotionally intelligent and psychologically mobile interviewees will frequently divulge personal information, and subsequently add, 'I don't know why I'm telling you this but . . .' or, 'I don't know why I told you, I've never told anyone else before'.

A problem with using the interview is that the interviewer can almost always force a response. Having acceded to the interview only very few people are able to resist the rule of the game that requires a response to a question. Given a response, even if it is intended as flippant or off-hand, a skilled interviewer can use it to force a subsequent reply:

Teacher: Don't expect me to tell you anything about the Headmaster, I won't say anything about the Head . . .
Interviewer: You just *have*,

Later,

Teacher: The Head is a well-meaning man.
Interviewer: You mean misguided?

Case Study and Action Research

The skilled interviewer has to be sensitive to the different stages of the interview. Initially the interviewee generally assumes that the interviewer has limited knowledge about him and that he cannot be entrusted with some kinds of information. At critical stages of the interview the interviewer may be able to reveal to the interviewee a knowledge of his situation that was unsuspected. If he or she is able to do this he may be able to move the interviewee into a new phase based on increased trust, recognition and unanticipated shared meanings.

Other social processes at work in the interview may work against the interviewer, for example the interview situation may set up social opportunities for the interviewee to release information not relevant to the research but which attempts to restrict the researcher in other activities related to the research.

Overall perhaps the main problem with the interview is that it releases more of the truth than the case study worker can handle. Consequently the basic value of the interviewer is respect for the privacy of the interviewee and a recognition that people own the facts of their lives.

The Report

Case study methods lend themselves to a variety of means of presentation, written reports, audio-visual recordings, displays and exhibitions. Generally these presentations should be devoid of indications of praise or blame from the point of view of the researcher. They should present contingency relationships only, leaving it to the audience to infer cause. They should attempt to be explicit about rationale and procedure, and the principles governing the selection and presentation of content. One consequence of this is to reduce the researcher's control over the content of the case study. The researcher may feel after a period of time that the study needs rewriting, but may be unable to rewrite because the procedures that were adopted prevent a reassertion of control over the data.

Wherever appropriate the case study should contain the expressed reactions (unedited and unglossed) of the principal characters portrayed to the report in its final draft form. It is implicit in the notion of case study that there is no one true definition of the situation. Within the confines of the study we act as though truth in social situations is multiple: the case study worker acts as a collector of definitions, not the conductor of truth.
[. . .]

Notes

1 Throughout this paper we use a distinction between 'researchers' on the one hand, and 'practitioners' on the other. This is a convention adopted to sharpen what, in fact, is an indistinct separation of roles. By 'practitioners' we mean teachers, head teachers, advisers, education officers, DES staff – all those who work in education. In other contexts researchers too may well be practitioners.
2 This theme has since been explored more fully in Norris (1977), especially by Helen Simons.
3 The section continues by raising the generalisation problems and only briefly mentions method: '. . . very often case studies are not representative and hence the results apply only to that group and to the specific situation involved. Nevertheless, a case study can be a useful starting point for a piece of research; it can also be used by students to gain the flavour of research without being involved in unnecessary complications.' (p. 20).
4 This idea provides the central theme for a research project funded by the SSRC and based at the Centre for Applied Research in Education, University of East Anglia (1977–79) 'Classroom Observation, the Practice of Advisers, Head Teachers and Teachers'.
5 Examples of such work are becoming available. See for example the Understanding Computer Assisted Learning Evaluation (CARE, Norwich 1974–7) and *The Case Studies in Science Education Project* (University of Illinois 1976–8).
6 For a more detailed account see Helen Simon's paper on interviewing in Norris (ed.) (1977).

References

BECKER, H.S. (1958). 'Problems of inference and proof in participant observation', *Am. Sociol. Rev.*, 23, 652–60.
BECKER, H.S. *et al.* (1961). *Boys in White.* Chicago: University of Chicago Press.
BECKER, H.S. (1964). 'Problems in the publication of field studies' in Vidich, A.J. (ed.) *Reflections on Community Studies.* New York: Wiley.
BECKER, H.S. *et al.* (1968). *Making the Grade.* New York: Wiley.
BEDFORD, S. (1968). *A Compass Error.* London: Collins.
BLYTHE, R. (1969). *Akenfield.* Harmondsworth: Penguin.
BRUGELMANN, H. (1974). 'Towards checks and balances in educational evaluation – on the use of social control in research design'. Unpublished paper, University of East Anglia: Centre for Applied Research in Education.
CASE STUDIES IN SCIENCE EDUCATION. Report available from Center for Instructional Research and Curriculum Evaluation, University of Illinois, Champaign, Urbana.
COLLIER, J. (1967). *Visual Anthropology: Photography as a Research Method.* New York: Holt Rinehart and Winston.
CRONBACH, L. (1974). 'Beyond the two disciplines of scientific psychology'. Paper read at American Psychological Association Conference, New Orleans.
DOLLARD, J. (1949). *Caste and Class in a Southern Town.* New York: Harper.
ELLIOTT, J. (1974). 'The Safari Solipsists' in Macdonald, B. and Walker, R. (eds.) *Innovation, Evaluation, Research and the Problem of Control,* 103–16.

(Safari Papers I), University of East Anglia: Centre for Applied Research in Education.

ENTWISTLE, N. (1973). Open University Course E341. *The Nature of Educational Research*. Block 1.

FREUD, S. (1953). *Standard Edition*, Vol. 2. London: Hogarth Press and the Institute of Psychoanalysis.

GRAEF, R. (n.d.) *The Space between Words – School* (BBC Film) Available from BBC Enterprises, Peterborough.

GUILFORD, J.P. (1954). *Psychometric Methods* (2nd Edition). London: McGraw-Hill.

HAMILTON, D. *et al.* (1977). *Beyond the Numbers Game: A Reader in Alternative Evaluation*. London: Macmillan.

HARGREAVES, D. (1967). *Social Relations in a Secondary School*. London: Routledge and Kegan Paul.

JAMES, W. (1980). *Principles of Psychology* (2 vols). New York: Henry Holt.

KAUFMAN, B. (1964). *Up the Down Staircase*. Englewood Cliffs, New Jersey: Prentice-Hall.

KURCHAK, M. (1974). 'The camera as a surgical instrument', *Take One*, 4, No. 1.

LABOV, W. (1973). 'The linguist as lame', *Language and Society*, April 1973.

LACEY, C. (1970). *Hightown Grammar: School as a Social System*. Manchester: Manchester University Press.

LEWIS, O. (1959). *Five Families*. New York: Basic Books.

MCCALL, G.J. and SIMMONS, J.L. (1969). *Issues in Participant Observation*. Reading: Mass.: Addison-Wesley.

MACDONALD, B. (1975). 'Evaluation and the control of education'. To be published in Tawney, D. (ed.) *Evaluation: The State of the Art*. London: Macmillan (in Press).

MALINOWSKI, B. (1967). *A Diary in the Strict Sense of the Word*. London: Routledge and Kegan Paul.

MEAD, M. (1975). *Blackberry Winter: My Earlier Years*. New York: Pocket Books.

NISBET, J. (1974). 'Educational research: The State of the Art'. Proceedings of the Inaugural Meeting of the British Educational Research Association, 1974, University of Birmingham.

NORRIS, N. (ed.) (1977). *Theory into Practice: SAFARI interim papers 2*. University of East Anglia: Centre for Applied Research in Education.

OETTINGER, A. (1969). *Run Computer Run*. Harvard: Harvard University Press.

PARLETT, M. and HAMILTON, D. (1972). 'Evaluation as illumination: a new approach to the study of innovatory programs', CRES Paper No. 9, University of Edinburgh.

POWDERMAKER, H. (1967). *Stranger and Friend*. London: Secker and Warburg.

RICHARDSON, E. (1973). *The Teacher, the School and the Task of Management*. London: Heinemann.

SCHUTZ, A. (1962–6). *Collected Papers*, 3 vols. The Hague: Nijhof.

SMITH, L.M. (1974). 'An aesthetic education workshop for administrators: some implications for a theory of case studies.' Paper read at AERA, Chicago, 1974.

SMITH, L.M. and GEOFFREY, W. (1968). *Complexities of an Urban Classroom*. New York: Holt Rinehart and Winston.

SPINDLER, G. (ed.) (1970). *Being an Anthropologist: Fieldwork in Eleven Cultures*. New York: Holt Rinehart and Winston.

THOMAS, W.I. (1951). (ed. by E.H. Volkhart) *Social Behaviour*. New York: Social Science Research Council.

Understanding Computer Assisted Learning. Report available from University of East Anglia: Centre for Applied Research in Education.

WALLER, W. (1932). *The Sociology of Teaching*. New York: Wiley.
WOLCOTT, H. (1967). *A Kwakuitl Village and School*. New York: Holt Rinehart and Winston.
YOUNG, M.F.D. (ed.) (1971). *Knowledge and Control*. London: Collier-Macmillan.

An Adversary's Account of SAFARI's Ethics of Case-Study[1]

D. Jenkins

For those who bewail its absence, honesty is a moral problem. For those who try to achieve it, it is a technical one.

(Vaughan, 1974)[2]

For the purposes of this paper I am assuming that the reader is familiar with the SAFARI Interim Papers: *Innovation, Evaluation, Research and the Problem of Control* (1974) and in particular Barry MacDonald's paper 'Evaluation and the Control of Education' and Rob Walker's paper 'The Conduct of Educational Case Study: Ethics, Theory and Procedures' in that volume. Indented quotations from Rob Walker's paper sprinkle my account. The text for the day might be:

The researcher is caught in the tension between meeting the obligations he owes his audience and the obligation he owes his subjects.

(Walker 1974, pp. 88–89)

But whereas SAFARI ethical statements begin rhetorically from the 'obligations to the subject' I want to begin elsewhere, the researcher's obligation to his audience and his own professionalism. Users of case study methods have encountered a number of difficulties in conducting their research. Walker's list of these difficulties includes the following crucial two:

problems of confidentiality of data; . . .
problems concerning publication, such as the need to preserve anonymity of subjects;

(Walker, p. 69)

This separation of the two problem areas has more than analytical convenience, as I shall try to show. There is a paradox at the heart of MacDonald's account of 'democratic evaluation' which manages *both* to offer subjects 'control' over the data *and* audiences 'the right to know'. He offers confidentiality to informants and gives them control over the use of the information they provide. The key concepts of democratic evaluation are 'confidentiality', 'negotiation', and 'accessibility'. The key justificatory concept is the 'right to know'.

The problem for a person aspiring to produce 'successful' case study in a sensitive area may thus be conceptualised as a 2 × 2 dichotomy

Access to sensitive data

low	high			
1	2	low	)	
			)	ability to
			)	release data
3	4	high	)	

The researcher begins in box 1, having low access to sensitive data and (concomitantly, since release depends on access) low ability to release it. But he wants to get to box 4, and enjoy both high access to sensitive data and high ability to release it. The internal logic of the 2 × 2 dichotomy suggests that anybody interested in defending himself or his institution against the intrusion or unsought consequences of a case study researcher has two ditches in which to fight; he might prevent access to the data or prevent its release. Symmetrically a case study worker needs to cross the same two ditches, first getting access to sensitive data and then effecting its release.

I follow SAFARI in taking it as read that there is an ethical problem at the heart of case study research. In 'Re-thinking case study: notes from the second Cambridge conference', Adelman, Jenkins and Kemmis (1976) write that 'case study research . . . because it is rooted in the practicalities and politics of real life situations, is more likely to expose those studied to critical appraisal, censure or condemnation . . . The limiting consideration is that the case study worker acknowledges that *others* must live with the consequences of his findings.' Responses to these ethical problems have been various. Some defend the 'right to know' as a spin-off from more general notions of public accountability. Others, like John Hayman (1976) begin by making moral assertions in the grey areas around the outside of privacy laws, and see the central issue as the rights of the individual. A third position is the SAFARI[3] one. At it crudest this involves two notions: the first is that of confidentiality which is recognised as 'facilitating access to the researcher' as well as 'protecting the confidants'. Some SAFARI statements in this area could be interpreted as containing an underlying and unacknowledged cynicism:

> The nature of case study is such that the participants can often only judge the full consequences of release of data in retrospect, when the full study is available. We have adopted the procedure of offering blanket confidentiality in order to gain faster access to relevant data and to protect informants from the need continuously to monitor what they say. Release of data is then progressively negotiated between case study worker and informants according to the context of publication and the audience being informed (p. 88).

The second notion is that of co-ownership of the data. All reports are to be 'negotiated' with those being studied.

> Democratic evaluation places the case study worker in the position of having to *negotiate* his interpretations with those involved in the study, rather than being free to impose them on the data (p. 72).

The purpose of these self-denying ordinances is said to be 'to redress the imbalance of power' between the research community and those in the schools who might be closely observed and reported upon.

Readers familiar with industrial relations theory might suppose 'co-ownership' to imply that the SAFARI team are proposing the introduction of a 'human relations' approach to educational research. The parties, now defined as equal, will collaborate naturally, as their barriers of mistrust, suspicion, and stereotyped perception are removed. Something of this flavour comes through at least during the initial field-work stage.

> Given an interviewer is both emotionally intelligent and psychologically mobile interviewees will frequently divulge personal information and subsequently add 'I don't know why I'm telling you this but' . . . (p. 90).

But rapport quickly gives way to a 'role negotiation' approach based on the specification of rights, duties, rules of conduct and principles of procedure. The unstated assumption, obviously, is that people have different and sometimes conflicting interests and that trust needs to be depersonalised into charters and stated obligations. SAFARI ethics is a technical rather than a moral edifice. The logic of the model requires sanctions, but none are available.

Rule-bound behaviour between antagonists paradoxically *frees* an aggressor operating within the rules. The Queensberry Rules in boxing, for example, at one level take the responsibility for limiting the hurt to an opponent away from the boxer. Limits are enshrined in the rules and in the right of a referee to intervene mercifully. Within these rules boxers are free to 'punish' their opponents. Perhaps SAFARI case study workers are similarly freed by a code of practice to go after the truth, confident that the fight is now fair. This is an attractive proposition and, in my view, could form the basis of a consistent and honourable position. But there are two good reasons why it poorly represents the SAFARI position, at least in so far as the rhetoric can be taken for reality.

In the first place SAFARI's whole tone is incompatible with the view that case study researchers should 'defeat their adversaries' and winkle out the truth. The SAFARI solipsists (Elliott, 1974) take a relativistic view of truth, and have no basis for sustaining the researcher's version of it over against any other.

> What we have attempted is to design a form of case study research in which the case study worker relinquishes some of his authority over interpretation in the attempt to gain greater credibility and influence (p. 93).

This much is admitted in the suggestion that reports ought to be *negotiated* for truth, accuracy and fairness. In essence SAFARI enjoins case study workers, in the words of St. Matthew, to be 'reconciled with their adversaries' rather than defeat them. The second reason is that the rules are unenforcable, not only in the absence of a machinery for enforcement, but because they represent at best a 'counsel of perfection'[4] and at worst a meaningless slogan. 'Co-ownership of the data' is an aspiration virtually impossible to realise in practice, given the nature of research and the nature of human understanding of complex situations. An earlier public morality that over-promised is now known retrospectively as Victorian hypocrisy. So what happens in practice to those seeking to follow SAFARI's ethical advice? The desert, as T.S. Eliot once said, is in the heart of your brother.

I now want to take up an adversary's position and argue for the most disreputable conclusion that appears to be compatible with all the evidence. I am not entirely sure that the case sticks for all its *prima facie* strength. It is more humane to consider the SAFARI case studies as hopelessly caught in the cross-fire between conflicting aspirations. But let us argue for the moment that the whole structure is manipulative. How might it be characterised?

Let me return to my original 2 × 2 dichotomy. The researcher who begins in box 1 but needs to get to box 4 could attempt to get there diagonally, which would involve a single 'ethical set'.[5] Instead the SAFARI case study worker chooses to employ a tricky 'knight's move', breaking the task in two, which he handles by employing two ethical systems. The trick is in the shift in the power-base between the first and the second.

Access to sensitive data

	low	high	
1		2	low)
			) ability to
			) release data
3		4	high)

SAFARI 'case study ethics' is in part a rhetorical device to facilitate performance of this questionable knight's move. Between boxes 1 and 2 we have
a gate labelled the *ethics of access*. Between boxes 2 and 4 we have a gate
labelled *the ethics of release*. Softly. Softly.

There are a number of potential advantages *to the researcher* in attempting
the knight's move. It will be clear that most of these spring from the facility of
separating the 'ethics' of access to data from the 'ethics' of its release.

1 The researcher makes it harder for the subject to find adequate models of
refusal at the first gate. Why fight in this ditch when the next one is so
impregnable – actual control and censorship over the 'joint' data?

> In the hands of a skilled interviewer most people are inexperienced and will
> reveal things they do not intend. Only by allowing retrospective control of
> editing and release of data to informants can the case study worker protect his
> subjects from the penetrative power of the research as well as checking his own
> misinterpretations or misunderstandings (p. 89).

2 The researcher is bidding for the privilege of being in the know. A rhetoric
suggesting that this privilege may not be cashable does little to weaken the
strength of the researcher's position in box 2. Sure he 'knows more than he
can say', but he is a *knower who wants to tell*. Contrast the weakness of a
teller who wants to know (a model closer to investigative journalism).

3 The victim who seeks protection in the first ditch between box 1 and box 2
can only fall back on some notion like 'confidentiality'. Yet information
given in confidence, either not for attribution or not for publication, is
typically given for one of two reasons, either as a weak pre-emptive strike
against the researcher's perceptiveness or as background data to the victim's
own rhetoric of justification. Given 'co-ownership of the data' and the promised 'ethics of release' has the concept of confidentiality anyway become
redundant, an early warning system to signal the unlikelihood of eventual
release? No; 'confidentiality' rides large in the SAFARI corporate mental life,
not for any functional reason at this stage in the knight's move *but because it
pre-empts the tone of the contact*, distorting it usefully away from the 'role
negotiation' model towards the deceptively-supportive 'human relations'
approach. It is the relationship that has become confidential, not the
data . . .

> One of the main reasons that fieldwork takes so long to conduct is . . . that the
> mutual trust required in research relationships takes time to create (p. 83).

4 The way is now open for *the cultivation of rapport* during transition from
box 1 and box 2. The researcher can not only argue that he can be entrusted
with secrets because release of data is off the current agenda. He can also
implicitly present himself as the knowledgeable quasi-insider, increasingly

unlikely to be fobbed off with just any old account. The wagon gathers pace.

> At critical stages of the interview the interviewer may be able to reveal to the interviewee a knowledge of his situation that was unsuspected. If he is able to do this he may be able to move the interviewee in to a new phase based on increased trust, recognition, and unanticipated shared meanings (p. 91).

5 Just as contraception presumably eases the classic problems posed to the seducer, so the SAFARI researcher is able to claim that his *safeguarding* procedures are part of his loving intent. But we are still between boxes 1 and 2. The seducer is prepared to wait. And the spy is allowed to screen himself, acting as guarantor to his own security risk.

> The basic value of the interviewer is respect for the privacy of the interviewee and a recognition that people own the facts of their lives (p. 91).

6 When our researcher reaches box 2, he turns his mind to the problem of getting to box 4 with his original objectives intact. It is at this point that he pulls out the second trick in his bag. *The ethics of consensus are surreptitiously replaced by the ethics of power.*

The *difference* between the ethical stances is more important than the 'apparent' content of each. The gap guarantees that tokens of esteem (the only coinage of the first negotiation) have a low exchange value in the second. Although officially frowned upon, various devices are standard to SAFARI investigators:

(a)   Manipulation of time-scales to allow insufficient time for reflection before some 'publication date'.

(b)   Negotiations of 'personalised' accounts, calculated to put at a disadvantage subjects reticent in suggesting alternative self portrayals.

(c)   Cynical employment of a cosmetic red-herring by which the task can be represented to the subject as 'improving' the account (Is your viewpoint adequately represented?) thus deflecting attention from the *fact* of release to its *form*, and inviting bogus co-authorship, thus making refusal psychologically improbable.

> In admitting the fragility of his own interpretations the case study worker can strengthen his account by mobilising the responses of participants as part of the final study (p. 87).

(d)   'Entrepreneurship' and *management* of the negotiation kept in the hands of the researchers.

(e)   Accounts negotiated for one audience (e.g. published *conference reports* read only by those having access to means of independent corroboration) can be treated as provisional negotiations for further release (e.g. as the basis of a chapter in a book by the researcher).

Ethical stances involve self-denial because the principled life does not allow a person to make an exception of himself. In the light of this, it is difficult to see SAFARI's self-serving manipulative device as ethical, although it exhibits (spuriously) some of the formal characteristics of 'principles of procedure'.

In conclusion two arguments can be launched against the SAFARI position. The first is that within its own terms it is beginning to look too much like a rhetorical con-trick, based on the devious knight's move described above. The second is that the whole notion of the 'imbalance of power' between the research community and those studied may be posed differently. Howard Becker took this line at the Second Cambridge Conference on Methods of Case Study in Educational Research and Evaluation, and I happily give him the last word:

> What I'm most concerned about is the way devices dreamed up to protect some hypothetical helpless teacher, for instance, from harmful exposure, end up by being used by powerful government agencies and personnel to keep the public from knowing what it has every right to know. It could even be argued that social research is a mechanism by which power imbalances leading to withholding of crucial information are righted.
>
> (Becker 1976)

Notes

1 This paper is also to appear in Simons, H., (Ed.), forthcoming, *Towards a Science of the Singular*, a collection of essays about case-study research in education.

2 This quotation opens an account by Dai Vaughan of his work with Roger Graef in the film series *The Space Between Words*. There are five films in the series (Family, School, Work, Politics, Diplomacy). Filmed by the same team each film aspires to reflect the institution operating as normally as possible. In attempting to make a 'film of record' the team work to a set of procedures which involve the minimum of interference by the film team. The films were originally transmitted on BBC-TV in 1972.

3 SAFARI, an acronym for Success and Failure and Recent Innovation, is a Ford Foundation sponsored research study conducted by Barry MacDonald. The SAFARI ethical position is elaborated in MacDonald, B. and Walker, R., (Eds.), 1974, *SAFARI, Innovation, Evaluation, Research and the Problem of Control: Some Interim Papers*, Norwich, Centre for Applied Research in Education, University of East Anglia.

4 In this respect it might be compared with 'neutral chairmanship' in the Humanities Curriculum Project. The term 'counsel of perfection' is a Catholic one, covering unattainable aspirations. It is possible, of course, for the 'ethical' SAFARI research worker to retreat to the weaker proposition that 'co-ownership of the data' is not a literal truth but a criterion helping to determine what might legitimately be done with it.

5 'Ethical set' means that the problems posed can be treated within a single interpretative framework.

References

ADELMAN, C., JENKINS, D. and KEMMIS, S., 1976. 'Re-thinking case-study – notes from the second Cambridge conference', *Cambridge Journal of Education* 6.3.

BECKER, H., 1976. private correspondence to the author, April 24th.

ELLIOTT, J., 1974. 'The SAFARI Solipsists' in MacDonald, B. and Walker, R. (Eds.), SAFARI, 1974, *Innovation, Evaluation, Research and the Problem of Control: Some Interim Papers*, Norwich, Centre for Applied Research in Education, University of East Anglia.

HAYMAN, J. JNR., 1976. 'Rights of Privacy and Research Needs: a Problem whose Time has Arrived', paper presented at the American Educational Research Association Convention, San Francisco, April.

MACDONALD, B. and WALKER, R., (Eds.), 1974. *SAFARI, Innovation, Evaluation, Research and the Problem of Control: Some Interim Papers*, Norwich, Centre for Applied Research in Education, University of East Anglia.

VAUGHAN, D., 1974. 'Space between shots', *Screen* 15:1.

WALKER, R., 1974. 'The Conduct of Educational Case Study: Ethics, Theory and Procedures' in MacDonald, B. and Walker, R. (Eds.), op. cit.

Democratic Evaluation as Social Criticism: Or Putting The Judgment Back into Evaluation

J. Elliott

In 'Evaluation and the control of education',[1] Barry MacDonald argued for evaluation procedures based on the concepts of 'confidentiality', 'negotiation', and 'accessibility'; the key justificatory concept for such procedures being the citizenry's 'right to know'. Since 'the citizenry' exist in a state of value pluralism the aim of the democratic evaluator is to represent 'the interests' of a range of social groups in his evaluation study. In other words MacDonald appears to assume that individuals in a pluralist society have the right to know *as* members of particular 'interest' groups rather than as members of the general public.

On an initial inspection the assumption appears to be a reasonable one. People could only have 'the right to know' as members of the general public if they had interests in common; if actions and policies benefited them under the description of 'members of the public' rather than that of 'members of group X'. The fact of pluralism appears to rule out the possibility of anything being in the public interest.

Of course, one could argue that the fact that people view what is good for them differently doesn't entail that there is no such thing as the common good. I once argued that MacDonald has tended to confuse *contingent* pluralism – the fact that groups disagree in their evaluations – with *epistemological* pluralism – the view that the truth of evaluations is relative to particular groups.[2]

Nevertheless, it might be argued, as I think MacDonald did subsequently, that this confusion makes little practical difference procedurally. Contingent pluralism requires that for practical purposes at least, the democratic evaluator must assume that people's interests are best assessed against their own criteria of 'good' rather than his own. In which case democratic evaluation aims to be an information service for people with differing conceptions of 'the good'. The criteria governing the selection and use of information about an educational policy and courses of action are not those of the evaluator who according to MacDonald should have 'no concept of information misuse'. Nor are they those of the general public. They are the criteria which define the 'interests' of different social groups within the larger society. Hence, MacDonald's view of the democratic evaluator's role as a neutral 'broker' (I almost said 'chairman') exchanging information between groups who want knowledge of each other.

Obviously, the 'broker' role is far from value-free. It is based on the view that evaluation ought to foster the interests of different groups because they have the right to know. The evaluation is described as democratic precisely because the right of different interest groups to know about each other is assumed to be a fundamental condition of a democratic society.

I want to argue that this assumption is false (later I shall also assert that it is cynical and destructive). If it is correct then every group in a democracy is obliged to foster the interests of every other group by providing them with information about their own activities. If group X has the right to know about group Y's activities and policies then group Y ought to inform group X of these matters. And this implies that group Y ought to foster group X's interests as well as its own. There is an obvious paradox here since it may not be in group Y's interests to inform group X who may use the information to harm them.

MacDonald's view of democratic society is wrong. As a member of a particular interest group democracy requires me to *tolerate* but not to actively promote interests which differ from my own.[3] If democracy as such does not require everyone to actively promote the interests of every social group, it does not ascribe to everyone as members of particular groups the right to know. It may be in my interests *as* a member of the local schools' parents association to know why pupils are being taught what they are, but if teachers *as* a group are not obliged to promote my interests I cannot have the right to know. Now of course, within particular democratic societies every group may hold the promotion of other groups' interests as an ideal for social living. But the point I want to make is that such an ideal is not a defining characteristic of democracy. The decision to release information about one group's activities to members of other interest groups can never be justified democratically on the grounds that people have an automatic right to know as members of particular interest groups.

The idea of democratic evaluation can only be salvaged if the notion of *public* as against *sectional* interests is restored in some way; in other words, if people have interests *as* members of the general public which are quite distinct from their interests *as* members of particular groups. I want to argue that they have, and that one can know what these are quite independently of any investigation of what people *think* is in the public interest.

MacDonald's difficulty stems from his assumption that pluralism is a basic presupposition of democratic life. Yet eighteenth century democracy was based on a view of society as unified in a knowledge of the common good.[4] It was because ordinary people were believed to be in a position to have such knowledge that they could be trusted to participate in the business of government. Government by the people does not presuppose the fact of pluralism. The latter is a problem for democracy rather than its source. It was in fact the emergence of liberalism as a political ethic which furnished a procedure for handling pluralism in a democratic context. Liberalism salvaged some idea of the common good in a pluralistic society by showing that since all groups desire to pursue their interests it is in everyone's interest to desire freedom from interference. *Freedom* was not simply in the interests of a particular group. It was in the interests of *all* members of society. And since everyone desires freedom it would be irrational for any person or group to pursue their interests at the expense of other people's. The principle of *equal liberty* defined 'the common good' or 'the public interest' in a liberal democracy. Rawls defines it as each person having 'an equal right to the most extensive liberty compatible with a like liberty for all'. On this principle people as members of the general public have the right to know if courses of action and policies result in inequalities of liberty. The emergence of liberal-socialism brought further refinements in the notion of the common good. These referred not so much to the equal freedoms of citizens – of personal conscience and thought, speech and assembly, etc. – but to social and economic inequalities. According to Rawls the principle covering these latter aspects is as follows:

> Social and economic inequalities are to be arranged so that they are both (a) reasonably expected to be to everyone's advantage, and (b) attached to positions and offices open to all.[6]

In other words justice does not require social and economic equality for its citizens but it does require *equality of opportunity* to secure social and economic advantages (i.e. status, income and wealth), and the distribution of these advantages to be in everyone's interests, albeit unequally.

Following Rawls I shall call the principle of 'equal liberty', and the principle of 'fair distribution of social and economic advantages' the *principles of justice*. Together they constitute a conception of the public interest which is not only compatible with the fact of pluralism but constitute a set of procedures for handling it. I want to argue, as Ernest House has recently, that *democratic evaluation* in education is a form of *social criticism* involving a critique of educational policies and courses of action in the light of principles such as these.[7] If information about such policies and actions is significant in the light of these principles then everyone has the right to know it as members of the public because it is in their interests in this capacity.

From the standpoint of democratic evaluation participants in educational situations have the right to privacy in matters which these two principles do not render matters of public concern.

The *democratic* evaluator cannot be a neutral broker transmitting information to different interest groups. His responsibility is to a single audience, the general public, and not a plurality of audiences. If this is so he must evaluate against those criteria which define 'the common good' or 'the public interest'. He cannot remain neutral on the question of information use. MacDonald is wrong in his assertion that democratic evaluation has no conception of 'information misuse'. The evaluator cannot escape responsibility for judgment against public criteria if he is to remain genuinely democratic.

I am aware that some may challenge me to justify the principles of justice as objective public criteria whose appropriateness is independent of what people happen to think of as 'the public interest'. This can be done I think in the way Rawls suggests.[8] He asks us to imagine a number of rational and mutually self-interested persons in an 'original position' of equal liberty in which people lack certain information about their social positions, talents and abilities. The 'original position' is a construct of a hypothetical situation of equal liberty in which people are ignorant of their different native endowments and the social positions attached to them. If asked to 'propose and acknowledge before one another general principles applicable to their common institutions as standards by which their complaints against these institutions are to be judged' people must, Rawls argues, agree that the two principles of justice express standards 'in accordance with which each person is willing to have his interests limited on the supposition that the interests of others will be limited in the same way'. In other words freed from the bias which a knowledge of social position and native endowments brings all men would recognise these principles as the most reasonable basis for organising their social life together.

If one accepts Rawls's line of thinking here then the principles of justice define the public interest not because they are accepted by everyone as members of the public but because they are the principles which everyone would accept in a situation where they are free from bias.

For the rest of this paper I will attempt to demonstrate that the conception of democratic evaluation I have constructed out of a critique of MacDonald's SAFARI[9] ethic provides a way out of a typical dilemma this ethic has posed for evaluators.

In his paper 'An adversary's account of SAFARI's "Ethics of case study" '[10] David Jenkins argued that MacDonald's SAFARI project does not specify an ethically consistent set of procedures at all, but two ethically inconsistent procedures which together form part of an overall manipulative strategy for securing the release of highly sensitive data. The strategy involves two moves. The first is that of securing access to sensitive data, via observation and interview, by promising confidentiality to participants (the ethics of access). Since confidentiality is promised, release can only be secured later by getting participants to release the evaluator from his promise. The second move involves the evaluator *negotiating* the release of data with participants, which by implication involves releasing him in part, from his original promise (the ethics of release). While the concept of *confidentiality* defines the ethics of access (move one), that of *negotiation* defines the ethics of release (move two). Jenkins argues that the difference between the two procedures lies in the power relations between the evaluator and the participant. Within the confidentiality ethic the power of the evaluator to use information is restricted. But within the negotiation ethic all kinds of manipulative devices, which restrict the participants' control over the data and increase the evaluator's control, become permissible. Jenkins refers to such standard devices as 'the manipulation of time scales' and that of 'representing the task as "improving" an account and thereby deflecting attention from the fact of release to its form'.

The thesis that within SAFARI's 'ethic' we have two ethically inconsistent procedures receives some practical support from Helen Simons. In her paper 'Building a social contract: negotiation, participation and portrayal in condensed field research'[11], she explores the practical dilemma of both giving participants control over data and negotiating its release within the context of condensed field work. She does not claim, as Jenkins does, that 'giving control' and 'negotiating release' are always ethically inconsistent. But she does claim that a practical dilemma exists within the time constraints of condensed field work. She argues that within these limits the evaluator is compelled to override the participant's right of control for the sake of securing release. Only an increase in the time scale allowed for negotiation might resolve the dilemma of making negotiation ethically consistent with control.

In my view the dilemma does not merely arise from practical constraints on the reconciliation of the two ethical procedures. It arises from the fact that SAFARI's procedures are based on two inconsistent ethical points of view. Jenkins is right, but he fails to characterise and explain the inconsistency adequately.

MacDonald argues that the key justificatory concept of democratic evaluation is 'the right to know'. However, while this right ethically justifies *negotiation as a procedure* it does not, I believe, *ethically* justify *promising confidentiality*. The key justificatory concept for the latter is 'the right to privacy'. This concept is conveniently ignored by MacDonald in his description of the key concepts of democratic evaluation and yet it is the only grounds against which *promising confidentiality* can be *ethically* rather than merely *technically* justified. If 'the right to know' is the sole justificatory concept as MacDonald claims then 'promising confidentiality 'lacks real ethical intent and becomes as Jenkins suggests, a manipulative, technical, device rather than an ethical stance. Perhaps in the SAFARI project we have no genuine ethic of access at all. All can be reduced to the ethics of release based on the right to know. However, if 'the right to confidentiality' expresses genuine ethical intent then SAFARI's (ethic) is indeed a case of moral schizophrenia, because it will assume that in relation to the same situation participants can have both the right to privacy and their 'audiences' the right to know. It is an irrational 'ethic' which cannot but fail to pose the kind of practical dilemma posed by Helen Simons's suggestion that the practical dilemma between 'giving control' and 'negotiation' might be resolved through extending the time scale for negotiation has a point. However, it will not resolve the underlying cause of the practical dilemma since this stems from the inconsistent beliefs of the evaluator. But it can alleviate some of the practical consequences of this condition. The participant may decide to release the evaluator from his promise of confidentiality before he is forced to break it by a thousand and one subtle 'negotiating' methods. This enables the evaluator to escape from the task of having to face the ethically inconsistent nature of his procedures.

Helen Simons's practical dilemma dissolves if we understand 'confidentiality' and 'negotiation' to define procedures which are applicable to different situations. The confidentiality ethic is appropriate in those situations where participants have the right to privacy and the negotiation ethic is appropriate in those situations where people have the right to know. The problem with MacDonald's SAFARI ethic is its dogmatic character. It is presumed as self-evident that participants always have the right to privacy and their 'audiences' the right to know. I want to argue that participants may be presumed to have the right to privacy unless their activities impinge on the public interest. In which case people as members of the public have the right to know and participants lose their right to privacy. When applied correctly no ethical inconsistency between these rights is involved because they apply to different situations.

Democratic evaluation appropriately involves an appraisal of the extent to which the presumption of privacy is justified. It certainly involves being taken into participants' confidence but always on the understanding that the promise of confidentiality is conditional upon them warranting the right to privacy in the light of the principles of justice. If they cannot justify their possession of this right, if their activities clearly infringe the principles of justice, then they are obliged to tell the truth about their activities to members of the public who now warrant the right to know. When an evaluator gains access to evidence which at least throws reasonable doubt on participants' rights to privacy the situation changes. Participants can no longer be presumed to possess that right. Evidence renders it at least problematic. The negotiation ethic should now supersede the confidentiality ethic. This involves evaluator and participants together assembling evidence and counter-evidence in the light of the principles of justice. The results of such negotiations need not depend on the power relations between evaluator and participants as they do in MacDonald's SAFARI 'ethic'. This is because the *negotiation* ethic is defined and governed by impartial principles of justice which can serve to establish a measure of agreement as to whether the public have the right to know or not. Any evidence of coercion constitutes a breakdown of this negotiation ethic. Checks on coercion and manipulation by an evaluator might be introduced in the form of (a) the use of observers and (b) the right of participants to seek 'a second opinion'.

I hope I have done enough to show that the contradiction in MacDonald's SAFARI ethic stems from a dogmatic *a priori* assertion of ethical rights. Once the task of democratic evaluation is construed as an appraisal of 'rights' in relation to a particular policy or course of action the tension between the right to know and the right to privacy disappears.

I should also have made it obvious that such an appraisal cannot be conducted without substantive criteria which express some conception of what constitutes 'the public interest' or 'the common good'. Both 'the right to know' and 'the right to privacy' can only be made intelligible in terms of such a conception. People have a right to privacy as members of a particular interest group because it is a guarantee of non-interference in their freedom to pursue their interests without interference. But this latter right of freedom of action only holds if it is compatible with those principles of justice which constitute the common good e.g. such as that of 'equal liberty'. Similarly people have 'the right to know' as members of the public if the pursuit of sectional interests infringes the principles of justice. MacDonald's SAFARI ethic can only escape internal inconsistency if it puts judgment back into evaluation.

One important implication of what I have said is that the public sponsors of evaluation have no right to dogmatically demand the release of evaluation reports. If the evaluator secures the confidence of participants and finds no evidence which is relevant to the public interest he is ethically bound to respect the participants' rights to privacy.

This essay is not just a product of 'armchair philosophy'. It developed from an initial attempt to clarify certain problems I experienced in trying to follow SAFARI procedures. These were:

1 Some of my interviewees agreed to release interview data to other staff which retrospectively I feel may not have been in their interests as members of staff in the school and which I ought to have kept confidential in spite of their willingness after 'negotiation' to release it.

2 One of my interviewees gave me confidential information which suggested that certain constraints were limiting her freedom to exercise her responsibilities to others within the school. I felt it was in her interests that this information should be released to other staff as soon as possible.

In other words I found myself intuitively making assessments about whether the others had the right to know and whether interviewees had the right to privacy. I realised that I was operating intuitively with certain criteria of information misuse; criteria which MacDonald claims the evaluator should not possess.

The fact that SAFARI procedures as I interpreted them restricted my control over use meant in practice that I had to deny my own intuitions. The inner conflict was intensified later by various letters from interviewees suggesting that the release of data I had negotiated between members of the interview group had resulted in harmful consequences for at least some members of that group.

In spite of the fact that the SAFARI ethic professed to give participants control over the data, the SAFARI worker will interpret it as biased in favour of open access to data and 'the right to know'. In other words he will tend if he follows the ethic to resolve the contradiction in favour of open access. My experience began to convince me that this preference for openness was wrong. I became even more convinced after reading House's 'Justice in evaluation'[12] and the final chapter of Dietrich Bonhoeffer's *Ethics*.[13] In this chapter Bonhoeffer tried to grapple with the problem of 'what is meant by "telling the truth"?' He argues that 'telling the truth' is not simply a matter of telling what one knows regardless of the situation. The following passage hit me particularly hard in the light of my experience as a SAFARI worker:

> It is only the cynic who claims 'to speak the truth' at all times and in all places to all men in the same way, but who, in fact, displays a lifeless image of the truth. He dons the halo of the fanatical devotee of truth who can make no allowance for human weakness, but, in fact, he is destroying the living truth between men. He wounds shame, desecrates mystery, breaks confidence, betrays the community in which he lives, and laughs arrogantly at the devastation he has wrought and at the human weakness which 'cannot bear the truth'. He says truth is destructive and demands its victims; and he feels like a god above these feeble creatures . . .

Now of course, it is this sort of attitude which SAFARI rhetoric condemns. Nevertheless, in its refusal to sanction any evaluation control over information use, it allows cynics freedom to destroy. And in its claim that people as members of particular 'interest' groups rather than as members of the public have 'the right to know' it positively supports this cynical stance, even when at the same time it schizophrenically supports participants' rights of privacy. But as Helen Simons has pointed out the inner contradictions will tend in fact to be resolved by pressuring for 'open access'.

In his chapter, Bonhoeffer argues that what constitutes truthful speech depends on the question:

> Whether and in what way a man is entitled to demand truthful speech of others . . . If my utterance is to be truthful it must in each case be different according to whom I am addressing, who is questioning me, and what I am speaking

about. The truthful word is not in itself constant; it is as much alive as life itself. If it is detached from life and from its reference to the concrete other man, if 'the truth is told' without taking into account to whom it is addressed, then this truth has only the appearance of truth, but it lacks its essential character.

In this essay I have only tried to explore Bonhoeffer's question at the interface between teachers and other groups in society. But it also needs to be explored in terms of intra-professional relations. For example, what sorts of things does a person in the role of headteacher have the right to know about the activities of his staff or the latter as teachers about the activities of individual staff? Here the criteria which ought to govern access to intra-professional information may be specifically educational rather than social and are perhaps more relevant to the early stages of case study work in schools when questions of intra-professional access to information are at stake. The problems I cited in relation to my own work pose such questions and could perhaps only be resolved by clarifying *educational*, rather than public, criteria for controlling information flow within educational institutions.

There may indeed be two distinct kinds of evaluation in education. One assesses people's right to know as members of the public (*social evaluation* of education) and the other assesses people's right to know as members of educational institutions (*educational evaluation*). Educational evaluation has a professional rather than a public audience and can be carried out independently. However, educational evaluation may be necessary if not a sufficient condition of social evaluation. In the process of determining whether or not the public have the right to know the evaluator has to assess the extent to which individual members of educational institutions have the right to know as educators about other members' activities. This means that the contents of a case study released for intra-professional inspection should differ from the contents of a case study released for public inspection.

Since 'telling the truth' is not context free what is appropriately said to people as fellow educators will differ from what is appropriately said to people as members of the public. Consequently, I am currently engaged in the laborious process of rewriting my SAFARI case study with a view to negotiating its public release.

References and Notes

1 Barry MacDonald, 'Evaluation and the control of education', in D. Tawney (ed.), *Curriculum Evaluation Today: Trends and Implications*, Schools Council, Research Studies, MacMillan, 1976.
2 John Elliott, 'The SAFARI solipsists', *Innovation, Evaluation, Research and the Problem of Control – some interim papers*, Centre for Applied Research in Education, University of East Anglia 1974.
3 See Pat White's remarks in her 'Education, democracy and the public interest', *Pro. Phil. of Ed. Soc. of Gt. Britain*, Vol V, No. 1., Jan. 1971, Basil Blackwell, Oxford.

4 Joseph Schumpeter's exposition of the classical doctrine of democracy in 'Two concepts of democracy', in Anthony Quinton (ed.), *Political Philosophy*, Oxford Readings in Philosophy, Oxford University Press, 1967.

5 John Rawls, 'The sense of justice', in Joel Feinberg (ed.), *Moral Concepts*, Oxford Readings in Philosophy, Oxford University Press, 1969, Ch. X.

6 John Rawls, *A Theory of Justice*, Oxford University Press, 1972. This second principle has been slightly reformulated since it was originally stated in 'The sense of justice'.

7 Ernest House, 'Justice in evaluation' mimeo, Centre for Instructional Res. and Curriculum, University of Illinois, Urbana-Champagne. In this paper House also explores the implications of Rawls's 'Theory of justice' for educational evaluation.

8 See op. cit. 5.

9 SAFARI is an investigation of the 'medium term' effects of several recently concluded curriculum development projects on the curriculum of the British Secondary School. It is staffed by Barry MacDonald (Director) and Rob Walker.

10 David Jenkins, mimeo, New University of Ulster, Coleraine, Northern Ireland.

11 Simons, H. 'Building a social contract: negotiation and participation in condensed field research', in N. Norris (ed.), *Theory in Practice*, SAFARI papers 2, Norwich, CARE, 1977.

12 See op. cit. 7.

13 Dietrich Bonhoeffer, *Ethics*, The Fontana Library of Theology and Philosophy, Collins, 1964. Part V.

Bread and Dreams or Bread and Circuses? A Critique of 'Case Study' Research in Education

P. Atkinson and S. Delamont

The 'SAFARI approach' . . . is less a methodology than a set of ethical principles translated as procedures for the design and conduct of research/evaluation
projects.

(Walker, 1981, p. 206)

It was in (the SAFARI Project) that MacDonald and Walker, along with other
colleagues, developed research designs which, for relatively low expenditure of
resources, allowed a high degree of penetration normally associated with
expensive and lengthy ethnographic studies.

(Kushner, writing in *Bread and Dreams*, 1982, p. 258)

The two quotes from researchers based at CARE (Centre for Applied
Research in Education, University of East Anglia) encapsulate the topics
which we address in this paper.[1] Starting from the position of committed
practitioners of interpretive research methods, particularly ethnography, in
this paper we draw attention to three major problems in the methodology
espoused by CARE, and its linked organizations in the USA and Australia.
The paper is divided into three sections: an introductory part where the
terms are defined; followed by sections on the inadequacies of methodology;
the contradictions in invocations of 'evaluation', 'naturalism', and 'democracy' in research; and the interrelations of generalization, comparison and
theorizing in case study. Planned educational change and curriculum innovation (*cf.* Stenhouse, 1975 and 1979) have become 'big business' and the
evaluation of educational programmes has likewise been a growth area.
With the development of this field of expertise and its professionalization,

debate concerning appropriate research techniques and objectives has also grown. It is to this debate – or at least to one corner of it – that our paper is addressed. Our own research in this area (Howe and Delamont, 1973; Atkinson and Shone, 1982) was closest in style to a variety of educational evaluation variously known as 'illuminative', 'naturalistic', 'holistic', 'responsive' or 'case-study' research. On the other hand, there are many aspects of the way in which such research has been conducted and justified with which we take issue. There are certainly other approaches to educational research with which we are even less in sympathy, but commentary on those is beyond the scope of this paper. It is precisely because our own methodological commitments and perspectives are similar to those of the illuminative and case-study researchers that we can offer an informed critique of what remains a contentious area in educational research.

Defining Terms: Our and Theirs

Although an early and influential paper in the field referred to 'illuminative' evaluation (Parlett and Hamilton, 1972), in recent years the term 'case study' has gained much greater currency, and we shall use the latter term to cover the general area. For reasons which we shall discuss at greater length below, it is hard to provide any hard-and-fast definition of 'case study' and related approaches to educational evaluation. But there is a number of connotations, which represent the shared presuppositions and preoccupations of the network or invisible college of its practitioners. (The college is rendered visible in various edited collections of papers and conference proceedings, to which reference will be made: it is located in various institutional settings, of which CARE is the major British centre.)

In general terms, the approach denies the applicability of so-called 'scientific' methods of inquiry, as exemplified for instance in experimental or quasi-experimental research designs. It rests on the belief that the innovation to be examined cannot be treated simply as a set of objectives, or as a variable or variables to be measured. Innovations 'on paper' may be transformed radically, in the course of their actual implementation. The 'reality' to be investigated, then, is a complex social reality of everyday life in institutional settings. The emphasis is firmly – even exclusively – on 'process' rather than 'product' or outcomes (*cf.* Simons, 1981). Simons provides a helpful characterization of the style:

> Studies of the process of learning and schooling will tend to be descriptive/ analytic, particular, small scale. They will record events in progress, document observations and draw on the judgments and perspectives of participants in the process – teachers, pupils, heads – in coming to understand observations and events in a specific context. Close description both of practice and the social

context is an important part of the study. Such descriptions provide opportunities for interpretations that elude other models of assessment or evaluation based on assumptions of comparability and elimination of variation. Such descriptions also provide opportunities for more of the complexity of educational experience to be grasped and articulated.

(Simons, 1981, p. 120)

The root metaphor of such a viewpoint is one of exploration and discovery. Rather than investigating the 'official reality' of the promoters of innovation, and confining attention to the stated objectives of the innovation itself, case-study or illuminative evaluators pay full attention to the unofficial and unforeseen aspects of the innovation and its implementation. Those who advocate the use of 'behavioural objectives' sometimes refer to them as necessary 'route-maps' to direct the evaluator; the practitioners of case-study would be more likely to point out that there always remains a good deal of uncharted territory. The task of evaluators, then, may not be that of retracing a predetermined route, but more akin to that of a 'search-party'.

It is remarkably difficult to provide anything approaching a definitive account of case-study approaches to educational evaluation. There is undoubtedly a package of approaches to which case-study workers would generally adhere, and we believe our remarks above have provided a faithful – if brief and sketchy – characterization of the main articles of faith. But close inspection of the authors' statements reveals the elusiveness of the notion itself.

In the first place, it has proved extraordinarily difficult for the practitioners themselves to furnish an adequate definition of their own enterprise. Indeed, on the basis of their own pronouncements, case-study evaluation would appear to be a 'paradigm' with none of the requisites of a paradigm – agreed subject-matter, methods, theories or exemplars. Given this, it is hardly surprising that such definitions that do appear are quite extraordinarily imprecise. A widely-quoted definition of case-study is that it is 'the study of an instance in action', and 'the study of a bounded system' (*cf.* Adelman, Jenkins and Kemmis, 1980). Such definitions (if they deserve the term) seem to be of symbolic value to the research network of devotees precisely insofar as they are vacuous and commit its members to remarkably little.

Confusion in this area is compounded when it is recognized that the unit of analysis ('case') can, in practice, mean just about anything:

The case need not be a person or enterprise. It can be whatever 'bounded system' (to use Louis Smith's term) that is of interest. An institution, a program, a responsibility, a collection, or a population can be the case.

(Stake, 1980, p. 64)

Stake goes on to protest that 'this is not to trivialize the notion of "case" . . .', but it certainly does render it so general and vague as to be of next to no methodological value. Likewise, the notion of a 'bounded system' is unhelpful. Naturally occurring social 'systems' are not self-evidently 'bounded'. Their boundaries are matters of *construction*, by actors and analysts. What counts as a 'case' is therefore much more problematic than 'case-study' researchers seem to allow for. The same is true of the even more vague idea of 'an instance in action'. Cases and instances are recognizable only as cases or instances of something, and the range of potentially relevant dimensions or criteria is immense. It is therefore quite meaningless for authors of the case-study persuasion to write as if the world were populated by 'cases' whose status and existence were independent of methodological and theoretical concerns.

To some extent, the imprecision of which this is but an example is a reflection of the origins of the case-study movement. From the earliest formulations, such as that by Parlett and Hamilton (1972), 'illuminative evaluation' (as they called it) was portrayed as much in negative terms as its positive attributes. That is, the authors were as keen to establish what they were *not*, and to establish an oppositional heterodoxy, as they were to provide a definitive account of their own position. This trend has continued in later publications emanating from the group, the members of which often characterize their work in terms of difference from other approaches to research. Parlett and Hamilton, for instance, distinguished their approach from the 'agricultural-botanical' paradigm, which they saw as the dominant model, based on the methods of field-experiments, psychometrics and the like. The movement has continued to identify itself in terms of oppositional and 'alternative' approaches, the proponents portraying themselves as renegade, heretical enfants terribles: on occasion they display the self-satisfaction of the heretical enthusiast.

Unfortunately, in the construction of this oppositional stance, the work of theoretical and methodological development has been neglected. In the early papers, appeals were made to traditions such as social anthropology as exemplars for the new paradigm. But as time has gone by, it has become apparent that for the most part case-study evaluators are content to invoke anthropology in a ritualized fashion. It has a totemic or fetishistic significance. But it is not apparent that the literature of case-study evaluation has been significantly affected by its authors' reading of British or American social/cultural anthropologists. (Some cultural anthropologists have become personally involved, and some individual authors, such as Louis Smith and Harry Wolcott must be exempt from this criticism.)

In short, precisely because of the failure of the researchers we are discussing to define their terms, we have difficulty in defining ours. Briefly we are criticizing a body of work which can be traced from the evaluation of the Humanities Curriculum Project and the Nuffield Resources for Learning Project, through UNCAL and SAFARI, to CARGO and *Bread and Dreams* (see Appendix and Walker, 1982 for details of these acronyms). Our criticisms apply to other projects conducted in the same general framework, notably Stake and Easley (1978) but we are concentrating on the work associated with MacDonald, Walker, Jenkins, Kushner, Norris and Stenhouse.

Our first area of criticism concerns methodology: or lack of it!

The Methodological Cop-Out

To some extent, the work of case-study practitioners has developed in parallel with more general scholarly interest in everyday life in schools and classrooms, and it draws eclectically on similar research methods. The methodology is likely to be based primarily on meaning-centred, qualitative data collection and analysis. Evaluation of this sort is not normally committed to any form of methodological purism (except in a negative sense, since some methods and research designs are ruled out). Rather, an eclectic approach is advocated, sometimes justified by appeal to between-method 'triangulation' (*cf.* Denzin, 1970; Webb *et al.*, 1966):

> In general, the techniques for collecting information for a case study are held in common with a wider tradition of sociological and anthropological fieldwork. Case study methodology is eclectic, although techniques and procedures in common use include observation (participant and non-participant), interview (conducted, with varying degrees of structure), audio-visual recording, field-note-taking, document collection, and the negotiation of products (for example discussing the accuracy of an account with those observed).
>
> (Adelman, Jenkins and Kemmis, 1980, pp. 48–49)

Appeal may also be made to the discovery of 'grounded theory' as advocated by Glaser and Strauss (1967) – see, for instance, Hamilton (1980, p. 81).

Case-study researchers protest that case-study methods are not thought of as a soft option. Hamilton (1980), for example, begins his paper by an explicit denial:

> Case study research is sometimes considered an immature science. It is claimed, for instance, that as an apparently non-technical mode of inquiry it is a suitable 'shallow end' activity for the statistically naive newcomer to educational research.
>
> This paper challenges such a viewpoint . . .
>
> (Hamilton, 1980, p. 78)

Nonetheless, such a message would appear to be implicit in the programmatic statements of many of the authors. Methodological sophistication is not a marked characteristic of the genre. Indeed, methodological and theoretical expertise may even be denied explicitly by particular advocates of the approach, as in Walker's (1981) remark with which we opened the paper.

As we have indicated, the methodological commitments are often adumbrated in a negative sense: the title of one collection of papers, *Beyond the Numbers Game* (Hamilton, *et al.*, [Eds.] 1977) captures this nicely. This negativity leaves little room for positive commitments, for instance:

> Case studies should not be equated with observational studies, participant or otherwise
>
> Case studies are not simply pre-experimental . . .
>
> 'Case study' is not the name for a standard methodological package . . .
> (Adelman, Jenkins and Kemmis, 1980, p. 48)

On the other hand, it is true to say that in practice a recognizable method-ological commitment is discernible, which corresponds fairly well to that connoted by the *ethnographic* approach. In the context of educational research generally, ethnographic research is a relatively new phenomenon, and has enjoyed something of a boom (*cf.* Delamont, 1984), although it is now a good deal less innovative than it was when Parlett and Hamilton first published their account. But in advocating a (vaguely) ethnographic approach, the case-study writers often seem in danger of reinventing the wheel: what is worse, they seem rather slapdash wheelwrights at that.

The published accounts betray alarmingly little acquaintance with the fact that qualitative and documentary methods have been in use by sociologists and anthropologists for many years, and – more significantly – that there has been a great deal of reflection and writing on the methodology of research of this sort. Shipman (1981) has drawn attention to such short-comings in the pages of what he calls 'parvenu evaluation'. He points out that 'the curriculum is but one subject for study through established research methods' (p. 111), and the claim for bespoke, supposedly innovative meth-ods in fact merely leads to the neglect of existing 'mainstream' research methods literature:

> Illuminative evaluation often seems . . . innocent of fifty years of debate within social science. Malinowski detailed the pros and cons of participant observation in 1922, a year after Anderson published his observational study of hobos in Chicago. The Chicago school was particularly active in using such methods and Thrasher published the first detailed account of the approach in 1928, based on a decade of work in the field. Discussing evaluation within education can be depressing because of the divorce from this long tradition within social science. It is possible to lecture and research in curriculum evalu-ation without realising that the tradition is there for us.
> (Shipman, 1981, p. 113)

In a similar vein, Spindler has written of the dangers inherent in the sudden fashion for ethnographic research in educational settings:

> To those of us who have long struggled to persuade educators that ethnographic studies would help illuminate the educational process and fellow

scientists that they should undertake ethnographic studies of this process, the
sudden wave of popularity is exhilarating. It is also alarming. Inevitably, any
movement that rapidly acquires many followers has some of the qualities of a
fad, and this is true of educational ethnography. It is not surprising that some
work called 'ethnography' is marked by obscurity of purpose, lax relationships
between concepts and observation, indifferent or absent conceptual structure
and theory, weak implementation of research method, confusion about
whether there should be hypotheses and, if so, how they should be tested,
confusion about whether quantitative methods can be relevant, unrealistic
expectations about the virtues of 'ethnographic' evaluation, and so forth.

(Spindler, 1982, pp. 1–2)

The dangers and pitfalls of which Spindler writes are all too obviously
present in the conduct and reporting of case-study evaluation.

In *Bread and Dreams*, for example, Kushner (1983, p. 258) claims that: 'A
combination of issues focusing intensive interviewing, selective observation
and the negotiation of accounts with participants made it possible to complete a school case-study on a base of seven days fieldwork'. The reader
wishing to pursue this extravagant claim is referred to Simons (1980): 'the
definitive collection of writings'. Simons (1980) contains little in the way of
methodological discussion or reflexivity. It is our contention that the case
study research tradition is seriously deficient due to both inadequate methods and a lack of methodological self-awareness.

The methodological self-awareness we are referring to here would not
imply a radical doubt over the essential purpose and value of ethnographic
work. On the contrary, it would recognize its value and importance even
more. It would treat the methods seriously, rather than adopting the essentially philistine attitude that 'anyone can do it'. This introduces our next
concern, the related issues of research, evaluation, 'democracy', and
naturalism.

Research, Evaluation, Democracy and Naturalism

We have called the case-study workers anti-intellectual and objected to their
lack of scholarship. This attitude may be justified, as in MacDonald (1974)
by the insistence on a basic difference between 'research' and 'evaluation'.
Thus the professional evaluator may simultaneously be invested with special
insight and experience on the one hand, and absolved from the theoretical
and methodological constraints of the 'researcher'. The distinction is
spurious. MacDonald bases his account on a crudely stereotyped distinction
between the 'pure' academic and the applied evaluator. He quite absurdly,
for instance, claims that academic researchers are insensitive to the social
and political context of their research, in contrast to 'evaluators'. This is the
product of a rhetoric of self-justification and congratulation on MacDonald's

part, rather than a reflection of research practice. No social or educational research is 'pure' in that sense; nor can 'applied' research escape the requirements of rigour and critical reflection.

It is true that this anti-intellectual or anti-academic tenor to such evaluation does, in various quarters, reflect a deliberate commitment on the part of the researchers. For some research workers, the task of evaluation is essentially a collaborative one, in which the evaluators and the practitioners (for example, the teachers) work together in generating shared perspectives, in reorganizing and accounting for the problems they encounter and so on. Thought of from this point of view the research process may be classed as a 'democratic' exercise. At the same time it may be suggested that a concern for 'theory' or 'methods' should be deprecated: it is seen as an essentially mystificatory exercise, in which 'experts' parade their superiority over practitioners. Expertise is seen as divisive, in contrast to the democratic ideal of collaborative partnership.

Walker, one of the leading representatives of the CARE tradition, is explicit about the 'democratic' implications of his own commitment to 'naturalistic' research. The research begins and ends within the everyday, 'natural attitude' of teachers, pupils and other participants:

> First it assumes that the research will start from the natural language of description of 'natural' observers and attempt to remain as close to them as possible. This is to say much more than that the researcher must simply avoid jargon and attempt to write lucidly . . .

> Second, it assumes that research will remain as close as possible to the organizational constraints facing 'natural' observers . . .

> Third, it assumes research will remain as close as possible to the kinds of resources normally available to 'natural' observers.
>
> (Walker, 1974, pp. 25–26)

The 'natural' observers Walker has in mind here would be teachers, pupils, teacher educators and advisors and inspectors. They all have practical interests and skills in observing, participating in and understanding classroom life.

There is thus an emphasis upon research as an essentially vernacular or demotic undertaking. Now it is perfectly true that ethnographic research explicitly rests upon the homology between everyday life and the methods used to study it. But that is not tantamount to an identity between the practical concerns of social actors and the theoretical concerns of sociological or anthropological analysis. Walker maintains that case-study work 'would start with, and remain close to, the commonsense knowledge of the practitioner . . .' In itself, that aim is hardly contentious. All ethnography must concern itself with subjects' common sense. But that is not in itself an argument for undertaking commonsense investigations. Quite the reverse: the successful unravelling and explication of mundane beliefs and actions demand the suspension of common sense, not its uncritical endorsement.

It is worth noting in passing that Walker's appeal to 'natural' observers contains some special pleading. He constructs the 'natural' observer as a sort of primitive innocent, whose natural state corresponds remarkably with Walker's preferred approach to research. For instance, part of the section referred to above continues in the following way:

> . . . it assumes research will remain as close as possible to the kinds of resources normally available to 'natural' observers. Incidentally, this may not imply 'simplicity' of technique since many practitioners can now obtain access to video-taped cctv but may find even small scale testing or survey programmes beyond their scope.
>
> (*ibid.*, p. 26)

There seems absolutely no reason to suppose (a) that, say, small-scale survey research is actually beyond the resources of practitioners, or that the administration of tests is not feasible for them: many in-service B.Ed. and M.Ed. dissertations attest to the contrary; (b) that the use and understanding of such techniques is beyond their commonsense understanding, even if they do not actually use them. We see no reason to suppose that a grasp of elementary research techniques of a 'traditional' sort is beyond the ken of all those involved in educational practice.

While Walker's pronouncements are intended to be 'democratic' in their effect, we believe their implications to be very different. It is intended to demystify the activities of research workers, to eliminate the sense of an elite and remote cadre of evaluation experts. MacDonald (for example, 1974) has also promoted a view of 'democratic' evaluation, contrasting it with what he refers to as 'bureaucratic' and 'autocratic' modes respectively. His stance derives from an explicitly political and ethical commitment to 'an informed citizenry': 'the evaluator acts as a broker in exchanges of information between groups who want knowledge of each other' (1974, p. 15). As he himself puts it, 'The key justificatory concept is "the right to know" ' (p. 18).

Smith *et al* (1981) have produced a typology of approaches to evaluation, based on MacDonald's position, and that of Lindblom and Cohen (1979), including the 'client/democratic' stance, which they characterize in this way:

> . . . the subjects or participants in the study have final control over entry, definition of problems, procedures, ownership, and release of data and interpretations, and so forth. They are the audience of the exercise. The negotiation process between the researcher/evaluator and the multiple individuals and subgroups involved in the program or activity is escalated in importance, focus, and time involvement. In an important sense, MacDonald is advocating political change in liberal, democratic, national states by exposing gaps between the realities of educational settings and the idealism most of us profess in our ideologies (p. 86).

It is evident, therefore, that contemporary case-study evaluation rests on two closely related presuppositions – appealing to a demotic naturalism and a democratic ethic. 'Naturalism' is invoked explicitly in numerous papers (for example, Kushner and Norris, 1980–81; Kemmis, 1980). Barton and Lawn (1980–81) have argued that the CARE version of 'naturalistic' inquiry and reportage is best understood as heir to the tradition of documentary social observation of which Mass Observation was a particularly pertinent exemplar. This tradition is an important one in British social thought, and the strengths of the CARE case study approach are its strengths. But the weaknesses are shared too. As Barton and Lawn argue, the commitment to naturalism does not remove problems of interpretation and theory, but can serve to mask them:

> We would also argue that if assumptions are not made explicit – that is, about the nature of society and the reflexive role of the individual – then the 'outsider', who may be a reader or researcher, is not encouraged to analyse critically or refute the view offered. It is offered as natural not evaluative (p. 21).

Case-study researchers explicitly draw upon models from naturalistic writing, including works of fiction, and may illustrate their own accounts with fictional accounts (*cf.* Walker, 1981). The critic will wish to point out that the most 'naturalistic' or 'realistic' literary account is the outcome of highly artful and conventional effort on the part of its maker. It is itself theory-laden:

> Naturalism in the novel, especially the novels of the late nineteenth century French school, used finely drawn individual characters, their real life settings and dialogue, to illustrate a thesis that was fashionable at the time – social Darwinism. The very fact that this thesis was part of the social norms of its audience probably made the novels 'feel' more naturalistic – they expected the situations to be like that. In retrospect, the detail and the observation seem at the mercy of the implicit thesis.
>
> (Barton and Lawn, 1980–81, p. 21)

Case-study evaluators are by no means alone in promoting a 'naturalistic' style with insufficient attention to its own conventional character (*cf.* Atkinson, 1982). Those who are responsible for the production of written accounts certainly should be aware of the nature of description and narration, as Walker (1981) advocates. But that is not an argument for substituting literary style for theory or method. And while the practitioners may reject epistemological orthodoxy or uniformity, there is a remarkable uniformity of style to their products. Rather than the straightforward, vernacular craft it is often claimed, case-study is a highly artful enterprise.

While we recognize the attractions in the 'democratic' argument, we dissent from the implications drawn from it. A denial of theory and method is, we believe, a denial of responsibility – of responsibility for one's research activities and conclusions. It suggests the paradox of a group of 'experts' in evaluation, part of whose stock in trade consists of a denial of expertise. It is clear, however, that they do have 'expertise': they do operate with distinctive methods and assumptions and the studies they undertake have clearly recognizable characteristics. A refusal to treat seriously issues of method is, we repeat, a denial of responsibility rather than a tenable position on the matter of evaluation.

It should be clear that we believe that in the context of case-study research a concern for ethics too often supplants equally important issues of theory and method. It is not our intention in the rest of this paper to attempt to remedy all the conceptual shortcomings of this self-proclaimed 'paradigm'. We shall concentrate on a restricted number of muddles. These are all concerned with the nature of the 'particular' and the 'general'. Here the character of case-study research is clearly exemplified, and the confusions reveal some of the methodological limits of the approach.

Generalization, Comparison and Theorizing

Our final themes are those of generalizing, comparing and theorizing. The proponents of case-study research often distinguish their enterprise from other research styles and approaches through a stress upon the unique, the particular, the 'instance'. The title of one of the edited collections encapsulates this: *The Science of the Singular* (Simons, [Ed.] 1980). We wish to argue that in their approach to 'cases', the authors are profoundly mistaken.

The paper by Hamilton (1980), from which the 'science of the singular' aphorism derives, represents a relatively sophisticated and well-informed defence of the case-study position. It is, however, flawed. Like too many statements deriving from this research network, it rests too glibly on crude stereotypes of research traditions: strangely – in the light of the apparent rejection of methodological orthodoxy – it insists on an extreme version of qualitative research and a thoroughgoing rejection of alternative approaches. The characterization of qualitative, ethnographic research is so extreme as to deviate from positions adhered to by most sociologists and anthropologists (though their disciplines are invoked).

Hamilton rests his argument on a series of contrasts between case-study and survey – proposing the latter as essentially positivist. Although it is not possible to rehearse all the counter-arguments here, it must be objected that the supposed opposition between 'naturalism' and 'positivism' is inadequate (*cf.* Hammersley and Atkinson, 1983), as is the assumption that survey research is to be equated with positivist assumptions (*cf.* Marsh, 1982).

The most contentious of Hamilton's distinctions concerns the nature of generalization and interpretation. It is claimed that survey research is concerned with generalization, and further, that this concern reflects a belief in the 'uniformity of nature'. Astonishingly, Hamilton maintains that survey researchers are so committed to such a belief that 'By this procedural logic (of the relation of a sample to a population) it is then quite acceptable to extrapolate from Scottish samples to US samples, from nineteenth century data to contemporary results, and so on' (Hamilton, 1980, p. 86). While sloppy reasoning of this sort no doubt takes place, we know of nothing in any formulation of 'positivist' social research remotely suggesting its legitimacy.

By the same token, it is suggested that 'generalization' is *not* a concern for the qualitative studies of particular institutions. The emphasis is all upon the unique characteristics of each, idiosyncratic 'case'. Referring to recent ethnographies of schools, Hamilton claims 'They treat each case as empirically distinct and, in contrast to survey analysis, do not automatically presume that different instances can be thrown together to form a homogeneous aggregate' (p. 79). Survey research does not 'automatically assume' that either, of course, and certainly does not 'throw together' instances in the insouciant way that phrase implies. On the other hand, qualitative research *does* aggregate 'instances'. Data are regularly collected into typologies, and at least an ordinal level of measurement is regularly invoked by fieldworkers in the claim that, say, things happen more or less frequently, are of more or less importance, are more or less disruptive and so on.

Likewise, it is simply not true that the traditions of qualitative research from which case-study research draws inspiration eschews generalization. We are certainly not dealing only with a series of self-contained, one-off studies which bear no systematic relationship to each other. The studies of social anthropologists, for instance, have consistently reflected the shared theories and methods of major schools and movements (such as structural-functionalism or culture-and-personality theory). The accumulated literature of anthropology represents the massively successful working-out of a number of related, evolving 'paradigms'. Anthropologists do document the particularities of given cultures and communities; but they do much more than that. The same can be said of relevant traditions in sociology, such as symbolic interactionism.

In fact, the development of ethnographic work in sociology and anthropology rests on a principle of *comparative* analysis. If studies are not explicitly developed into more general frameworks, then they will be doomed to remain isolated one-off affairs, with no sense of cumulative knowledge or developing theoretical insight. Regrettably, this failing of 'illuminators' renders their work a rather pale version of qualitative research. This is particularly noticeable in the extent to which their focus remains fixed on the particular research setting, with little attention to other educational settings, and practically none to social settings of other sorts. They neglect the insights which may be gained from similar ethnographic work in such institutions as hospitals, prisons, hostels, therapeutic communities, old peoples' homes and so on. Yet all these settings – as well as many others – exhibit the same general processes as the evaluator may wish to understand in an educational programme: they too may be marked by inter-professional conflict, by tension between staff and inmates, by competing definitions of the institutional goals, by upheavals consequent upon planned innovations and so on. If one is to adopt an essentially ethnographic approach to research, then the work will remain inadequate unless such comparative perspectives are employed (Delamont, 1981; Wolcott, 1981).

This point concerning comparative perspectives relates directly to the issue of the generalizability of such research and its 'findings'. The analytic approach to such studies should be conceived of in terms of *formal* concepts – or, as Lofland (1971) calls them, *generic* problems. These formal concepts are abstract, ideal-typical, notions which characterize features, problems and issues which may be common to a range of different concrete settings. A well known example of this sort of concept is Goffman's (1968) formulation of the 'total institution' which he uses to portray features which are common to a wide variety of apparently diverse organizations (mental hospitals, monasteries, military camps, etc.). Thus Goffman's primary analysis of the mental hospital is developed through explicit and implicit comparison with these other institutions, which are shown, in *formal* terms, to have common features.

The development of such formal concepts thus frees the researcher from the potential strait-jacket of restricting attention only to the particular setting directly available to study. Indeed, the emphasis is, if anything, reversed. Ethnographers in sociology have sometimes been taxed with the charge of devoting too much attention to 'trivial', 'exotic' or 'bizarre' settings of everyday life, but these settings are used to illustrate and display the *formal* properties of social life. As Rock (1979) puts it:

> The career of the high school teacher, the organization of a ward for tuberculosis patients, the moral history of the taxi-dancer, the career of a mental patient, and transactions between police and juvenile delinquents present materials for the dissection of elementary social forms. They are explored to illuminate a simple grammar of sociation, a grammar whose rules give order to the allocation of territorial rights, the programming of timetables, and the meeting of diverse groups. More important, it is a grammar which is intended to provide recipes for an understanding of the abstract properties of social life.

It is the case, we recognize, that evaluators are not primarily in the business of generating sociological or social psychological theory as such. Walker (1982, p. 200) says there is 'a general consensus amongst those in the field that even if theoretical progress is possible or desirable (both points being at issue), it will only emerge gradually as a residual accumulation . . .' But theory in this context is not a self-contained, de-contextualized activity. While the formal concepts are derived from concrete instances and settings, they are only recognizable, and are only realized in their concrete manifestations. There is a constant interplay between 'theory', 'method' and 'findings'. At the same time, if evaluators are unwilling to grapple with the formal concepts and theories, then their work is doomed to be little more than a series of one-off, self-contained reports, all of which return to 'square one', conceptually speaking.

Theory cannot be left to accumulate, any more than the issue of generalization can be avoided. Yet here, too, we find the writings of the case-study exponents confused.

Robert Stake (1980) has attempted to come to terms with the issue of generalization. His approach to the problem serves, we argue, further to highlight the weaknesses of a commitment to naturalistic case-study inquiry, as currently proposed. Stake's key concept is 'naturalistic generalization':

> What becomes useful understanding is a full and thorough knowledge of the particular, recognizing it also in new and foreign contexts.
>
> That knowledge is a form of generalization too, not scientific induction but *naturalistic generalization*, arrived at by recognizing the similarities of objects and issues in and out of context and by sensing the natural covariations of happenings. To generalize this way is to be both intuitive and empirical, and not idiotic.
>
> (Stake, 1980, pp. 68–69)

In some ways such a formulation seems similar to our own emphasis upon the importance of generic analytic categories. The stumbling block is that Stake repeatedly insists on the tacit, the experiential and the private. Likewise he repeatedly contrasts such notions with the 'scientific', 'propositional formulations' and the like. Again, his views parallel the well-worn distinction between 'science' or 'positivism' and 'naturalism'.

Stake suggests that what he calls naturalistic generalizations will be of more value to the users or consumers of research. He invokes Howard Becker:

> Sociologist Howard Becker spoke of an irreducible conflict between sociological perspective and the perspective of everyday life. Which is superior? It depends on the circumstance of course. For publishing in the sociological journals, the scientific perspective is better; but for reporting to lay audiences and for studying lay problems, the lay perspective will often be superior.

In these formulations, Stake confuses a number of issues. The way in which a study is *reported* (for example, to a 'lay' audience) should not be mistaken for a methodological principle in deriving and warranting knowledge. Likewise, tacit knowledge pervades all reasoning in the natural and social sciences. But that is no excuse for the failure to develop explicit formal analysis, as Stake advocates.

Furthermore, the appeal to 'naturalistic generalization' seems to pass on to the consumers of research the right and capacity to define what is to count as knowledge. This is comfortable for Stake if the hypothetical user can be constructed in such a way as to want and to appreciate 'naturalistic' inquiry, 'vicarious experience' and the like. As with MacDonald's 'democratic' ideal, it translates into research practice provided researcher and other participants operate within a morally consensual framework, or the researcher can impose his or her definition of what counts as evaluation.

Concluding Remarks

The criticisms we make here are not new or unique (Parsons, 1976; Shipman, 1981). We raised these issues with Parlett and Hamilton (1972) in 1971 and 1972, and have debated them with people from CARE since. In 1978 one of us wrote:

> Paradoxically, the relative shortcomings of the 'illuminative' approach mean that its proponents are, in the last analysis, as limited as the practitioners of the denigrated 'agricultural-botany'. Without an adequately formulated body of theory or methods, the illuminators have been, and will be, unable to progress and generate a coherent, cumulative research tradition. They cannot transcend the short-term practicalities of any given programme of curriculum innovation. They merely substitute one variety of atheoretical 'findings' – based mainly on observation and interview – for another – based mainly on test scores.
>
> (Delamont, 1978)

We see no reason to dissent from that verdict here.

Notes

1 The arguments in this paper have been discussed with a variety of colleagues since 1970. We have debated them with Clem Adelman, Len Barton, David Hamilton, Barry MacDonald, Malcolm Parlett, Bob Stake and Rob Walker and the late Lawrence Stenhouse in print and face to face. We gave versions of this paper at the 1981 conference of the SfAA in Edinburgh and the 1982 BERA conference at St. Andrews, and received useful feedback. We have both conducted evaluations of educational innovations (Howe and Delamont, 1973; Atkinson and Shone, 1982), and conducted fieldwork in educational institutions.

We are grateful to Mrs Mytle Robins for typing this version of our paper.

References

ADELMAN, C., KEMMIS, S. and JENKINS, D. (1980). 'Rethinking case study: notes from the second Cambridge conference', in Simons, H. (Ed.) – see below.

ATKINSON, P. (1979). *Research Design in Ethnographic Research*, Course DE304, Block 3, Unit 5, Milton Keynes, The Open University.
ATKINSON, P. (1982). 'Writing ethnography', in Helle, H.J. (Ed.) *Kultur und Institution*, Berlin, Dunker and Humblot.
ATKINSON, P. and SHONE, D. (1982). *Everyday Life in Two Industrial Training Units*, Köln, IFAPLAN.
BARTON, L. and LAWN, M. (1980/81). 'Back inside the whale' and 'Recording the natural world', *Interchange*, 3, 4, pp. 2–26.
DELAMONT, S. (1978). 'Sociology and the classroom', in Barton, L. and Meighan, R. (Eds.) *Sociological Interpretations of Schools and Classrooms*, Driffield, Yorks, Nafferton Books.
DELAMONT, S. (1981). 'All too familiar?', *Educational Analysis*, 3, 1, pp. 69–84.
DELAMONT, S. (Ed.) (1984). *Readings in Classroom Interaction*, London, Methuen.
DENZIN, N. (1970). *The Research Act*, Chicago, Aldine.
GOFFMAN, E. (1968). *Asylums*, Harmondsworth, Penguin.
GOFFMAN, E. (1971). *The Presentation of Self in Everyday Life*, Harmondsworth, Penguin.
HAMILTON, D. (1980). 'Some contrasting assumptions about case study research and survey analysis', in Simons, H. (Ed.) – see below.
HAMILTON, D. et al. (Eds.) (1977). *Beyond the Numbers Game*, London, Macmillan.
HAMMERSLEY, M. and ATKINSON, P. (1983). *Ethnography: Principles in Practice*, London, Tavistock.
HOWE, J.A.M. and DELAMONT, S. (1973). 'Pupils' answer to computer language', *Education in the North*, 10, pp. 73–78.
KEMMIS, S. (1980). 'The imagination of the case and the invention of the study', in Simons, H. (Ed.) – see below.
KLAPP, O. (1958). 'Social types', *American Sociological Review*, 23, pp. 674–680.
KUSHNER, S. (1982). 'The research process', MacDonald, B. et al. (Eds.) *Bread and Dreams*, Norwich, CARE.
KUSHNER, S. and NORRIS, D. (1980–81). 'Interpretation, negotiation and validity in naturalistic research', *Interchange*, 11, 4, p. 26–36.
LINDBLOM, C. and COHEN, D. (1979). Usable Knowledge, New Haven, Conn., Yale U.P.
LOFLAND, J. (1971). *Analysing Social Settings*, Belmont, California, Wadsworth.
MARSH, C. (1982). *Survey Research*, London, Allen and Unwin.
PARLETT, M. and HAMILTON, D. (1972). *Evaluation as Illumination*. Occasional paper No. 9, Centre for Educational Research in the Educational Sciences, University of Edinburgh. Reprinted in Hamilton, D. et al. (1977) – see above.
PARSONS, C. (1981). 'A policy for educational evaluation', in Lacey, C. and Lawton, D. (Eds.) *Issues in Evaluation and Accountability*, London, Methuen.
RAWLINGS, B. (1980). 'The production of facts in a therapeutic community', in Atkinson, P. and Heath, C. (Eds.) *Medical Work: Realities and Routines*, Farnborough, Gower.
ROCK, P. (1979). *The Making of Symbolic Interactionism*, London, Macmillan.
SHIPMAN, M. (1981). 'Parvenu evaluation', in Smetherham, D. (Ed.) *Practising Evaluation*, Driffield, Yorks, Nafferton Books.
SIMONS, H. (Ed.) (1980). *Towards a Science of the Singular*, Norwich, CARE.
SIMONS, H. (1981). 'Process evaluation in schools', in Lacey, C. and Lawton, D. (Eds.) *Issues in Evaluation and Accountability*, London, Methuen.
SMITH, L.M. et al. (1981). 'Observer role and field study knowledge', *Educational Evaluation and Policy Analysis*, 3, 3, pp. 83–90.

SPINDLER, G. (1982). 'General Introduction', in Spindler, G. (Ed.) *Doing the Ethnography of Schooling*, New York, Holt.

STAKE, R. and EASLEY, J. (Eds.) (1978). *Case Studies in Science Education*, University of Illinois, Urbana-Champaigne, CIRCE.

STAKE, R. (1980). 'The case study method in social inquiry', Simons, H. (Ed.) – see above.

STENHOUSE, L. (1975). *An Introduction to Curriculum Research and Development*, London, Heinemann.

STENHOUSE, L. (1979). *Curriculum Research and Development in Action*, London, Heinemann.

WALKER, R. (1974). 'Classroom research: a view from Safari', MacDonald, B. and Walker, R. (Eds.) *Innovation, Evaluation Research and the Problem of Control*, Norwich, CARE.

WALKER, R. (1981). 'Getting involved in curriculum research: a personal history', in Lawn, M. and Barton, L. (Eds.) *Rethinking Curriculum Studies*, London, Croom Helm.

WALKER, R. (1982). 'The use of case studies in applied research and evaluation', in Hartnett, A. (Ed.) *The Social Sciences in Educational Studies*, London, Heinemann.

WEBB, E. *et al.* (1966). *Unobtrusive Measures*, Chicago, Rand McNally.

WOLCOTT, H.F. (1977). *Teachers versus Technocrats*, Centre for Educational Policy and Management, Eugene, Oregon, University of Oregon.

WOLCOTT, H.F. (1981). 'Confessions of a "trained" observer', in Popkewitz, T.S. and Tabachnick, B.R. (Eds.) *The Study of Schooling*, New York, Praeger.

Appendix

One difficulty for 'outsiders' working on the products of the case-study researchers is the scattered, fragmentary and unpublished source material. We have listed below mimeoed, lithoed and other 'semi-published' materials which we have read in order to produce this paper.

The output of CARE, University of East Anglia, is available from CARE by mail order.

ADELMAN, C. and GIBBS, I. (1979). *A Study of Student Choice in the Context of Institutional Change*, Report to the DES.

ELLIOTT, J. and MACDONALD, B. (Eds.) (1975). *People in Classrooms*, Norwich, CARE.

JENKINS, D. *et al.* (1979). *Chocolate Cream Soldiers*, Coleraine, New University of Ulster.

MACDONALD, B. and WALKER, R. (Eds.) (1974). *Innovation, Evaluation Research and the Problem of Control: Safari Papers 1*, Norwich, CARE.

MACDONALD, B. *et al.* (1975). *The Programme at Two*, Norwich, CARE.

MACDONALD, B. (Ed) (1978). *The Experience of Innovation*, Norwich, CARE.

MACDONALD, B. *et al.* (1981). *Evaluators at Work*, Köln, IFAPLAN.

MACDONALD, B. *et al.* (1982). *Bread and Dreams*, Norwich, CARE.

NORRIS, N. (Ed.) (1977). *Theory in Practice: Safari Papers Two*, Norwich, CARE.

SIMONS, H. (Ed.) (1980). *Towards a Science of the Singular*, Norwich, CARE.

STAKE, R. and EASLEY, J. (Eds.) (1978). *Case Studies in Science Education*, University of Illinois at Urbana-Champaigne, CIRCE.

WALKER, R. (1981). *The Observational Work of Local Authority Inspectors and Advisors*, Norwich, CARE.

WOLCOTT, H.F. (1977). *Teachers Versus Technocrats*, Eugene, Oregon, Centre for Education Policy and Management.

The reader may also wish to consult *Interchange*, Vol. 11, No. 4, 1980–81, a special issue on 'The social observation tradition in British educational research'.

Index

256